PRIMITIVISM
AND THE IDEA OF PROGRESS

IN ENGLISH POPULAR LITERATURE OF
THE EIGHTEENTH CENTURY

PRIMITIVISM
AND THE IDEA OF PROGRESS.

IN ENGLISH POPULAR LITERATURE OF
THE EIGHTEENTH CENTURY

BY

LOIS WHITNEY

OCTAGON BOOKS

A DIVISION OF FARRAR, STRAUS AND GIROUX

New York   1973

Reprinted 1965
by special arrangement with The Johns Hopkins Press

Second Octagon printing 1973

OCTAGON BOOKS
A Division of Farrar, Straus & Giroux, Inc.
19 Union Square West
New York, N. Y. 10003

Library of Congress Catalog Card Number: 65-25874
ISBN 0-374-98531-6

Printed in U.S.A. by
NOBLE OFFSET PRINTERS, INC.
NEW YORK, N.Y. 10003

To

RONALD SALMON CRANE

THE PUBLICATION OF THIS BOOK

WAS MADE POSSIBLE

BY GRANTS IN AID OF RESEARCH

FROM

THE JOHN SIMON GUGGENHEIM MEMORIAL FOUNDATION

AND

THE AMERICAN COUNCIL OF LEARNED SOCIETIES

AND BY A GRANT IN AID OF PUBLICATION

FROM

THE LUCY MAYNARD SALMON FUND FOR RESEARCH

OF VASSAR COLLEGE

ACKNOWLEDGMENTS

I have acknowledged on the previous page my very great indebtedness to the Guggenheim Memorial Foundation, the Council of Learned Societies, and the Salmon Fund of Vassar College for generous assistance in financing the research work that went to the making of this book and the publication of the results; I should like here to make acknowledgment of other aid no less appreciated. Most of the material for this study was gathered at the British Museum where my search for unclassified popular documents of the eighteenth century was greatly facilitated by the resourcefulness and courtesy of the librarians. I should like also to express my gratitude to the libraries of Vassar College, Harvard University, and the University of Chicago for their willing coöperation in opening their stacks to me and borrowing books difficult of access in this country.

I am indebted to many friends for their helpful suggestions and interest, but more especially I have the very deepest sense of obligation to Professors Arthur O. Lovejoy and Ronald S. Crane for their encouragement and inspiration at the inception of this piece of research and for their patient, critical reading of text and proof at its completion.

L. W.

FOREWORD

The complex of inter-related ideas to which the historians of literature and philosophy have given the name of ' primitivism ' is at once a philosophy of history and a theory of values, moral or aesthetic or both. The two elements of it are, indeed, logically separable, and have sometimes occurred separately in the history of Western thought; and the motives which have led to the acceptance of the one are not necessarily those which have generated the other. But from at least the fifth century B. C. they have, for sufficiently comprehensible reasons, usually been associated.

As a philosophy of history primitivism is, of course, the belief that the earliest condition of man and of human society, *l'homme tel qu'il a dû sortir des mains de la Nature*, was the best condition. And this belief, though it encountered opposition from the outset and in nearly all subsequent periods, remained, on the whole, for more than twenty-two centuries probably the most widely prevalent preconception about past terrestrial history, among Western peoples. Man has, throughout a great part of his historic march, walked with face turned backward; and a nostalgia for his original state, which tradition and piety had pleasingly idealized, has persistently beset him. That heaven lay about him in his racial infancy has — if one may judge by the prodigious frequency of its iteration in literature — been one of the commonest and most tenacious of man's faiths. The motivation of this ' chronological primitivism ' — as the editors of this series propose to call it — has been various and complex, and cannot be adequately discussed in this brief preamble to a study of an especially important late phase of the general history of primitivism; to attempt

xi

here to analyze its psychological sources and its logical
or pseudo-logical connections with other long prevalent
preconceptions is the less necessary because many of the
most potent and constant of them appear clearly in Miss
Whitney's pages.

But two or three very summary remarks about the
relations of this aspect of primitivism to other tendencies
are perhaps worth setting down. The conviction of the
superiority of man's original state is, in the first place,
capable of being, as it historically has been, combined
with different assumptions as to what has been the course
of human history since its beginning. Frequently in ancient
times and down to the seventeenth century it has been
associated with the doctrine of an inevitable and progressive decline or enfeeblement not only of man but of
nature. This doctrine and chronological primitivism,
indeed, have often been merely two sides of a single
idea — that illustrated by Seneca's dictum that " it is not
to be doubted that the world produced better things when
it was not yet worn out " (*neque . . . dubium est, quin
meliora mundus nondum effetus ediderit*). The energies
of Nature were at their highest in its vernal prime; they
have necessarily diminished with the lapse of centuries;
the earth doth wax old as doth a garment; and the worst
is yet to come. But chronological primitivism has been
equally compatible with the belief in the essential constancy of nature's processes and in the immutability of
human nature and behavior — once man's primeval perfection or innocence had been lost. And it has also been
compatible with the conception of past history as undula-
tory — a succession of advances and retrogressions, in no
phase of which, however, has the excellence of the first
stage been wholly recaptured. Again, more than one out-
look upon the future, either near or remote, has been

conjoined with the primitivistic idealization of man's remotest past. This has not always — though it has doubtless most often — been merely an emotional nostalgia. For those who did not accept the doctrine of a necessity, in the nature of things, of a more or less continuous degeneration, chronological primitivism has sometimes been also a practical program of reform — of reform through reversion. The happiness and goodness which man had once known could be recovered, easily and simply, by returning to his original mode of life and to the original and normal constitution of society. That such an ideal state had already existed was the more reason for believing that it could exist again, if, after so long an estrangement from them, a corrupted race could but be brought back to nature's ways — that is to say, the ways which are really most 'natural' to man. Thus the primitivism of regretful retrospection was not inconsistent with a certain belief in the possibility of progress — provided the goal of progress was conceived as, in its essentials, identical in kind with the starting-point from which man set out. In the moods which have accompanied it, therefore, chronological primitivism has, at different periods and in different minds, run the gamut from the gloomiest pessimism to the most cheerful and exuberant meliorism. But with one idea — a relatively rare though by no means an unexampled one before the past two centuries, which already shows signs of decreptitude — this sort of primitivism is, of course, fundamentally incongruous: the idea of a general *law* of progress, of a necessary sequence of stages of human development in the past continuing into the future, of which, with perhaps minor fluctuations, the later embody more of value than the earlier. The incongruity of the two ideas has not always, indeed, as Miss Whitney abundantly and amusingly shows, prevented

them from being equally ardently embraced by the same
minds and inculcated in the same writings.

It would be hard to determine whether, on the whole,
chronological primitivism or what may be distinguished
from it as cultural primitivism gained most from their
early established, though not congenital, union. That the
latter, at all events, has had independent roots of its own
in human nature and in philosophic reflection is manifest
upon any survey of the history of this dual phenomenon.
And the roots of cultural primitivism are likewise various
and even incongruous. Common to them all, indeed, is the
conviction that the time — whatever time may, for a given
writer, be in question — is out of joint; that what is
wrong with it is due to an abnormal complexity and
sophistication in the life of civilized man, to the patho-
logical multiplicity and emulativeness of his desires and
the oppressive over-abundance of his belongings, and to
the factitiousness and want of inner spontaneity of his
emotions; that ' art,' the work of man, has corrupted
' nature,' that is, man's own nature; and that the model
of the normal individual life and the normal social order,
or at least a nearer approximation to it, is to be found
among contemporary ' savage ' peoples, whether or not
it be supposed to have been realized also in the life of
primeval men. Civilized man has been almost continu-
ously subject to moods of revolt against civilization, which
in some sense is, indeed, profoundly contrary to his
nature; and in the serious preachers of primitivism this
revolt has been chronic and intense. But the belief in the
superiority of the simple life of ' nature ' has been the
manifestation sometimes of a hedonistic, sometimes of a
rigoristic and even ascetic, conception of the nature of the
good, and sometimes of a mixture of both. Some men
have turned to primitivism because they loved indolence

and ease, others because they — at least in imagination —
loved hardship and austerity; and the latter have probably
been the more numerous. The 'return to nature,' in
some or all respects, has been the program alike of those
who would escape from the restraints of accepted moral
codes and of those who deplored the moral laxity of a
luxurious society; and even Christian moralists have sometimes, however oddly, pointed to the noble savage as a
better exemplar of the evangelical virtues than was often
to be found among those who had been reared under the
Christian teaching and had supernatural means of grace
at their disposal. Throughout Western history, again,
cultural primitivism has been the form oftenest taken by
communism and equalitarianism; the thesis that man's
lapse from the 'natural' order took place when private
property in land was introduced and inequalities of economic condition thus began is one of the early and most
persistent elements in the literary expressions of primitivism. But the discrimination of the sources, the diverse
doctrinal affiliations, and the protean manifestations, of
cultural, as of chronological, primitivism is much too large
an undertaking to be attempted in this prefatory note.
Upon these matters, too, Miss Whitney's study — within
the limits of the period with which she is concerned —
seems to me to throw much new light.

Now in the eighteenth century, especially in its second
half, primitivism reached at once a climax and a crisis.
Never before had manifestations of cultural primitivism
in literature been quite so abundant — though this was
partly because, with the increase of readers, the multiplication of popular journals, and the vogue of the didactic
or 'philosophical' novel, all current ideas and intellectual
fashions were being more copiously reiterated in print
and more assiduously and widely popularized than in any

preceding age. Never before, in modern times, had the praise of the simple life been sounded quite so eloquently, and with so moving an air of conviction, as by Rousseau; and never before had quite such seemingly engaging models of the noble savage and the life according to nature been available for primitivistic uses as after the French and British voyages of exploration among the Polynesian peoples in the 1760's and 1770's. And primitivistic premises had seldom, if ever, been so seriously, boldly and vigorously employed in polemic against the existing economic or political order, or against certain elements of the moral tradition of the West, as they were by Lahontan, Rousseau, Morelly, Diderot, and other writers of the period. The new fashion of ' sensibility,' also, as Miss Whitney shows, had a natural, though not an exclusive, affinity with primitivism. Nor, in general, had the sacred word ' Nature ' — with its vast ambiguity — begun to lose its magic, until very late in the century; on the contrary, the use of it to designate the norm of thought and taste and practice for man had, I think — though this is saying much — never before been so constant, or applied so insistently or in such diverse fields. Rare indeed was the eighteenth-century author who could write five pages without invoking the sanction of ' Nature ' for whatever opinion he happened to be advocating; not very numerous were those who could refrain from sprinkling it freely through every page. And yet, just this time when so many factors tended to give fresh vitality and vogue to primitivism was also the time when the movement of events and new tendencies of thought were working against it more potently than ever before, so that fairly early in the following century it became, not, indeed, extinct, but plainly (at least for a time) obsolescent. Of the two major changes which were thus

undermining the primitivistic tradition, one was in the
realm of philosophic and scientific theory, the other in
that of economics and technology. Throughout the century, the conception of 'progress' as a general law holding good throughout the historic process, and in each of
its aspects, was finding increasingly frequent expression
among the more original and seminal minds of the age.
It was clearly affirmed of the world in general before it
received equally unequivocal application in the special
sciences. Leibniz had roundly declared, about the beginning of the century, that "a perpetual and unrestricted
progress of the universe as a whole must be recognized."
Akenside and Young in verse, Buffon and Kant in prose,
had outlined a sort of cosmic evolutionism; the theory
of the transformation of species was propounded before
the end of the third quarter of the century by Maupertuis,
Diderot and Robinet; the descent of man from, *i. e.*, his
original identity with, one of the species of anthropoid
apes, was affirmed by Rousseau and Monboddo; the idea
of what is now termed 'social evolution,' of the essentially 'progressive' character of man and human society
had, as Mr. R. S. Crane has recently shown, been making
headway since the late seventeenth century even in the
most orthodox circles; the *fact* of progress in the sciences
and the applied arts was becoming ever more apparent,
and the Baconian dream of the transformation thereby of
the conditions of human existence was gaining an increasing hold upon the imagination of the educated public;
and from the mid-century 'perfectibility' was a beloved
neologism which summed up this new and stirring conception of man's nature and his prospects. The opposition
to chronological primitivism, in some or all of its forms
and degrees, thus took on an unprecedented vigor, and
spread over a more extended front than before, at the very

moment when cultural primitivism, at least, was receiving certain new reenforcements.

But, most of all in England, cultural primitivism as such was also patently at variance with the new economic developments of the period. "There was never from the earliest ages," Dr. Johnson wrote in 1757, " a time in which trade so much engaged the attention of mankind, or commercial gain was sought with such general emulation." The expansion of British commerce, the establishment of new manufactures in which England was rapidly to gain world-preeminence, the growth of great industrial areas, the beginning of the transfer of the centre of economic interest, and of the seat of economic and eventually of political power, from agriculture to machine industry— these were manifestly hostile (as Mandeville's ironic eye had already prophetically discerned) to those traditional ' virtues ' which were most fully expressed in the ideal of the ' simple life according to nature.' The ethics of the limitation of desires, the doctrine of the necessarily corrupting effect of luxury, the ancient denunciation of the *amor sceleratus habendi*, were not only inimical to the interests of rapidly increasing classes whose fortunes were linked with the tendencies which the primitivists decried; they were also in conflict with a new, essentially economic form of national pride and even piety. Trade and commerce became, more frequently than in any earlier time, the theme of the rhapsodical effusions of poets. Yet the age-old tradition, in literature if not in practice, gave ground slowly and never completely — partly because the very growth of an industrial civilization, with its complexity, its laboriousness, its aesthetic uglinesses, and its further intensification of economic inequalities, lent at times a heightened appeal to the primitivist's picture of the life of the child of nature. The opposition between

the two tendencies was less often a conflict between different minds than a fluctuation of moods within the same
minds — witness the numerous eighteenth-century writers
who, like Thomson, yearn on one page for

> the blissful groves
> Where nature lived herself among her sons,
> And innocence and joy forever dwelt,

and who turn on the next to celebrate the glorious tri-
umphs of Britain's commerce and the blessings " of
wealth, of trade, of cheerful toiling crowds."

These brief and necessarily much over-simplified observations may at least serve the purpose for which they
were designed — to suggest, by way of introduction, the
special interest and importance of the theme with which
Miss Whitney has dealt so clarifyingly and with so much
enlivening concrete detail. She has chosen for her topic
the period in English literature in which primitivism and
the ideas opposed to it were most closely and most nearly
equally at grips; and she has illustrated the interplay and
conflict of the two tendencies, not alone from a few eminent authors who are still read, but still more from the
multitude of now-forgotten popular writers who — as
such writers usually do — much better exemplify the complex and varied working of these and related ideas in the
general mind of the age.

I cannot conclude without some comment on the method
which Miss Whitney has, in the main, followed in her
treatment of the subject; for it is, I think, a method still
too little practised by those who deal with the history of
ideas. What most distinguishes it is that it is, in fact, more
largely concerned with the analysis of the connections, the
' elective affinities' and interactions, the historical working-
out of the implications, of specific ideas, or the fusions

and disintegrations of old and of new — but in either case widely current — thought-complexes, than with the exposition of the ' systems' of doctrine — which are usually systems only in a Pickwickian sense — of individual writers or of schools or parties. The latter sort of exposition has, of course, its legitimate and, indeed, indispensable place in the historiography of thought; and it is much the simpler, easier and safer way of writing that history. But it does not, in truth, tell the real story clearly, vividly and effectively. For it is not the systems of philosophers, as systems, that are the dynamic factors in the general movement of thought. It is *separate* conceptions — presuppositions, dialectical motives, individual dogmas, or alluring catchwords, detached from their original contexts — that play this part. In the history of ideas, *ideas* should be the units dealt with, the *dramatis personae*; and it is in the presentation of *their* vicissitudes and relations, as they severally pass through many minds of different types, that the real significance and living movement of the piece lie. Because of her careful discrimination of the several unit-ideas which are the protagonists in the story and her exhibition of the complexity of their inter-relations and the kaleidoscopic diversity of the patterns which they formed, Miss Whitney has, I think, not only much illuminated an important phase in the history of English thought — one of the great, confused transitions from old to new ways of thinking — but has also given to this a degree of dramatic interest, as well as, sometimes, of a humorous piquancy, which only such an analytic method makes possible.

ARTHUR O. LOVEJOY

THE JOHNS HOPKINS UNIVERSITY
JUNE, 1934

CONTENTS

INTRODUCTION

I was first led to undertake the following study by a casual reading of some eighteenth-century novels. They were novels now almost forgotten which in their day were highly popular — *Ethelinde; or, the Recluse of the Lake; Emmeline, the Orphan of the Castle; The Young Philosopher; Marchmont; The Old Manor House*—all by Charlotte Smith. I was astonished at the curious mixture of ideas that I met there — theories of the superiority of primitive man and of man's natural goodness all huddled together with theories of perfectibility, sometimes two antagonistic points of view in the same sentence. The primitivistic ideology bade men look for their model of excellence to the first stages of society before man had been corrupted by civilization; the idea of progress represented a point of view that looked forward to a possible perfection in the future. The primitivistic teaching, again, extolled simplicity; the faith in progress found its ideal in an increasing complexity. The former system of thought, finally, taught an ethics based on the natural affections; the latter system was built on an intellectualistic foundation. Here in the pages of Charlotte Smith were ideas existing amiably side by side which by all the rules of logic ought to have annihilated each other. Yet this fictional form, confused as it was, must have been one of the forms in which the current of thought of the time reached the widest reading public, if it reached the public at all.

Two questions were raised in my mind: were Charlotte Smith's novels indicative of any widespread attempt, at this period so rich in controversy, to popularize these currents of thought, and if so, was the confusion of ideas that I found here of common occurrence? Only a very slight further investigation enabled me to answer both questions

1

with at least a tentative affirmative. Such being the case, would it not be enlightening, I asked myself, to investigate further the popular literature of the period — the fictional best-sellers, the cheap tracts, the popular poems — with the purpose of getting some conception of what the people who read these books must have thought about the issues which were occupying the leaders of thought of the time? In other words, I wanted to see what the history of ideas of the eighteenth century would look like if it were written, not in terms of what the philosophers actually said, but in terms of what the public thought they said — a far different matter, but equally important after all, since it is only after ideas reach the public that they become a real social force. I wanted to see what happened to ideas in the course of their dissemination, and I wanted to watch the complex pattern of overlapping waves of different and often warring tendencies, the confusion of one ideology with another.

Obviously it would be impossible to rewrite in one volume the whole history of eighteenth-century popular philosophy. I have limited myself, therefore, to the two ideologies which I saw conjoined and confused in the novels of Charlotte Smith, primitivism and the idea of progress, and I have studied their popular expression for the years between 1750, or thereabouts, and 1815, since that is the period in which these two antagonistic systems of thought came together most interestingly.

Fortunately my materials have been plentiful. The novel, for instance, in this period took itself with extreme serious-ness. Never did it less deserve the criticism it so frequently met with at this very time, that it was a species of litera-ture almost beneath the contempt of the mature person and dangerous to the morals of the young — ' just calcu-lated to kill time — to attract the attention of the reader for an hour, but leave not one idea on the mind.' On the contrary, the majority of the minor novelists of that troubled period took their work with such pedagogic earnestness as radically to impair the artistic value of their compositions. The very titles display a seriousness of purpose that, combined with the prolixity of the novels themselves, would today be considered an almost certain guarantee against their sale: *The Triumph of Benevolence*, four volumes; *Traits of Nature*, five volumes; *Liberal Opinions upon Animals, Man, and Providence, in Which are Introduced Anecdotes of a Gentleman*, six volumes;— *Memoirs of Modern Philosophers; Vaurien, or Sketches of the Times Exhibiting Views of the Philosophies, Religions, Politics, Literature, and Manners of the Age; Whatever is Just is Equal, but Equality not Always Just; Ellinor, or the World as It Is; Caleb Williams, or Things as They Are; Man as He Is; Hermsprong, or Man as He Is Not; Sketches of Modern Life, or Man as He ought not to Be.* The prefatory warning of R. C. Dallas, the author of *Percival, or Nature Vindicated*, would seem to us unnecessary: ' They who, allured by the title of Novel, take up this book with an avidity for an uninterrupted chain of incidents, will be disappointed. To improve the heart, as well as to please the fancy, and to be the auxiliary of the Divine and the Moralist, are the best praises of the best novel writers.'

To such an extent, in fact, had the novel become a rec ognized vehicle for the popularization of current thought both radical and conservative that not only did I find it profitable to look to the novels as well as the treatises of such recognized propagandists as Godwin, Holcroft, Bage, and Mary Wollstonecraft for a complete expression of their ideas, but I found without much difficulty a whole host of literary ' middlemen ' who were instrumental in

retailing the ideas of the period to the public.   Mrs.
Charlotte Smith, Mrs. Inchbald, Mrs. Mary Robinson,
Mrs. Etc. etc.,' writes the exasperated author of *Pursuits
of Literature*, 'though all of them are ingenious ladies,
yet they are too frequently *whining* or *frisking* in novels,
till our girls' heads turn wild with impossible adventures,
and now and then are tainted with democracy.' Some idea
of the extent of this popularization of ideas through fiction
may be gathered from the remark of a character in *The
Force of Prejudice*, an anti-radical novel of 1799. Ingle-
bert, father of the hero, deploring the wide currency of
the 'pernicious scepticisms' and 'sophistical delusions'
of Hume and Gibbon, Voltaire and Rousseau, and Goethe
— surely an eclectic assortment — remarks with question-
able grammar, 'and those unaccustomed to the higher
pursuits of literature, in which Hume and Gibbon moved,
were accessible through the medium of novels, in which
were dissiminated [sic] the most dangerous principles: —
principles which corrupt the heart and debase the understanding. . . .'

Drama was not slow in catering to the public that made
of the novel called *Memoirs of Modern Philosophers* a
best seller. Like the novel, the drama had its *Art and
Nature*, its *Every One Has His Fault*. Necessarily less
polemical than the novel, however, the drama quite wisely
held chiefly to the field of a rather sparkling social satire
with the noble savage as a frequent vehicle. With the
use of didactic poetry as a means of propagating and
popularizing theories on every subject from the raising of
broccoli to the latest utilitarian doctrine, students of
English poetry of the second half of the century are only
too painfully familiar. Further, not only did pamphlets
abound, but with the increase in the number of periodicals
towards the end of the century there came about an in-

creased opportunity for the spread of ideas through the vehicle of the special article and the essay. 'We are no longer in an age of ignorance,' one reads in *Pursuits of Literature*, 'and information is not partially distributed according to the ranks, and orders, and functions, and dignities of social life. All learning has an index, and every science its abridgment. I am scarcely able to name any man whom I consider as wholly ignorant. We no longer look exclusively for learned authors in the usual place, in the retreats of academic erudition and in the seats of religion. Our peasantry now read the *Rights of Man* on mountains and moors and by the way side; and shepherds make the analogy between their occupation and that of their governors. Happy indeed, had they been taught no other comparison. Our *unsexed* female writers now instruct us or confuse us and themselves in the labyrinth of politics, or turn us wild with Gallic frenzy.'

It is only by a study of all these vehicles of popularization that it is possible to arrive at an adequate understanding of the actual modification of thought in its transmission from philosopher to layman. Society at large did not read Berkeley or Hume, Hartley or Helvétius, but society at large did attend the theatre, subscribe to the magazines, buy pamphlets, and read novels — and even poetry it seems, at least in rather larger amounts than at present. It is to this literature therefore that I have looked for the form in which the thought of the times became a social force; and I have been continually amazed by the results of my search.

Plentiful as the materials have been, however, the following study is not in any sense designed as a compendium of all the popular literature illustrative of primitivism and progressivism in the period covered. I have omitted many pertinent documents because they have already been adequately treated elsewhere, and other material because it is in process of being studied by other scholars. I have attempted to select from the available material popular documents that are as fresh but at the same time as thoroughly representative as possible, and that tell as clearly as any the story of the gradual degeneration and confusion of these two ideologies. To get a proper perspective on the popular literature, I have analyzed the net-work of background ideas of primitivism in Chapter I, and of the idea of progress in Chapters V and VI. I have tried to determine what theses of the various schools of thought of the century lent themselves to the former point of view and what to the latter, and what were the probable sources of confusion between the two ways of thinking.

CHAPTER I

Philosophical Backgrounds of Eighteenth-Century Primitivism

I

No small part of the interest of the life-history of an idea as it passes through a succession of human minds comes from the fact that the idea has frequently so changed its whole temperament and complexion in the course of only a few generations as to become not only uncongenial to its blood relations but a positive scandal to the family tree. Such is the case with the idea that primitive men — the Indians, the South Sea Islanders — are good, wise, and benevolent. That the thought complex which in the late seventeenth century was favorable to the persistence of an age-old admiration for the uncultivated mind and heart [1] had a common origin not only with the glorification of reason in the philosophy of the Enlightenment, but with the high spirituality and mysticism of the Platonists, and with the aesthetic virtuosity of the moral sense school, is one of the anomalies of the history of primitivism. How it all came about I shall try to make clear in the following pages. I hope that the reader will bear with me in this chapter while I subject what is already familiar material to a slightly different alignment from the usual one — an alignment which will be necessary to explain what would otherwise be incomprehensible in the survey of the more popular literature of the eighteenth century to follow.

I shall begin with several quotations from Charron

---

[1] For a history of this idea in antiquity, see the forthcoming volume, *Primitivism in Antiquity*, the first volume of a proposed documentary history of primitivism edited by A. O. Lovejoy, G. Boas, R. S. Crane, and G. Chinard.

7

which will serve as a convenient statement of certain underlying principles still widely current in the thought of the late seventeenth and early eighteenth centuries. In the third chapter of the second book of his *Of Wisdome*, Charron writes:

(a) Now the paterne and rule to be honest, is this nature it selfe, which absolutely requireth that we be such, it is, I say, this equity and vniuersal reason which shineth in euery one of Vs . . . and so he is an honest man essentially, and not by accident and occasion; for this law and light is essential and naturall in Vs, and therefore it is called Nature and the law of nature. He is also by consequent an honest man, alwaies and perpetually, vniformly and equally at all times and in all places: for this law of equity, and naturall reason is perpetuall in vs, *Edictum perpetuum, A perpetuall edict*, inuiolable, which can never be extinct nor defaced, *Quam nec ipsa delet iniquitas; vermis eorum non moriatur, which neither iniquity it selfe may deface; their worme shall neuer die.* vniuersall and constant in all things, and alwaies the same, equall vniforme, which neither time nor place can alter nor disguise. . . .[2]

(b) Men are naturally good, and follow not euill, but for profit or pleasure.[3]

(c) Doubtlesse, Nature in euery one of vs is sufficient, and a sweet mistris and rule to all things, if we will hearken vnto hir, employ and awaken hir; and wee need not seeke elsewhere, nor begge of Arte and the Sciences, the names, the remedies, and the rules which we haue need of. . . . We see ignorant people, idiots, and simple men, leade their liues more sweetly and cheerefully, resist the assaults of death, of want, of sorrow, more constantly and contentedly, than the wisest men and most actiue. And if a man marke it well, he shall finde among pesants and other poore people examples of patience, constancie, equanimitie, more pure than all those that are taught in Schooles; they follow

----

[2] Pierre Charron, *Of Wisdome. Three Bookes* . . . , trans. Samson Lennard, London [1615?], p. 272.

[3] *Ibid.*, p. 275.

simplie the reason and conduct of nature, they trauell quietly and contentedly in their affaires, not enflaming or eleuating themselues, and consequently more soundly.[4]

(d) But we doe not only not hearken vnto it, [the law of nature] . . . but also . . . we endeuour to auoid it, we suffer it to sleepe and to cease, louing better to begge elsewhere our first rudiments, to runne to studie any arte, than to content our selues with that which is bred within us. . . . From this generall and Vniversall alteration and corruption it is come to passe, that there is nothing of Nature knowen in vs. If we must say what the lawes thereof are, and how many they are, we are much hindred. The ensigne and marke of naturall law is the vniuersitie of approbation: for that which Nature shall haue truely ordeined for vs, we with a common consent shall follow without doubting; and not only euery nation, but euery particular person.

Now there is not anything in the world which is not denied and contradicted, not by one nation but by diuers: and there is not any thing so strange and vnaturall in the opinion of diuers, which is not approved and authorised in many places by common vse.[5]

(e) there are some that haue their particular nature, that is to say, their temper and temperature so good and pleasing . . . that they find themselues without endeuor, and without arte or discipline, whollie carried and disposed to goodnesse and honestie, that is to say, to follow and conforme themselues to the vniuersall nature, whereby they are tearmed well-borne; *gaudeant bene nati.*

This kind of naturall and easie honestie, and as it were borne with vs, is properly called goodnesse, a qualitie of a soule well borne and well gouerned, it is a sweetnesse, facilitie, and debonaire mildnesse of nature: . . . We should rather call this kind of goodnesse innocencie, as men call little children sheepe, and the like, innocent creatures. But an actiue, valiant, manly, and effectuall goodnesse is that I require, which is a readie, easie, and constant affection vnto that which is good, right, iust, according to reason and nature.[6]

[4] *Ibid.*   [5] *Ibid.,* pp. 275-77.   [6] *Ibid.,* pp. 278-79.

(f) . . . it is certaine, that in the like thing the naturall is
more worth than the acquired; that it is far more noble, more
ecsellent and diuine to worke by nature than by Art, easily, equally,
vniformedly, than painfully, vnequally, with doubt and danger.[7]

Analyzing and summarizing these passages we find in
(a) and (c) an almost complete statement of the philosophy of the Enlightenment in regard to the laws of
nature; that is, that they are (1) eternal — a ' perpetuall
edict'; (2) immutable — ' constant in all things, and
alwaies the same'; (3) universal and uniform; (4) simple
and easy of comprehension; and (5) knowable by all
men by the light of nature so that ' wee need not begge
of Arte and Sciences . . . the rules which we have need
of.' These five principles, stated with varying emphases
and in diverse combinations are fundamental not only to
the rationalistic philosophy of the Enlightenment and the
theology of the deists,[8] but are found, with a slightly
different genesis and some modification, in the more
mystical philosophy of the Cambridge Platonists. They
form the starting point for many diverse lines of reasoning, some of which eventuated in radical primitivism, some
in a theory of progress. A number of the corollaries,
important from the primitivistic point of view, are already
made explicit by Charron. One important corollary is that
since there is a natural tendency towards goodness among
men (cf. b) and a light of nature by which even the
most ignorant may know natural law, the laws of nature
may often be more graciously followed among ' pesants '
and ' simple men ' than among more learned people (c).
The complement to this corollary is the generalization that

[7] *Ibid.*, p. 281.   Much of all this was obviously derived from
Montaigne.
[8] See A. O. Lovejoy, ' The Parallel of Deism and Classicism,' *Mod.
Phil.*, XXIX (1932), 281-99.

:ivilized men have so degenerated that they no longer
readily recognize or follow the laws of nature (d). But
a third corollary provides for a few ' beautiful souls '
even in our modern civilization who are so good by nature
that they follow the laws of nature unconsciously (e).
This type of goodness Charron prefers to call ' innocencie.'
A fourth favorite inference was the idea that what is
natural is to be preferred to what is acquired by art (f).
If one expands Charron's brief ' natural goodness ' to
include a natural tendency towards benevolence and a recognition of benevolence as one of the primary laws of
nature, one has the foundation of much of the later
primitivistic thought. It will, however, be worth our while
to follow somewhat more fully the late seventeenth-century line of reasoning about the law of nature to see to
what extent it is responsible for the complex network of
the thought of the eighteenth century.

II

We might take as our starting point any one of the five
principles found in Charron, for so mutually dependent
are they that, at whatever point one starts, the rest follow
logically. If, for example, one admits that there are
eternal and immutable truths — and the stress of controversy in the mid-seventeenth century made the belief
that there were such particularly acceptable both to the
Platonist and the more purely rationalistic philosopher —
and if these truths are uniform for all times and all places,
they must of necessity be simple, fundamental, and
broadly applicable. Again, if they are binding on all
nations at all times, they must be such as to be readily
discoverable and recognizable, and man must be supposed
to have the faculty within him for such discovery and recognition without the necessity of any special revelation.

In this mutual dependence among the five principles out
lined by Charron lay their strength and philosophica
attractiveness. Perhaps it will be best to make the foca
points of our discussion the two principles which are th
most fruitful in further developments, namely, that th
laws of nature are simple and easy of comprehension an
that they are readily knowable by all men by the light o
nature.

The clearness and simplicity of eternal and immutabl
truths and their self-evidence are among their most uni
versally recognized characteristics. ' Nay, the very essenc
of truth,' writes Cudworth, ' . . . is this clear percepti
bility and intelligibility.' [9] And Whichcote writes eve
earlier: ' nothing is more knowable than the great in
stances of natural truth. . . . Things of natural knowl
edge, or of first inscription in the heart of men by God
these are known to be true as soon as ever they ar
proposed.' [10] This immediacy of recognition of trutl
' without any further discourse or reasoning ' [11] furnishec
an excellent soil for primitivism. If eternal and immutabl
truths which offered the requisite basis for right livin₉
were indeed so clear, simple, and self-evident as both th
Platonists and the deists professed to believe,[12] there wa
nothing logically to interfere with the supposition tha
primitive man could know and follow the laws of natur

[9] The True Intellectual System of the Universe, London, 1845, III, 34
Cf. Joseph Glanvill, ' The Agreement of Reason and Religion,' in Essay
on Several Important Subjects in Philosophy and Religion, London, 1676
p. 26.
[10] Benjamin Whichcote, Works, Aberdeen, 1751, III, 20-22. Cf
Henry More's definition of ' Common Notions ' in ' The Immortality o
the Soul,' Bk. I, Ch. II, Axiome III, in Philosophical Writings of Henr
More, ed. F. I. MacKinnon, N. Y., 1925, p. 61.
[11] More, ibid.
[12] Cf. Matthew Tindal, Christianity as Old as Creation: or, the Gospel
a Republication of the Religion of Nature, London, 1731, pp. 214, 215-19

as well as civilized man. On this point many divines, even those who were the farthest from being primitivists themselves, gave admirable support to the primitivists. A number of them, especially among the Platonists, following ancient precedent,[13] appealed to the 'consent of nations' to demonstrate the fact that there is so universal an applicability and acceptance of natural law that all kinds and conditions of men 'do tacitly and spontaneously conspire in a dutiful observation of the most radicall and fundamental Lawes of *Nature.*'[14] For, as Culverwel writes further, 'As face answers face, so does the heart of one man the heart of another, even the heart of an Athenian, the heart of an Indian. . . . Then look upon the diversities of Nations, and there you will see a rough and barbarous Scythian, a wilde American, an unpolisht Indian, a superstitious Egyptian, a subtile Ethiopian, . . . and many other heaps of Nations . . . and tell me whether it must not be some admirable and efficacious Truth, that shall so over-power them all, as to passe currant amongst them, and be own'd and acknowledg'd by them.'[15]

The universal recognition of identical laws of nature was of course explained by the theory that all men are adequately provided with a faculty for finding out the laws of nature for themselves. The intricate differences in theory regarding this faculty, variously called 'the candle of the Lord,' 'the light of nature,' and reason, need not greatly concern us except as they tended to produce later important divergences of thought.

Among the earliest Platonists, notably Whichcote,

[13] Cf. Henry More, *An Antidote against Atheism,* London, 1653, Bk. I, Ch. X, pp. 32-34.
[14] Nathanael Culverwel, *An Elegant and Learned Discourse of the Light of Nature, with Several Other Treatises,* London, 1654, p. 67.
[15] *Ibid.,* pp. 68-69.

Glanvill, and More (in his earliest writings), the laws of nature are thought of as innately part of man's mental equipment. Such a theory forms quite naturally the simplest possible basis for primitivism, and Whichcote himself draws the primitivistic inference. His line of reasoning is that God has implanted the ' principles of natural light ' in man, and has made it natural to him to follow them as long as his mind retains its primitive cast. Many men have so corrupted their minds, however, with ' ill use, custom, and practice ' that they no longer recognize the laws of nature.[16] Hence one seldom finds real goodness among civilized men but must look for it among primitive men. — ' A thing to be admired, that *nature* should bestow *that* on the *Scythians*, which the *Grecians*, long instructed by precepts of philosophers, had not attained! that formed manners should be transcended by uneducated barbarity? — Hence it appears that the condition of *human nature* is not so very *rude* as some report; since so much is found in the uncivilized parts of the world.' [17]

With More the case is somewhat different. Starting with a by no means crude theory of innate truth,[18] he comes in

[16] *Op. cit.*, III, 53; II, 15, 64.

[17] *Ibid.*, IV, 257-58. See also Joseph Glanvill, *op. cit.*, pp. 5, 15-18, 20-21.

[18] *Antidote against Atheism*, p. 13: ' But the Mind of Man more free, and better exercised in the close observations of its own operations and nature, cannot but discover that there is an active and *actuall Knowledge* in a man, of which these outward Objects are rather the re-minders then the first begetters or implanters. And when I say *actuall Knowledge* I do not mean that there is a certain number of *Ideas* flaring and shining to the *Animadversive Faculty* like so many *Torches* or *Starres* in the *Firmament* to our outward sight, or that there are any *figures* that take their distinct places, or are legibly writ there like the *Red letters* or *Astronomical Characters* in an *Almanack*; but I understand thereby an active sagacity in the Soul, or quick recollection, as it were, whereby some small businesse being hinted unto her, she runs out presently into a more clear and larger conception.' See also *id.*, pp. 17-19.

the *Explanation of the Grand Mystery of Godliness* not
only to a somewhat more elaborate description of the
operation of reason,[19] its dependence on the testimony of
sense and its use of the ' Book of Nature,' of revelation,
and records,[20] but to a sense that the mystery of divine
truth ' ought to be *competently Obscure and Abstruse.*' [21]
He questions both the adequacy of reason and the clearness and simplicity of eternal and immutable truth.[22] All
of this leads directly away from primitivistic thought, and
even more so does the mystical and highly spiritual theory
of the ' boniform faculty' of the *Enchiridion Ethicum.* The
spiritual love, the ' Peace and Tranquillity of the Mind:
nay a state of such Serenity, as hath no other motions than
those of Benignity and Beneficence,' [23] there described
could only be the result of the finest and highest type of
intellectual development. Yet far as More's thought and
intention in the idea of the boniform faculty are from
primitivism, the thought of the *Enchiridion Ethicum,* in
so far as it is related to the eighteenth-century ethics of
benevolence, leads us right back to primitivism by a different route — a route which we shall survey later. And
even in the *Enchiridion Ethicum* itself, More gives so much
ground to the other side as to admit that the boniform
faculties is ' common to all men. For it is not above the
Talent of the meanest to love God, and his neighbour very
heartily.' [24] And he admits further that the mind left to

[19] *Theological Works,* London, 1708, p. 35 ff.
[20] *Ibid.,* p. 288.
[21] *Ibid.,* p. 2.
[22] *Ibid.,* p. 319. See also pp. 88, 90, and the criticism of the extreme
rationalistic point of view in the *Psychozoia,* C. II, st. 87-99. See especially st. 98, l. 4, ' Onely the spirit can the spirit own.' See also John
Smith, *Select Discourses,* Cambridge, 1673, pp. 3, 13-15.
[23] *Enchiridion Ethicum. The English Translation of 1690. Repro-
duced from the First Edition.* The Facsimile Text Society, N. Y., 1930,
p. 159.   [24] *Ibid.,* p. 8.

nature's care is better than the mind perverted by wrong teaching.[25]

We need not inquire into the various theories of the operation of the reason in its search for the truths of natural law without the help of innate ideas, tempting as many of these theories are.[26] The question of importance is the adequacy of the reason for arriving at truth by its own exertions. Any epistemological individualism obviously had to overcome the difficulty of the wide-spread contemporary disagreement as to what these eternal and immutable truths specifically were, and the further difficulty of man's evident reluctance to follow the laws of nature when he knew, or ought, according to the primitivists, to know quite plainly what they were. In fact one of the amusing anomalies of late seventeenth and early eighteenth century thought is that while there is probably no other period in the history of English thought more highly controversial, there is no other period in which so many thinkers are agreed that there are only a few simple, self-evident and immutable truths easily knowable by even the humblest intellect. Obviously there was a sad discrepancy between fact and theory which at least some of the philosophers were realists enough to see. As More wrote in his *Psychozoia*:

> For reasons use
> Back'd with advantage of all sciences,
> Of Arts, of tongues, cannot such light transfuse
> But that most learned men do think amisse
> In highest points divided as well you know, I wisse.[27]

[25] *Ibid.*, pp. 88-89. Cf. ' Platonick Song of the Soul: Psychathanasia, or The Immortality of the Soul,' *Philosophical Poems*, Cambridge, 1647, p. 75.

[26] See, for instance, the discussion of Cudworth's theory of knowledge in John H. Muirhead, *The Platonic Tradition in Anglo-Saxon Philosophy*, London, 1931, pp. 39-46.

[27] C. II, st. 94, ll. 5-9.

There were two possible ways out of the difficulty. One might take the very plausible view that since the reason is the instrument for the perception of truth, the more highly perfected the instrument and the more intelligently it is used, the more perfectly will it formulate for itself the laws of nature. Present disagreement is therefore not an indication of falsity in the theory but is a result of imperfection in the instrument. Progressive enlightenment will come from progressive refinement of the intellect. This line of thought about reason is of course directly anti-primitivistic and leads into a conception of progress. One sees its later crystallization into a theory of progress in such a book, for instance, as Ethan Allen's *Reason the Only Oracle of Man*, where, with these same premises about the light of nature, the author argues that a gradual perfection of reason will bring about a progressive knowledge of natural law and hence a general progress in society.[28] This conception of progressive enlightenment, either in the individual or in society, is adopted by many of the seventeenth and early eighteenth century thinkers, even by those who have other somewhat contradictory views.[29] It is explicitly the point of view of John Sergeant in his *Method of Science* (1696) where he argues that present disagreement about truth is due merely to logical fallacies in reasoning. Likewise Collins starts with the same premises about the self-evidence of truths,[30] but concludes that perfection of knowledge in either the physical or moral law must come by a gradual development of the power of reason: ' It was by a gradual Progress in *Thinking,* that Men got so much Knowledge in

[28] Bennington, 1784. See especially, Ch. V, Sect. I, p. 177 ff.
[29] Cf. Whichcote, *Works,* I, 69.
[30] Anthony Collins, *A Discourse of the Grounds and Reasons of the Christian Religion*, London, 1737, p. xvii, p. 100. (First ed., 1724.)

Astronomy, as to know that the Earth was an *orbicular Figure*, and that it moves about the Sun. It was by that means, that we are arriv'd at a Demonstration of the Existence of but one God, and at that strict and philosophical Notion of him, as a Being destitute with respect to all our Discoveries.' [31]

Such a point of view seems to us so obvious as to be almost axiomatic. If one comes to examine it however in relation to the presuppositions with which most of the rationalists started, one sees that it does not harmonize very well with the idea of the simplicity and self-evidence of the law of nature or with the democratic and leveling tendency of the whole network of *Aufklärung* thought. It was especially embarrassing to the deists, who wanted to get rid of the necessity of revelation but who were too humane to leave all but the most highly cultivated peoples in religious darkness. Few of the deists were willing to sacrifice their fundamental principle of uniformitarianism for a logical theory of progress; few of them were willing to question with More the simplicity of divine truth or the adequacy of pure reason to arrive at it. They preferred another way out of the difficulty. The compromise most commonly adopted was the view that while man as originally created with all his faculties unimpaired and uncorrupted was capable of knowing divine truth and naturally inclined to follow it, he has now so degenerated as to need either intellectual regeneration or, according to the orthodox opponents of deism, the special help of revelation.

As to the original adequacy of reason and its present inadequacy we have already seen what Whichcote had to say on the subject. Joseph Glanvill makes the same point: ' These [Principles of Truth] are the same that they ever were, though we discern them not so clearly as the

[31] *Ibid.*, p. 8.

Innocent State did.' [32] Culverwel follows Salmasius in
the argument that one only finds the recognition and the
practice of the law of nature among men unspoiled by art.
'Those Nations,' he writes, 'that have more of Art and
Improvement amongst them, have so painted Natures
face, have hung so many Jewels in her eare, have put so
many bracelets upon her hand; they have cloth'd her in
such soft and silken raiment, as that you cannot guesse at
her so well, as you might have done, if she had nothing
but her own simple and neglected beauty: you cannot
taste the Wine so well, because they have put Sugar into
it, and have brib'd your palate. So that the learned
Salmasius will scarce go about to fetch the Law of Nature
from the Jewes principally; you see he chooses to fetch
it rather from a Scythian, from a Barbarian; there he shall
see it without any glosses, without any Superstructures,
without any carving and gilding.' [33] Pufendorf safeguards
his generalization about the power of reason to find out
the law of nature by the phrase 'when unperverted,' and
calls in the help of 'natural Rectitude' as a guide to the
'apprehending Faculty' in things moral.[34] Toland, likewise, establishes the sufficiency of the reason for the perception of moral law but is forced to admit that our
reason is now so corrupt that 'We are too prone to frame
wrong Conceptions and erroneous Judgments of things.' [35]

[32] 'The Agreement of Reason and Religion,' *op. cit.,* Essay V, p. 17.
See also pp. 15-16.

[33] *Op. cit.,* pp. 72-73. But cf. 'All men in the world have not equall
abilities, opportunities, advantages of improving their Reason, even in
things natural and moral, so that Reason it self tells us, that these are
in some measure necessitated to believe others.' *Ibid.,* p. 153.

[34] *Of the Law of Nature and Nations.* . . . Done into English by
Basil Kennett. . . . London, 1729, Bk. II, ch. III, xiii, p. 132, and Bk.
I, ch. III, iii, p. 25. Latin ed., 1692.

[35] *Christianity not Mysterious,* London, 1696, p. 57.

A regeneration of the reason will again enable us to perceive divine truth.[36]

In the anti-deist Clarke one finds perhaps the most clear-cut compromise: (1) Men were originally fully capable of finding out the law of nature for themselves by their reason: 'Indeed in the original uncorrupted State of Humane Nature, before the Mind of Man was depraved with prejudicate Opinions, corrupt Affections, and vicious Inclinations, Customs, and Habits; right Reason may justly be supposed to have been a sufficient Guide, and a principle powerful enough to preserve Men in the constant Practice of their Duty.'[37] (2) Men are now 'strangely *corrupted*' so that they are incapable of discovering moral law: 'The greater part of Mankind are not only *Unattentive*, and basely *Ignorant*; but commonly they have also, through a careless and Evil Education, taken up *early Prejudices*, and many *vain and foolish Notions*; which prevent their natural Understanding, and hinder them from using their Reason in *moral Matters* to any effectual purpose.'[38] (3) They now need the special teaching of revelation.[39] Tindal, the champion of deism against the attack of Clarke, is 'concern'd, and griev'd, to see a Man, who had so great a share of the Light of Nature, imploy it to expose that Light.'[40] Tindal finds no inadequacy in the light itself if it is only given a chance to operate. It does not even need the aid of revelation, for men were of necessity 'created in a state of innocence capable of knowing, and doing all God requires of them.'[41] Christianity has merely sought to restore 'the true primitive, and natural Religion, implanted in Mankind from the Creation.'[42]

---

[36] *Ibid.*, p. 64.

[37] *A Discourse concerning the Being and Attributes of God* . . . , London, 1716, p. 196.

[38] *Ibid.*, p. 276.

[39] *Ibid.*, pp. 154-55.

[40] *Op. cit.*, p. 350.

[41] *Ibid.*, p. 344.

[42] *Ibid.*, p. 348.

It is chiefly owing to this compromise that a rationalism which might at first view be thought to lead logically to an interest in progress through the development of intellect, furnished so much ground for the glorification of primitive and natural man and for theories of degeneration.

III

There is another line of thought to be found in the discussions of the law of nature which is of interest in the development of primitivistic theories, and that is the widespread recognition of benevolence as one of the primary laws of nature. Interestingly enough the theory of benevolence is the one important point which it is necessary to add to the passages from Charron with which we started. The explanation is obvious: most of the discussions of benevolence (that were not direct appeals for charity), in fact most of the expressions at this time of this whole related scheme of ideas that we have been surveying, were evoked by the *Leviathan*. It is doubtful whether in a period such as this, which so generally assumed reason, rather than feeling, to be the dominant factor in the moral and social life of man [43] there would ever have been so much stress laid on benevolence and compassion if it had not been for the aspersions cast on human nature by Hobbes. So much enthusiasm for qualities that one more commonly associates with the emotional than the intellectual life does indeed consort rather oddly

[43] I am using the above circumlocution to avoid if possible the confusion which comes from using the term ' rationalist ' both in the above sense and also in the narrower sense as a term characterizing the thinkers who subscribed to the complex of ideas of the enlightenment described at the beginning of the chapter. I shall probably not be able completely to avoid using ' rationalist ' in these two senses. Confusion arises from the fact that a philosopher may subscribe, as we shall see in the case of Hutcheson, to uniformitarianism and still be an anti-rationalist in ethics.

with the allegiance to reason of most of the divines and philosophers of the period. We shall not comprehensively analyze the attacks made on Hobbes, but shall consider only the reasoning about benevolence which is important in our particular problem. The bearing of the discussion of benevolence on the development of primitivistic thought is clear. If benevolence can be shown to be ' natural ' to man, the goodness of primitive man who lives 'naturally' is almost axiomatic, and the contemporary lack of benevolence confirms the theory of degeneration. The discussion of benevolence in the late seventeenth and early eighteenth centuries is of the utmost importance in the development of eighteenth-century primitivistic theories because it enabled the latter to survive even after their rationalistic foundation had been discarded for an ethics based on feeling. It may be noted in passing that the theory of benevolence not only led to primitivism, but by virtue of the particular turn which it took through its association with its related rationalistic principles it led by another channel, that of utilitarianism, into theories of progress. Of which later.

There were several ways in which writers of this rationalistic period retained so much emphasis on benevolence in their systems of thought as to approach an ethics of feeling. There was in the first place, as Professor R. S. Crane has pointed out, a definite anti-Stoical strain in the thought of the period which, while it does not go over into anti-rationalism, at least acknowledges the importance of the passions as well as the reason in the moral life of man. Professor Crane has called attention to the following extract from the sermons of Charles Hickman: ' Nay, tho' it were a possible thing for a Man to force his nature, and divest himself wholly of his Passions, yet 'tis a question whether the thing were desirable or no. They are the proper season of our Souls, which would be very insipid, and flat without them: The proper motive to encourage, and stir us up to good works, without which (as our Constitution now stands) our Reason would be too weak to support our Vertue, and Man at best would be but a heavy, sluggish, unactive Creature. But to this a *Stoick* may object, that our Passions incline us to evil works, as well as to Good: That they lead us into dangers, and betray us unto sin, and therefore 'tis fit they should be rooted out.' This objection Hickman answers at length and then concludes: ' It is not a sign of *Goodness* in Man, to have no Passion in him, for such a Man is apparently Good for nothing at all. He does not hate his Brother, 'tis true: But then he does not love him neither. He does not oppress his Neighbour perhaps; but withal, he neither pities, nor relieves him. . . .' [44]

In the next place the theologians and philosophers kept benevolence well within their rationalistic systems of thought either by making a recognition of the duty of benevolence towards one's fellowmen part of the intellectual equipment implanted in men's minds by God, or by assuming, not without classical precedent, that reason would naturally lead men to benevolence as one of the primary laws of nature. As to the first, it will be noted that Whichcote speaks of ' that universal benevolence, that God by his own right-hand did sow in the nature of men, and did plant when he made man upon earth, that universal benevolence, which spirits the intellectual world.' [45] The attitude is brought out even more clearly by Culverwel: ' There is no jarring in pure intellectuals; if men were tun'd and regulated by Reason more, there would be more Concord and Harmony in the world. As

[44] *Fourteen Sermons*, London, 1700, pp. 252-65. The theme recurs in several familiar passages of Pope's *Essay on Man*.

[45] *Op. cit.*, II, 222.

man himself is a sociable creature, so his Reason also is a sociable Light. This Candle would shine more clearly and equally if the windes of passions were not injurious to it.' [46] This conception of benevolence as an intellectual quality merged in many writers almost unconsciously into the more typical eighteenth-century view of man as controlled in his natural state by the feeling of pity and compassion. 'Pity, Compassion, and a Fellow-feeling,' writes William Colnett, 'are such natural Passions to Mankind, and so woven into their constitution. . . .' [47] And even the rationalistic Tindal falls into the same vein — 'Man, as our Divines maintain against Hobbs, is a social creature, who naturally loves his own species, and is full of pity, tenderness, and benevolence' — while in the next breath he speaks of reason as leading men into universal love.[48]

The second alternative, the assumption that reason, 'which is the proper nature of man,' will inevitably lead one to the idea that benevolence is one of the primary laws of nature is frequently to be met with.[49] It is, in fact, often combined with the first alternative, as in William Gould's sermon, *The Generosity of Christian Love*: 'God hath fastened on all the Creatures not onely a private desire to satisfie the demands of its own Nature, but a general Charity and feeling of Communion as sociable parts of the Universe or Common Body. . . . Thus the Law and Light of Nature preach down the sordid pursuit of a Private Interest, and proclaim the Excellency of that

---

[46] *Op. cit.,* p. 140.

[47] *A Sermon Preach'd before the Societies for Reformation of Manners* . . . , London, 1711, p. 5.

[48] *Op. cit.,* p. 49. Cf. Joseph Glanvill, *Catholick Charity Recommended in a Sermon,* London, 1669, p. 10.

[49] E. g. Clarke, *op. cit.,* p. 107; and Pufendorf, *op. cit.,* p. 137, where one gets a thoroughly rationalistic statement of the same idea.

Love which *seeketh not her own* as most heroically generous.' [50]

There developed in this line of thought a utilitarian strain which is of the greatest interest in connection with the development of eighteenth-century ethics. Take Richard Cumberland, for example. He argues elaborately that man has a natural tendency towards benevolence by virtue of his physique, his intellect, and his affections.[51] But side by side with this argument is the reasoning used by some of the later utilitarians that there is a natural identification of private and public interests — that the promotion of the good of the whole will naturally make for the good of the individual. The individual is led by his reason to see that benevolence toward his fellows will mean the highest happiness for himself. Cumberland derives all natural laws from this one: ' The greatest Benevolence of every rational Agent towards all, forms the happiest State of every, as of all the Benevolent, as far as is in their Power; and is necessarily requisite to the happiest State which they can attain, and therefore the common Good is the supreme Law.' [52] Cumberland is followed in both lines of thought by Samuel Parker.[53] Parker asserts that the principles of love and tenderness are implanted in man,[54] but to make benevolence doubly sure he reasons that God first designed the happiness of all and then to ensure its realization so ordered things as to make every man's individual happiness depend on his honest and sincere

[50] London, 1676, pp. 12-13.
[51] *A Philosophical Enquiry into the Laws of Nature,* London, 1727, pp. 122-63. (Latin ed., 1672.)
[52] *Ibid.,* p. 41. See also p. 47. And Culverwel, *op. cit.,* ' Mt. Ebal,' p. 87; and Isaac Barrow, *Works,* London, 1830-31, II, 227.
[53] See his acknowledgment of his dependence on Cumberland in *A Demonstration of the Divine Authority of the Law of Nature, and the Christian Religion,* London, 1681, p. ix.
[54] *Ibid.,* pp. 54-55.

endeavours to promote that of the community: ' the most likely way to improve or secure his own private weal is to consult and promote the common good.' [55] He does not see that if man were really as compassionate by nature as he has asserted, man would not need—indeed could not feel—the instigation of private interest. Here we have side by side the two lines of thought, the former of which led directly into primitivism of the most emotional type,[56] and the latter of which contributed to the idea of progress, or more accurately, contributed to the formulation of a mechanism whereby the progress of society was to be ensured. The relation of the latter line of thought to eighteenth-century utilitarianism is even more strikingly brought out in Tindal's statement of it, with its addition of the pleasure-pain test: ' In a word, As a most beneficent disposition in the supreme Being is the source of all his actions in relation to his Creatures, so he has implanted in Man, whom he has made after his own image, a love for his species; the gratifying of which in doing acts of benevolence, compassion, and good will, produces a pleasure that never satiates: as on the contrary, actions of ill-nature, envy, malice, etc. never fail to produce shame, confusion, and everlasting self-reproach.' [57]

[55] *Ibid.*, p. 18.

[56] Cf. Whichcote, *op. cit.*, II, 222-23; William Claggett, *Humanity and Charity of Christians*, London, 1687, p. 5; Isaac Barrow, *op. cit.*, p. 232; John Scott, *The Christian Life*, London, 1681, pp. 36-38. Many of these men have been mentioned by R. S. Crane in a list of references to early discussions of benevolence in his review of Wm. E. Alderman, ' Shaftesbury and the Doctrine of Benevolence in the Eighteenth Century,' *Phil. Quart.*, XI (1932), 204.

[57] *Op. cit.*, p. 17. For a list of references to treatments of the theory that seeking the good of the species will bring the greatest happiness to men and that the good of the individual is the good of the species, see R. S. Crane's review of W. E. Alderman, ' Shaftesbury and the Doctrine of Benevolence in the Eighteenth Century,' *Phil. Quart.*, XI (1932), 205.

IV

So far I have omitted all reference to Shaftesbury from the discussion, even though I have included not only his contemporaries but some writers also whose works appeared after the *Characteristics*. I have purposely reserved all discussion of Shaftesbury's ethics until we were in a position to see its relation to the thought preceding or contemporary with him and to the development of thought after his time. There is very little that is new in the *Characteristics*. Shaftesbury sums up most of the ideas that we have been surveying and adds little more than new emphases and alignments. And it must be admitted, too, that there is very little that is clearly or straightforwardly thought through in his work. But perhaps because of this very eclecticism and confusion, and because of the popularity of the *Characteristics*, Shaftesbury provided an excellent soil for a rich diversity of thought to follow. For this reason he is of even greater importance to the study of the popular dissemination and perversion of certain ideas than some of the more vigorous and original minds that preceded him. By discussing him in relation to Hutcheson who succeeded him I shall try to show in what sense he was a pivotal figure.

The central pre-occupation of eighteenth-century moralists was with two related questions, forced on them by Hobbes. The first concerned the principle of approbation in man — what is his means of distinguishing between right and wrong? — and the second concerned motive — what determines his action? Hobbes had answered the first question with a theory of egoistic hedonism and the second with the principle of self-interest. The answer of the rationalists to both questions was, as we have seen, extremely simple: by reason man both informs himself about right and truth and convinces himself of the wisdom

of following them. Now Shaftesbury, like the Platonists
and rationalists, rejects at the outset both the pleasure-pain
test of right and wrong and the principle of self-interest.
His reasons for rejecting the latter are indeed as cogent
an answer to the rationalists as to Hobbes. Both schools,
of thought, Shaftesbury thought, over-simplified human
nature. ' There are more wheels and counter-poises in this
engine than are easily imagined,' he wrote. ' 'Tis of too
complex a kind to fall under one simple view, or be
explained thus briefly in a word or two. . . . But here,
my friend, you must not expect that I should draw you
up a formal scheme of the passions, or pretend to show
you their genealogy and relation: how they are interwoven with one another, or interfere with our happiness
and interest. . . . Modern projectors, I know, would
willingly rid their hands of these natural materials, and
would fain build after a more uniform way.' [58] This opposition to an exclusive principle of self-interest Shaftesbury
held to consistently from his first published writing, his
Preface to the *Discourses* of Whichcote,[59] to his last.
In regard to the pleasure-pain test, he says flatly that
' pleasure is no rule of good.' [60] There is no stability in
a judgment based on pleasure; what displeases us in one
mood, pleases us in another, and pleasure brings satiety
and disgust. ' Either, therefore, " that is every man's
good which he fancies, [i. e. which gives him pleasure]
and because he fancies it and is not content without it,"
or otherwise, " there is that in which the nature of man
is satisfied and which alone must be his good." ' [61] ' The

[58] ' An Essay on the Freedom of Wit and Humor,' *Characteristics of
Men, Manners, Opinions, Times, etc.,* ed. J. M. Robertson, London, 1900,
I, 77-78.

[59] *Op. cit.,* III, vi-viii.

[60] ' Soliloquy or Advice to an Author,' *loc. cit.,* I, 200.

[61] ' The Moralists,' *loc. cit.,* II, 149.

tutorage of fancy and pleasure, and the easy philosophy of taking that for good which pleases me, or which I fancy merely, will in time give me uneasiness sufficient.' [62] But having first rejected the pleasure-pain test, Shaftesbury then tacitly acknowledges its importance. He does so in the first place by the great stress he puts on pleasure: the pleasure to be derived from the ' natural, kindly, or generous affections ' and the misery from their absence; [63] second, by his gradation of pleasures, with the mental pleasures, identified with or growing out of the natural affections, at the top; [64] third, by his identification of philosophy with the study of happiness, much in the spirit of the utilitarian moral arithmetic: ' If philosophy be, as we take it, the study of happiness, must not every one, in some manner or other, either skilfully or unskilfully philosophise? . . . And therefore this still is philosophy, to inquire where, and in what respect one may be most a loser; which are the greatest gains, the most profitable exchanges," since everything in this world goes by exchange.' [65] Thus while Shaftesbury nominally rejects egoistic hedonism he gives more specific precedent than the other men we have been considering to the later utilitarians who wanted to combine a pleasure-pain test with the principle of the greatest good for the greatest number.

The more constructive side of Shaftesbury's thinking and his relation to the rationalistic solution of the problem of approbation is difficult of analysis, partly because of contradictory statements and partly because of a confusion in his use of terms. The term ' affection,' for instance, he uses in a variety of contemporary senses, and it is sometimes difficult to tell which he intends in a given

[62] ' Miscellany IV,' loc. cit., II, 280.
[63] ' Concerning Virtue and Merit,' loc. cit., I, 292 ff.
[64] Ibid., p. 294.
[65] ' Moralists,' loc. cit., II, 150-51.

instance. He seems to use it oftenest in the sense of
' inclination or disposition of the mind toward something,'
as in the phrase ' affection or aversion '; [66] but again he
uses it to designate moral qualities, as in ' good qualities
and affections, as love to his kind, courage, gratitude, or
pity.' [67] And he sometimes seems to distinguish it from
mental tendencies as in ' his inclinations and affections, his
dispositions of mind and temper.' [68] But in spite of the
uncertainty of interpretation, one may say in general that,
with a very much fuller appreciation of the importance
of the feelings and passions in determining human behavior than most of his immediate predecessors, he
nevertheless, in his earliest writing at least, is inclined to
attach almost as much importance as they to the reason.
The question is of importance because an ethics of benevolence based on feeling leads directly into a sentimental
type of primitivism, whereas an ethics based on the
rationalistic principles of the Enlightenment leads only to
a rationalistic type of primitivism, if any.

Let us follow the course of Shaftesbury's thought. Our
actions, he asserts in the ' Essay concerning Virtue and
Merit,' are determined by our affections and passions,
either the natural affections leading to the good of society
as a whole, or the self-affections leading to private good.[69]
But actions, even those determined by the social affections,
cannot be called virtuous, unless there is in them an element of reflection.[70] ' And thus we find how far worth
and virtue depend on a knowledge of right and wrong,
and on a use of reason, sufficient to secure a right application of the affections.' [71] But confusion comes with

[66] *Op. cit.*, I, 277.
[67] *Ibid.*, p. 266.
[68] *Ibid.*, p. 280.
[69] ' Essay concerning Virtue and Merit,' *loc. cit.*, I, 285 ff.
[70] *Ibid.*, p. 253.   [71] *Ibid.*, p. 255.

Shaftesbury's introduction of the sense of right and wrong which determines our choice. In one passage he does indeed make this moral sense practically analogous to the reflective power and dependent on the development of reason: ' Let us suppose a creature who, wanting reason and being unable to reflect, has notwithstanding many good qualities and affections, as love to his kind, courage, gratitude, or pity. 'Tis certain that if you give to this creature a reflecting faculty, it will at the same instant approve of gratitude, kindness, and pity; be taken with any show or representation of the social passion, and think nothing more amiable than this, or more odious than the contrary. And this is to be capable of virtue, and have a sense of right and wrong.' [72] On the other hand Shaftesbury is so eager to establish this sense of right and wrong as a ' natural ' sense that he sometimes speaks of it as existing prior to and independently of the faculty of reason. ' Sense of right and wrong therefore being as natural to us as natural affection itself, and being a first principle in our constitution and make, there is no speculative opinion, persuasion, or belief, which is capable immediately or directly to exclude or destroy it. That which is of original and pure nature, nothing beside con-trary habit and custom (a second nature) is able to dis-place. And this affection being an original one of earliest rise in the soul or affectionate part, nothing beside contrary affection, by frequent check and control, can operate upon it, so as either to diminish it in part or destroy it in the whole.' [73] He does not quite call the moral sense innate, but insists that it comes from nature: ' if you dislike the word innate, let us change it, if you will, for instinct, and call instinct that which Nature teaches, exclusive of art,

[72] *Ibid.*, p. 266.   [73] *Ibid.*, p. 260.

culture, or discipline.' [74] Even under the terminology of
the doctrine of taste, this sense, he argues, is natural and
instinctive with man, existing prior to culture and art.
' Is there then . . . a natural beauty of figures? and is
there not as natural a one of actions? . . . No sooner are
actions viewed, no sooner the human affections and passions discerned (and they are most of them as soon discerned as felt) than straight an inward eye distinguishes,
and sees the fair and shapely, the amiable and admirable,
apart from the deformed, the foul, the odious, or the
despicable. How is it possible therefore not to own
" that as these distinctions have their foundation in
Nature, the discernment itself is natural, and from Nature
alone "?' [75] Finally in ' Miscellany III ' taste is treated
in one passage as quite distinct from both reason and
conscience: ' Thus we see, after all, that 'tis not merely
what we call principle, but a taste which governs men.
They may think for certain, " this is right, or that
wrong ": they may believe " this a crime, or that a sin;
this punishable by man, or that by God ": yet if the
savour of things lies cross to honesty; if the fancy be
florid and the appetite high towards the subaltern beauties
and lower order of worldly symmetries and proportions,
the conduct will infallibly turn this latter way. Even conscience, I fear, such as is owing to religious discipline, will
make but a slight figure where this taste is set amiss.' [76]
This anti-intellectual temper is in accord with his advice
to Michael Ainsworth: ' But be persuaded, in the mean
time, that wisdom is more from the *heart*, than from the
head. *Feel* goodness, and you will see all-things fair and
good.' [77]

[74] ' Moralists,' *loc. cit.,* II, 135.
[75] *Ibid.,* p. 137.
[76] ' Miscellany III,' *loc. cit.,* II, 265.
[77] *Letters of the Earl of Shaftesbury,* n. p., 1746, p. 26.

Thus we see two divergent tendencies in Shaftesbury, the one to identify the moral sense with reason and make its development dependent on the development of the reflective principle, and the other to stress feeling more than reason and to make the moral sense exist prior to the development of reason and be independent of it and superior to it in power. This conflict in ideas Shaftesbury never faced squarely; he adhered now to the one point of view and now to the other without, apparently, grappling with the fundamental principle at stake. The most that can be said is that he leaned rather more toward the former alternative in his early writing than in his late.

Hutcheson, unlike Shaftesbury, starts out with a clear-cut opposition to the rationalists. He objects to the point of view of the school of Clarke in the first place because the approach to the good by the way of reason is too difficult and uncertain for the generality of mankind:

The weakness of our Reason, and the avocations arising from the Infirmity and necessity of our Nature, are so great, that very few of Mankind could have form'd those long Deductions of Reason, which may show some Actions to be on the whole *advantageous* to the *Agent*, and their Contrarys *pernicious*. The *Author* of *Nature* has much better furnish'd us for a virtuous Conduct, than our Moralists seem to imagine, by almost as quick and powerful Instructions, as we have for the preservation of our Bodys: He has made Virtue a *lovely Form*, to excite our pursuit of it; and has given us *strong Affections* to be the Springs of each virtuous Action.' [78] But his principal ground of objection is more fundamental: that reason is not and cannot in the nature of things be an exciting force. Our actions are determined by our affections and passions and

[78] *An Inquiry into the Original of Our Ideas of Beauty and Virtue*, London, 1725, pp. vi-vii.

even our approbation presupposes a moral sense antecedent to reason. ' All the possible Reasons,' he writes,
' must either presuppose some *Affection*, if they are exciting; or some *moral Sense*, if they are justifying.' [79] Men
may make use of reason to ' compare the Tendencys of
Actions, that they may not stupidly follow the first
Appearance of *publick Good*,' but on the other hand
any mistake which they make will be due not to ' any
Irregularity in the *moral Sense*, but in the *Judgment* or
Opinion.' [80] The idea, held by Shaftesbury, that an act
cannot be called virtuous in which there is no element of
reflection, Hutcheson reduces to an absurdity.[81] He is even
more frankly hedonistic than Shaftesbury, although he at
times has some difficulty in keeping his hedonism dis-
entangled from the principle of self-interest, to which he
was unalterably opposed.[82] He goes so far in his moral
arithmetic as to reduce his moral principles to algebraic
equations, such as the following: ' When in comparing
the *Virtue* of two Actions, the *Abilitys* of the *Agents* are
equal, the *Benevolence* is as the *Moment of publick Good*,
produc'd by them in like Circumstances: or $B = MxI$.' [83]
Professor W. R. Scott has pointed out how Hutcheson
later modified this ethical system to meet the criticism that
his moral sense was a mere instinct by developing a theory
that morality consists neither altogether in feeling nor in
reason, but in will. He also transformed his moral sense

[79] *An Essay on the Nature and Conduct of the Passions and Affections*,
London, 1742 (first edition 1728), pp. 224-25. Cf. *Inquiry*, Treatise
II, Sect. II.

[80] *Inquiry*, p. 186.

[81] *Essay on the Passions*, pp. 234-35, and *Inquiry*, pp. 175-76: ' I
know not for what Reason some will not allow that to be *Virtue*, which
flows from *Instincts*, or Passions,' etc.

[82] See, for instance, *Inquiry*, p. 177.

[83] *Inquiry*, pp. 168-69.

into a moral faculty.[84] But it was his first recognition of
the affections and passions as the exciting force which was
of importance in leading the way from the rationalistic
presuppositions of the seventeenth century towards the
ethics of feeling in Hume.

V

To return to Shaftesbury, I have already pointed out
in another connection a second fundamental contradiction
in his ethical doctrines.[85] His attempt to establish the
moral sense as natural to man, existing in him prior
to education or refinement, led inevitably to certain other
primitivistic presuppositions and inferences. If a moral
sense is natural to us, our untutored ideas and reactions
may be more trustworthy than those acquired by education. Thus, ' Men's first thoughts in this matter [moral
principle of honesty] are generally better than their
second: their natural notions better than those refined by
study or consultation with casuists.' [86] ' For even rude
Nature itself, in its primitive simplicity, is a better guide
to judgment than improved sophistry and pedantic learning.' [87] Again, if the moral sense is natural to man it
must be universal and perhaps in even better operation
among some more primitive nations that have not been
corrupted by luxury than among civilized nations. Thus
Shaftesbury speaks of ' that simplicity of manners and
innocence of behaviour which has been often known
among mere savages, ere they were corrupted by our commerce, and, by sad example, instructed in all kinds of

[84] *Francis Hutcheson, His Life, Teaching, and Position in the History
of Philosophy,* Cambridge, 1900, pp. 213-14.
[85] ' Thomas Blackwell, A Disciple of Shaftesbury,' *Phil. Quart.,* V
(1926), 208-11.
[86] ' Freedom of Wit and Humour,' *loc. cit.,* I, 88.
[87] ' Soliloquy,' *loc. cit.,* I, 215.

treachery and inhumanity. 'Twould be of advantage to us to hear the causes of this strange corruption in ourselves, and be made to consider of our deviation from nature.' [88]

But Shaftesbury was really not so interested in the primitivistic line of development from his premises as he was in another line. He had needed the principle that the moral sense — even a sense of the beauty of virtuous action — was natural to men for his refutation of the self-interest principle; but having vigorously established the former he virtually turned his back on it and its consequences for the more congenial contemplation of the refinement of taste and the development of virtuosity. Unconsciously, with the working out of the idea that a life may have the grace and symmetry of a work of art, Shaftesbury is betrayed into a flat contradiction of his former position that a taste for moral beauty is instinctive with us. He now reasons that ' a taste or judgment, 'tis supposed, can hardly come ready formed with us into the world. Whatever principles or materials of this kind we may possibly bring with us, whatever good faculties, senses, or anticipating sensations and imaginations may be of Nature's growth, and arise properly of themselves, without our art, promotion, or assistance, the general idea which is formed of all this management and the clear notion we attain of what is preferable and principal in all these subjects of choice and estimation will not, as I imagine, by any person be taken for innate. Use, practice, and culture must precede the understanding and wit of such an advanced size and growth as this. A legitimate and just taste can neither be begotten, made, conceived, or produced without the antecedent labour and pains of criticism.' [89] Not only does Shaftesbury thus contradict

---

[88] ' Soliloquy,' *loc. cit.,* I, 226-27. See also ' Essay concerning Virtue and Merit,' *loc. cit.,* I, 291-92.   [89] ' Miscellany III,' *loc. cit.,* II. 257.

his former assertion of the naturalness of the moral sense but in his preoccupation with moral refinement he so far forgets his central principle that the social affections make man's chief end the good of society as to make the artistic life an end in itself.[90]

It is obvious that this last phase of the thought of Shaftesbury, with its emphasis on progressive refinement, is more congruous with a theory of progress than with primitivism; and as a matter of fact there are hints that he had some glimmerings of the idea of evolution even outside of the human species: ' The vital principle is widely shared and infinitely varied, dispersed throughout, nowhere extinct. All lives, and by succession still revives. . . . New forms arise, and when the old dissolve, the matter whence they were composed is not left useless, but wrought with equal management and art, even in corruption. . . . The abject state appears merely as the way or passage to some better.' [91] He speaks in another place of ' the revolutions of past ages, the fleeting forms of things.' [92]

But Shaftesbury has no clear and consistent theory of progress in the human species. The most that one finds in his work is the familiar picture of the rise and fall of nations — ' from woods and wilderness, to cities and culture, again into woods; one while barbarous, then civilized, and then barbarous again; after, darkness and ignorance, arts and sciences, and then again darkness and ignorance as before.' [93] Indeed he was fundamentally too

---

[90] ' Philosophical Regimen,' in *Life, Unpublished Letters, and Philosophical Regimen of Anthony Earl of Shaftesbury,* London, 1900, pp. 48 ff. Prof. Scott, *op. cit.,* pp. 182-83, has pointed out this contradiction in Shaftesbury.

[91] ' Moralists.' *loc. cit.,* II, 110-11.

[92] *Ibid.,* p. 123.

[93] *Philosophical Regimen,* p. 70. The sentence which Mr. Bonar points

loyal to some of the fundamental assumptions of primitivism, if not to primitivism, to grasp any real conception of perfectibility. Simplicity was his great god. He returned to the principle of simplicity as a norm and standard over and over again.[94] Now, as we shall see, it was not until thinkers were willing to leave the safe haven of simplicity and face squarely the prospect of increasing complexity that any real theory of progress and infinite perfectibility was possible. To Shaftesbury the worst that could happen to man was ' a loss even of simplicity, a quitting of that uniform, self-same, divine, and simple principle, for a various, manifold, compound, and changeable one, a composition, mere composition.' [95]

Thus Shaftesbury, starting with a sense of right and wrong that is natural and universal, gradually develops the notion of moral excellence as dependent upon a refined taste for beauty, proportion, and grace in the moral life, consonant with and partly growing out of a taste for those qualities in physical nature and in art, a notion which leads him into an aristocratic exclusiveness that paved the way for the fashionable cultivation of sensibility throughout the century. Hutcheson, on the other hand, is again more single-minded and consistent. This greater consistency was probably partly due to his separation at the outset [96] of the sense of the beauty or deformity in external objects from the sense of beauty or deformity in human actions. He names the former for clearness the Internal Sense, and the latter the Moral Sense. He was thus able to discuss the one without necessarily involving

out (*Moral Sense*, London, 1930, p. 44) as indicating an idea of progress refers only to the development of the individual, not to progress in the species.

[94] See especially the section on Simplicity in the *Philosophical Regimen*.
[95] *Philosophical Regimen*, p. 159.
[96] *Inquiry*, p. vi.

the other in the same conclusions. But his consistency was probably largely due also to his greater and more uniform emphasis on the pre-rational and unreflective nature of the moral sense which we noted before. At any rate Hutcheson keeps more constantly in mind than does Shaftesbury the two corollaries to the idea of the natural-ness of the moral sense: its universality and its uniformity. The universality of the moral sense is proved, he reasons, by the fact that both universal experience and history show that in all nations there are certain actions or affections that always win approbation. The uniformity is proved by the fact that it is always the quality of '*kind Affection*' which wins this approbation.[97] This emphasis on uni-versality and uniformity gives to Hutcheson's moral phi-losophy a much more democratic note than one finds in Shaftesbury. He is never tired of reiterating the statement that 'This moral sense diffuses itself through all con-ditions of life, and every part of it. . . .'[98] The natural moral faculty of the mind and the benevolent affections 'are so common to all mankind, that there are scarce any entirely deprived of any of them,'[99] although humanity, Hutcheson admits, is now so depraved that 'altho' nature has given us all some little sparks as it were to kindle up the several virtues; and sown as it were some seeds of them; yet by our own bad conduct and foolish notions we seldom suffer them to grow to maturity.'[100] Altogether, the ethics of Hutcheson furnishes an admirable basis for sentimental primitivism, first, by the preference that he gives to feeling over reason as the exciting force in action; second, by his insistence on the superior power in human

---

[97] *Essay on the Passions*, pp. 280-81.
[98] *Introduction to Moral Philosophy*, Glasgow, 1753 (second Eng. ed.), p. 19.
[99] *Introduction to Moral Philosophy*, p. 32.
[100] *Ibid.*, p. 33.

nature of the benevolent affections, so that the natural
state of man could be described by him as ' a State of
*Good-will, Humanity, Compassion, mutual Aid, propa-
gating and supporting Offspring, Love of a Community
or Country, Devotion, or Love and Gratitude to some
governing Mind* '; [101] and finally by his emphasis on the
universality and uniformity of this disposition in man
before he had been corrupted by civilization. That
Hutcheson did not himself draw any more specific primitivistic inferences than these, that he actually talked of
savage and barbarous tribes of unbenevolent disposition,
did not in the least disturb his more sentimental followers.

VI

To carry the story of eighteenth-century ethics one step
further before we close, we see in Hume the perfect anti-
thesis to a rationalistic ethics, and that in spite of the fact
that it was his primary purpose to found a *science* of
morals. Hume had an even more potent reason than
Hutcheson for founding an ethical system on feeling
rather than on reason: the doubt that he had thrown on
the ability of reason to do more than form simple perceptions. Gone is the possibility, after this, of basing a
morality on the laws of nature discovered by the reason;
gone the possibility of the old duality of passion and
reason and the supposition that virtue arises only from the
victory of reason over passion. 'Reason is, and ought only
to be the slave of the passions, and can never pretend to
any other office than to serve and obey them.' [102] Reason
is, with Hume, an inert force, incapable of affecting our
passions. ' As long as it is allow'd, that reason has no
influence on our passions and actions, 'tis in vain to pre-

[101] *Essay on the Passions*, p. 201.
[102] *A Treatise of Human Nature*, London, 1739, II, 248.

tend, that morality is discover'd only by a deduction of reason. An active principle can never be founded on an inactive; and if reason be inactive in itself, it must remain so in all its shapes and appearances, whether it exerts itself in natural or moral subjects. . . . Moral distinctions, therefore, are not the offspring of reason. Reason is wholly inactive, and can never be the source of so active a principle as conscience, or a sense of morals.' [103] The distinction of right and wrong is based on feeling alone. ' " Morality " is more properly felt than judg'd of.' [104] To have the sense of virtue, is nothing but to ' *feel* a satisfaction of a particular kind from the contemplation of a character. The very *feeling* constitutes our praise or admiration. We go no farther; nor do we enquire into the cause of the satisfaction. We do not infer a character to be virtuous, because it pleases: But in feeling that it pleases after such a particular manner, we in effect feel that it is virtuous.' [105] Thus Hume's moral sense, in contrast to Shaftesbury's and like Hutcheson's earlier version of it, is based purely on feeling and makes reason, at most, only ancillary. But I shall postpone a more detailed discussion of some phases of Hume's ethics until a later chapter where we can consider it in connection with utilitarianism.

[103] *Ibid.*, III, 5-7.   [104] *Ibid.*, p. 26.   [105] *Ibid.*, p. 28.

CHAPTER II

SIMPLICITY VERSUS LUXURY AND DEGENERATION

I

Before we turn to the more general history of primitivism in eighteenth-century popular literature there is an interesting side eddy to be taken into consideration. As we have seen in the first chapter, the theory of progressive degeneration, which had been an inherent part of primitivism from the time of the first fables of the golden age to the present, but which had been more than once challenged by the 'modernists' of the seventeenth century, was given fresh impetus by the complex of ideas constituting the dominant philosophy of the Enlightenment. It was a logical inference from the uniformitarianism of that philosophy: God has endowed all men, so ran the reasoning, with intelligence sufficient to find out the uniform and eternal laws of nature; if civilized man fails to discover and follow the laws of nature as perfectly as primitive man, it is because his mind and heart have become corrupted by the vices of civilization. This line of argument of the deists and free thinkers was vigorously met, it is true, by a group of Anglican divines in the first half of the eighteenth century. Professor R. S. Crane has pointed out [1] the successive steps by which John Edwards (*A Compleat History or Survey of All the Dispensations and Methods of Religion* . . . , 1699), William Worthington (*An Essay on . . . Man's Redemption*, 1743), and Edward Law (*Considerations on the State of the World*, 1745) worked out, in response to uniformitarianism and its attack on revealed religion, a theory of prog-

[1] 'Anglican Apologetics and the Idea of Progress, 1699-1745,' *Modern Philology*, XXXI, Feb. and May, 1934.

ress in religion which in the hands of the last named
writer at least was integrated into a comprehensive scheme
of history in which progress became a general law of
human life.

In spite, however, of this vigorous antidote, from within
the established Church, to the idea of progressive degeneration, in spite of the fact that the progress of science
in the seventeenth century had favored a general theory of
progress, in spite of the agitation of the question through
the quarrel of the ancients and the moderns, the idea
of degeneration remained one of the popular favorites
in the eighteenth century. Of the popular currency of the
idea about the middle of the century we have the testimony of Chesterfield: 'If we give credit to the vulgar
opinion, or even to the assertions of some reputable
authors, both ancient and modern, poor human nature
was not originally formed for keeping: Every age has degenerated; and from the fall of the first man, my unfortunate ancestor, our species has been tumbling on, century
by century, from bad to worse, for about six thousand
years.' [2] Further testimony is found later in *The Lounger*,
edited by Mackenzie and others, in an article called
'Comparison of Ancient with Modern Times, Much to
the Advantage of the Latter.' This purports to be an
attack on the current doctrine of degeneration of mankind
'both in mental and corporeal endowments.' 'With these
people,' writes the author, 'all science is held to be upon
the decline, arts are retrograde; the greater virtues absolutely annihilated; and morality itself tending fast to
utter extinction.' [3] In reality the article is an ironical

---

[2] *The World*, II (1756), 1181 ff., reprinted in *London Magazine*,
XXV (1756), 491. See also *The World*, I (1764), 449 ff.; also the
Sentimental Magazine, I (1773), 67.
[3] *The Lounger*, I, No. 19 (1787), 172, British Essayist edition. The
article is attributed here to Fraser Tytler.

defence of the idea of degeneration and shows that mankind has only progressed in the refinement of cruelty.

II

One of the main factors in keeping alive the theory of
degeneration in eighteenth-century thought was its usefulness in the popular opposition to the new economic
theories supporting luxury. To review the situation briefly,
England was growing in prosperity during the eighteenth
century; commerce was expanding; industry, with the
invention of machinery, was pushing rapidly forward;
wealth and its concomitant, luxury, were national factors
to be reckoned with. Statesmen and economists were finding it to the interests of the nation, as Kaye has pointed out
in his edition of Mandeville,[4] to displace the popular idea,
inherited from classical thought, that luxury in a nation
goes hand in hand with corruption. Mandeville sums up
in the *Fable of the Bees* the current notions on the subject:
' It is a receiv'd Notion, that Luxury is as destructive to
the Wealth of the whole Body Politic, as it is to that of
every individual Person who is guilty of it, and that a
National Frugality enriches a Country in the same manner
as that which is less general increases the Estates of private
Families. . . . What is laid to the Charge of Luxury
besides, is, that it increases Avarice and Rapine: And
where they are reigning Vices, Offices of the greatest
Trust are bought and sold; the Ministers that should
serve the Publick, both great and small, corrupted, and
the Countries every Moment in danger of being betray'd
to the highest Bidders: And lastly, that it effeminates and
enervates the People, by which the Nations become an
easy Prey to the first Invaders.' [5] With a brutal directness

[4] Bernard de Mandeville, *Fable of the Bees*. With a commentary . . .
by F. B. Kaye, Oxford, 1924, I, xcvii ff.   [5] *Ibid.*, I, 108, 115.

that must have disconcerted the people who wanted to maintain national prosperity without admitting luxury, Mandeville asserted that ' Great Wealth and Foreign Treasure will ever scorn to come among Men, unless you'll admit their inseparable Companions, Avarice and Luxury: Where Trade is considerable Fraud will intrude.' [6] Only in a state of society, contends Mandeville, where there is a fertile soil and happy climate, a mild government and more land than people, may men ' be as Virtuous as they can, without the least Injury to the Publick,' [7] but in this state of society man will be a ' lumpish Machine, without the Influence of his Passions,' like a ' huge Wind-mill without a breath of Air.' [8] We can easily see, says Mandeville further, that ' no Societies could have sprung from the Amiable Virtues and Loving Qualities of Man, but on the contrary that all of them must have had their Origin from his Wants, his Imperfections, and the variety of his Appetites: We shall find likewise that the more their Pride and Vanity are display'd and all their Desires enlarg'd, the more capable they must be of being rais'd into large and vastly numerous Societies.' [9] Mandeville's ingenious apology for luxury, the details of which we need not pursue, fired the opening gun of a controversy on the subject which was waged throughout the century.[10] Setting aside the economic theories developed in defence of luxury, let us follow the series of agitated replies to these theories.

[6] Remark Q, *ibid.,* I, 185.
[7] *Ibid.,* p. 183.
[8] *Ibid.,* p. 184.
[9] ' A Search into the Nature of Society,' *ibid.,* pp. 346-47.
[10] Mandeville's own answer to the attacks on his point of view that appeared before the sixth edition of 1732 may be found in Remark Y, *ibid.,* I, 248 ff.   For an excellent summary by Kaye of the more philosophical attacks on *The Fable of the Bees,* see II, 401-17.   See also Paul

The *London Magazine* seems to have felt itself especially appointed to combat what it considered the materialistic tendency of the age. In September, 1754, ' Civis ' writes in this periodical that ' Amongst the many reigning vices of the present age none have risen to a greater height than that fashionable one of luxury, and few require a more immediate suppression, as it not only enervates the people, and debauches their morals, but also destroys their substance.' [11] He does not so much regret the spread of luxury among the higher classes as among the lower, and advocates the revival of the Elizabethan sumptuary laws for apprentices.[12] Another writer in January, 1756, professes that he is not fond of ' those common place declamations against the degeneracy of the present times ' but nevertheless deplores a present indulgence in luxury so great as to ' threaten the undermining of our constitution and the downfall of our state. . . . Our riches may perhaps be greater than formerly, but I am sure that our virtue is less.' [13] He gives examples of ancient states to prove that ' certain ruin has followed wherever luxury has prevailed.' [14] In September of the same year the *London Magazine* reprints a satire on luxury from *The Connoiseur*.[15] In May, 1758, ' Britannicus ' describes in detail ' to what a degree this pestilence hath spread itself through the nation,' [16] and predicts certain ruin if measures are not quickly taken. 'Aurelius' in December, 1764, is somewhat more temperate in tone, but says that ' A little rational consideration will enable us to discover the

Sakmann's *Bernard de Mandeville und die Bienenfabel-Controverse*, Freiburg, Leipsic, und Tübingen, 1897.
   [11] *London Magazine*, XXIII (1754), 409.
   [12] *Ibid.*, p. 410.
   [13] *Ibid.*, XXV (1756), 15-16.
   [14] *Ibid.*, p. 15.
   [15] *Ibid.*, XXV (1756), 439-40.
   [16] *Ibid.*, XXVII (1758), 223.

kindred links between luxury, rapine, meanness, extrava-
gance, misery, idleness, vice and guilt: for they are of
one family, as scandalous as pernicious, and alike fatally
destructive in their effects.' [17] Another correspondent in
April, 1768, finds Biblical texts to oppose the ' depravity
of the age ' due to luxury.[18] The writer of 'New Thoughts
upon Luxury ' in November, 1772, preaches simplicity
and cites the example of the early Romans who ' did not
think themselves dishonoured by putting their hand to
the plough with their slaves.' [19] In February, 1773, the
magazine prints a ' Lively Portrait of the Fashionable
Luxuries,' [20] and in October, 1774, an ' Essay on Luxury '
in which luxury is said to have poisoned the whole
nation.[21] Finally in December, 1779, appeared a somewhat more extensive essay, ' On Avarice and Luxury, and
their Influence on the Happiness of a Trading People,'
in which the primitivistic implications are made explicit.
Appeal is first made to ' nature ': ' How few our wants!
How easy, and at what small expence are all our natural
desires satisfied! and yet how numerous are our wishes;
and what a vast train of appetites have we created consequent of these, that have no foundation in our nature,
and very remote, if any influence at all, upon our real
felicity.' [22] Comparison is made with the ' brute creation '
that, guided by instinct and natural desire, has happiness.
' But man, anxious to be unhappy, industrious to multiply
woe, and ingenious in contriving new plagues, new torments, to embitter life, and sour every present enjoyment,
has inverted the order of things, has created wishes that
have no connexion with his natural wants, and wants that
have no connexion with his happiness.' [23] Then follows

[17] *Ibid.*, XXXIII (1764), 620.
[18] *Ibid.*, XXXVII (1768), 683-84.
[19] *Ibid.*, XLI (1772), 539.
[20] *Ibid.*, XLII (1773), 68-70.
[21] *Ibid.*, XLIII (1774), 481.
[22] *Ibid.*, XLVIII (1779), 537.
[23] *Ibid.*

the inevitable appeal to primitive man: ' It must have been a considerable time before this vice was known amongst mankind: artless, innocent nature must have been for many ages, and is, to this day, in some remote corners of the earth, an utter stranger to this unnatural inmate. Reason might awaken their fears for futurity, and their caution might teach them, as well as some of the brute creation, to provide against want in times, places, and seasons, where a present supply of the necessaries of life could not be expected. But this caution went no further: this caution begot industry, and prompted them to labour, a thing absolutely necessary as a regimen, and as essential to the health and support of our constitutions as nourishment itself.' [24] The author describes the gradual growth of industry, the development of trade and commerce, and along with them the pernicious love of wealth for its own sake. But even this ' green sickness of the soul ' is not so pernicious as the love of wealth for the sake of luxury, the gratification of the senses: ' Wherever these two daemons, Avarice and Sensuality, take possession of the soul, the whole man is debased, and every principle of moral virtue is eradicated from the mind.' [25] This series of articles may be taken as indicative of the amount of agitation of the issue at the time and as representative of the doctrine which assumed the progressive degeneration of mankind, and found the source of it in luxury and the remedy in a return to primitive simplicity.

This line of reasoning often led to a special primitivistic strain in authors the rest of whose thought is not primarily primitivistic. Henry Brooke, for instance, who is largely anti-primitivistic in his basic philosophy, falls into a radically primitivistic position when he touches on

[24] *Ibid.*, p. 538.   [25] *Ibid.*, p. 539.

luxury, predicting 'the necessity of our growing worse and worse, till the pinnacle of art shall put a limit to desire, till invention shall be exhausted, and not longer prolific of new wants and additional wishes in man. But so long as untried allurements, so long as untasted pleasures, so long as new objects can be set up to our imagination in our eager pursuit after happiness on earth, our wishes will inflame our impatience to reach the prize; in proportion to that impatience our endeavours will be exerted; in proportion to such exertion, the fence of law and morals will be broke through or trampled down; and in proportion to the insufficiency of moral restraints, all sorts of fraud and violence, of licentiousness and corruption, of debauchery and profligacy, must prevail throughout the world.' [26]

Richard Price, again, who has usually been enrolled among the progressivists (a classification, however, which we will see in a later section some reason for modifying) becomes purely primitivistic when, in his discussion of the principles of insurance and annuities, he discusses the effect of luxury on human life. Luxury and the false refinements of 'civil society' bring inevitably in their train vices which as inevitably are responsible for 'that black catalogue of diseases which ravage human life.' [27] The solution is to live 'according to nature.' 'Let us then value more the simplicity and innocence of a life agreeable to nature; and learn to consider nothing as savageness but malevolence, ignorance and wickedness. The order of nature is wise and kind. In a conformity to it consists health and long life; grace, honour, virtue and joy. But nature turned out of its way will always punish. *The wicked shall not live out half their days.* Criminal

[26] *The Fool of Quality*, N. Y., 1860, I, 297-98.
[27] *Observations on Reversionary Payments*, London, 1771, p. 275.

excesses embitter and cut short our *present existence*; and
the highest authority has taught us to expect, that they
will not only kill the *body*, but the soul; and deprive of an
EVERLASTING EXISTENCE.' [28]

Perhaps commoner is the more moderate view of John
Brown in his *Estimate of the Manners and Principles of
the Times*, 1757, that the first effects of commerce are
salutary and useful and that it is only the final stage of
wealth and luxury that brings corruption. 'If we view
Commerce in its first stages,' he writes, 'we shall see,
that it supplies mutual Necessities, prevents mutual Wants,
extends mutual Knowledge, eradicates mutual Prejudice,
and spreads mutual Humanity. If we view it in its middle
and more advanced Period, we shall see, it provides Conveniences, increaseth Numbers, coins Money, gives Birth
to Arts and Science, creates equal Laws, diffuses general
Plenty and general Happiness. If we view it in it's third
and highest Stage, we shall see it change it's Nature and
Effects. It brings in Superfluity and vast Wealth; begets
Avarice, gross Luxury, or effeminate Refinement among the
higher Ranks, together with general Loss of Principle.' [29]
He does not therefore advocate as others had done a return to primitive simplicity or even an attempt to check
the exorbitant trade and wealth of England in an attempt
to bring back her former integrity of manners and principles. He confesses that England is in a dilemma. 'If
our Commerce be maintained or increased, its Effects bid
fair to destroy us: If Commerce be discouraged and
lessened, the growing Power of our Enemy [France]
threatens the same Consequence.' [30] His only solution is
a compromise: 'That Commerce and Wealth be not dis-

[28] *Ibid.*, pp. 275-76.
[29] *Op. cit.*, London, 1757, 2nd ed., pp. 152-53.
[30] *Ibid.*, p. 217.

couraged in their *Growth*; but checked and *controuled in their Effects.*' [31]

III

There is, of course, very little new in these assertions of the inseparability of luxury and degeneration. The idea that virtue and happiness inevitably accompany the austerities of primitive life, a corollary of classical denunciations of luxury, was to be found in the earliest sixteenth-century travel-literature and comes down uninterruptedly into the eighteenth century. What the discussion of luxury — together with actual economic and social dissatisfactions — did help to bring about, however, by forcing the mind into a re-evaluation of cultural refinement, was a renewed burst of enthusiasm for simplicity, the simplicity of life according to nature. In the value set on simplicity, propaganda against luxury joins hand with one of the leading ideas of the philosophy of the Enlightenment.

In the midst of sentimental passages in novels and poems designed for the world-weary of the eighteenth century, it is refreshing to pick up the charming letters of Lord Edward Fitzgerald to his mother and get a version of the popular enthusiasm for primitive simplicity never designed for the reading public. The letters help to restore our faith in the genuineness of an enthusiasm that seems often in its conventionalized expressions to be little more than a literary fashion. There can be no doubt of the sincerity of Lord Edward Fitzgerald, whether he is writing from the wilds of the new world, where he was adopted by the Bear Tribe of Red Indians,[32] or praising his friend Thomas Paine,[33] or renouncing his hereditary title in a burst of

[31] *Ibid.*
[32] Gerald Campbell, *Edward and Pamela Fitzgerald*, London, 1804, p. vii.
[33] Thomas Moore, *Life and Death of Lord Edward Fitzgerald*, 1831, I, 170-1.

revolutionary enthusiasm.[34]   Gallant soldier, loyal Irish-
man, and organizer of the Irish rebellion of 1798, he lived
his thirty-six years so richly and rewardingly that one
wonders why he should ever have been tempted to aban-
don that life with its warm personal ties for the simple
life of the North American Indian. He made two journeys
to America, one in 1781 and the second in 1788-89. The
letters I quote were written during the second visit. The
first is written from New Brunswick, a country ' almost
all in a state of nature, as well as its inhabitants,' who
' ought to be the happiest people in the world but they
do not know it.' [35]   On September 2, 1788, Lord Edward
writes to his ' Dearest, dearest Mother,' ' I know Ogilvie [36]
says I ought to have been a savage, and if it were not that
the people I love and wish to live with are civilized people,
and like houses, etc., etc., I really would join the savages;
and, leaving all our fictitious, ridiculous wants, be what
nature intended we should be. Savages have all the real
happiness of life, without any of those inconveniences, or
ridiculous obstacles to it, which custom has introduced
among us.' [37]   And then he adds playfully, ' To bring
things home to one's self, if *we* had been Indians, instead
of its being my duty to be separated from all of you, it
would on the contrary, be my duty to be with you, to make
you comfortable, to hunt and fish for you. . . .   There
would then be no devilish politics, no fashions, customs,
duties, or appearances to the world, to interfere with one's
happiness.' To be sure, he adds, the poor ladies would
have to join in the work. ' Now the dear Ciss and Mimi,
instead of being with Mrs. Lynch, would be carrying wood

---

[34] Campbell, *op. cit.*, p. vii; and I. A. Taylor, *Life of Lord Edward
Fitzgerald*, London, 1903, pp. 133-51.

[35] Moore, *op. cit.*, I, 78.

[36] His step-father, formerly his tutor.

[37] *Ibid.*, I, 91.

and fetching water, while ladies Lucy and Sophia were cooking or drying fish. As for you, dear mother, you would be smoking your pipe. Ogilvie and us boys, after having brought in our game, would be lying about the fire, while our squaws were helping the ladies to cook, or taking care of our papouses: all this in a fine wood, beside some beautiful lake, which, when you tired of, you would in ten minutes, without any baggage, get into your canoes and off with you elsewhere.' [38] And again, concerning his perilous voyage down the Mississippi to New Orleans, he writes, ' I should like to give you an account of my voyage, but it would be too long: it has done me a great deal of good. I have seen human nature under almost all its forms. Everywhere it is the same, but the wilder it is the more virtuous.' [39]

Heighten this whimsical playing with the idea of the simple life and subtract the humor, and it becomes in the hands of the anonymous author of *The Adventures of Emmera; or, the Fair American*, a novel of 1767, something like this: ' In a word, I rendered myself as complete a master of European manners as I was able; and it was the reflections I drew from that knowledge which induced me to seek for more natural ideas and purer practice in a country just on the verge of cultivation — for I laid it down as a maxim, that a country must abound in the necessaries of life before the superfluities could deluge it with luxury and vice. . . . Never can I allow the vain sophistry of modern times to influence my judgment so vilely as to render it more agreeable to reside in the midst of the most frightful vices, the most consuming debauchery, the most disgusting immorality — merely because this horrible detail is tinsell'd over with the varnish of riches, arts, elegance and dissipation — rather than pass

[38] *Ibid.*, pp. 91-92.　　　　[39] *Ibid.*, p. 158.

through life amidst simplicity and innocence, labour, health and chearfulness — Reflect one moment on the contamination of European refinements — What a contrast!'[40] Sir Philip Chetwyn, the son of the speaker of these sentiments, runs across Emmera, the fair American, just at the moment when her father is dying. He finds in her the ideal of simplicity and virtue. She has been bred to an abhorrence of the evils of the world and a love of the simple life of solitude among the friendly Indians. Her debates with Sir Philip on the relative advantages of solitude and social life form the main substance of the book. After an unsuccessful attempt to live in England, Emmera convinces Sir Philip that the life of nature is best. 'Oh! Sir Philip,' cries Emmera, 'my blood runs cold to think of the intolerable wickedness in the world, and amongst people that think themselves refined in their understandings and polished in their ideas! These are the people that call the Americans savages! Virtuous and amiable people! I have quitted the neighbourhood of men to become the companion of brutes!'[41] And Sir Philip concludes: 'The most unusual strength of reason in my amiable wife, has long drawn a most striking comparison between society and retirement — A comparison, founded in the clearest observation, the most judicious remarks, the most humane attention to the interests of mankind: Can I, who have been the constant witness to the truth of her conclusions — who have tasted such genuine happiness in her favourite solitude — Can I be blind to the voice of reason, sense and understanding! — Nothing could ever speak stronger to me than the experience I have had — I embrace with joy that life I know to be happy —'[42]

This phase of primitivism has been so often illustrated

[40] London, 1767, I, 7-9.   [42] Ibid.. pp. 195-96.
[41] Ibid., II, 185.

that there is little need to dwell on it further.[43] I shall confine myself, therefore, to mentioning a few examples either neglected or only slightly treated by other writers on the subject.

Both Mr. Fairchild and Mr. Bissell mention Charlotte Lennox's *Euphemia,* but both pass over what to me is the most interesting point. Except for an example or two of fashionable sensibility transferred to the savage, and examples of Indian gravity and eloquence,[44] Mrs. Lennox's picture of the Indians, colored presumably by her early recollections of them in American frontier posts, is not a thoroughly primitivistic one. 'The whole fashion of their lives,' she writes, ' is of a piece, hardy, poor, and squalid; and their education, from their infancy, is solely directed to fit their bodies for this mode of life, and to form their minds to a capacity of enduring and inflicting greatest evils.' [45] She is a degree too honest to deal otherwise with her early impressions, however fashionable the opposite point of view was. Mr. Fairchild has noted the disparity between the praise of the savage, guarded as it is, in *Euphemia* and her earlier unidealized picture of him in *Harriot Stuart,* 1751,[46] but there is another shifting of her point of view that has more significance. It is when Mrs. Lennox comes to theorize about the values of civilization that she belies most strikingly her early impressions, and chooses for quotation from the work of Abbé Raynal those passages that contrast, to the disparagement of civilization, the simplicity of savage life with the ener-

---

[43] Cf. H. N. Fairchild, *The Noble Savage,* N. Y., 1928; C. B. Tinker, *Nature's Simple Plan,* Princeton, 1922; and Benjamin Bissell, *The American Indian in English Literature of the Eighteenth Century,* New Haven, 1925.

[44] *Op. cit.,* London, 1790, IV, 69, 176.

[45] *Ibid.,* III, 25.

[46] *Op. cit.,* pp. 158-59.

vating complexities and the injustices of life in cultivated society. The quotations are apparently taken, with the change of only a few words, from the English translation of Raynal's history of the Indies: *A Philosophical and Political History of the Settlements and Trade of the Europeans in the East and West Indies*, translated from the French . . . by J. Justamond, M. A., London, 1776.[47] The passage which Mrs. Lennox quotes is as follows:

" It is in the nature of man, says that sensible and elegant writer," pursued he, " that we must look for his means of happiness. What does he want to be as happy as he can be? — present subsistence; and if he thinks of futurity — the hopes, and certainty of enjoying that blessing. The savage who has not been driven into, nor confined within the frigid zones by civilized societies, is not in want of this first of necessaries; if he lays in no stores, it is because the earth and the seas are reservoirs, always open to supply his wants — fish and game are to be had all the year, and will supply the want of fertility in the dead seasons.

" The savage indeed, says the elegant writer whose words I quote, has no house well secured from the access of external air, or commodious fireplaces; but his furrs answer all the purposes of the roof, the garment, and the stove. He works but for his own occasions; sleeps when he is weary, and is a stranger to watchings and restless nights. War is a matter of choice with him; danger, like labour, is a condition of his nature, not a profession annexed to his birth — a national duty, not a domestic servitude.

" The savage is serious, but not melancholy; his countenance seldom bears the impression of those passions and disorders, that leave such shocking and fatal traits on ours. He cannot feel the want of what he does not desire; nor can he desire what he is ignorant of. Most of the conveniences of life are remedies for

[47] Cf. Anatole Feugère, *Un Précurseur de la Révolution, L'Abbé Raynal*, Angoulême, 1922, especially Ch. IV, sect. I, ' Le Goût de L'Exotisme,' p. 99 ff., and Ch. V, ' L'Art d'Utiliser les Hommes: Raynal et ses Collaborateurs,' pp. 176 ff.

evils he does not feel. He seldom experiences any of that weari-
ness that arises from unsatisfied desires; or that emptiness and
uneasiness of mind, that is the offspring of prejudice and vanity.
In a word, the savage is subject to none but natural evils."

My philosopher, observing I listened to him with pleasure,
went on with his quotations. "What greater happiness than this,
says the Abbé, does the civilized man enjoy? His food is more
wholesome and delicate than that of the savage; he has softer
clothes, and a habitation better secured against the inclemencies
of the weather. But should he live under a government, where
tyranny must be endured under the name of authority — to what
outrages is not the civilized man exposed! If he is possessed of
any property, he knows not how far he may call it his own; when
he must divide the produce between the courtier, who may attack
his estate; the lawyer, who must be paid for teaching him how
to preserve it; the soldier, who may lay it waste; and the collector,
who comes to levy unlimited taxes." [48]

'It must be confessed,' Mrs. Lennox adds at the end,
'this picture though a little overcharged, is not ill drawn.'
Now had she followed Raynal also in his description of
the American Indian, the general tone of her own description of the Indians would have been quite different, for
Raynal has much to say of their regard for each other,[49]
their innate benevolence,[50] and of their power of reason
'which had not been misled by prejudice, or corrupted by
passions,'[51] but which served, without government, to
establish harmony and security among them. It is quite
clear that it is only when she is roused by the consideration
of luxury and its consequences that she is willing to throw
in her lot unreservedly with the primitivists. There could
be no better testimony to the popularity of the line of

[48] *Op. cit.*, III, 29-32. Cf. Raynal, *op. cit.*, V, 130-33.
[49] *Ibid.*, IV, 439.
[50] *Ibid.*, pp. 440-43. Cf. also the description of the 'Caribs,' III,
274 ff., and the Brazilians, III, 134 ff.
[51] *Ibid.*, IV, 438.

reasoning which linked primitivism with the attack upon luxury.[52]

A poem of 1779 which I have not seen mentioned in writings on primitivism, speaks for itself in the title: *The Injured Islanders, or the Influence of Art upon the Happiness of Mankind*. Like the poem, *Otaheite*, 1775, it takes its inspiration from the idyllic life of that island, but is an even more clear-cut presentation of the simplicity-luxury issue. It is an address of Oberea, the queen of Otaheite, to Captain Wallis, imploring him to return and restore her to her rightful power and the islanders to their former peace and happiness. She contrasts the present state of the island with its former condition, ' Ere Lux'ry taught Ambition to be great — ':

> Canst thou forget, how cheerful, how content
> Taheitee's Sons their Days of Pleasure spent!
> With rising Morn they sought the healthful Stream,
> And walk'd, or work'd till sultry Noon-tide came,
> Then social join'd, from vain Distinctions free,
> In Mirth convivial round the spreading Tree,
> While tuneful Flutes, and warbling Wood-notes near,
> In rival Strains still charm'd the list'ning Ear:
> At grateful Eve they mix'd the artless Tale,
> The Jest, the Dance, the vegetable Meal;
> Paid the last visit at some Fountain's Head,
> To cleanse, and cool them for the peaceful Bed;
> Deem'd the bright Sun declin'd for them alone,
> These Isles the World, and all the World their own.
>   Where smiles the Land where fewer Ills assail?
> Where fewer Fears, or Passions can prevail?
> No Serpents here their poison'd Volumes wreathe;
> No tainted Gales with fell Diseases breathe;

[52] It should be noted that Raynal's work as a whole is much more than a simple invective against luxury, in its far-reaching analysis of the European situation. He even sees that certain types of luxury are a wholesome incitement to industry. *Ibid.*, V, 50 ff.

> No varying Arts to multiply Desires,
> No Av'rice chills, and no Ambition fires;
> Each Blessing granted as our Wishes rise,
> We live, and love—the Fav'rites of.the Skies. . . .[53]

Arts and industry seem contrary to the real interests of man. What can be their ultimate benefit?

> Say to what tend these forward Views that raise
> Presumptuous Mortals to their Maker's Ways?
> To what can Arts, or Industry aspire?
> What proud Ambition's utmost Aims desire?
> But cheerful Ease, that wants nor Toil nor Skill;
> The Sun can give it, and the cooling Rill,
> Prolifick Earth the balmy Blessing shows
> In Fruit-clad Hills, and Valleys of Repose,
> Such as in Pomp of vary'd Dies display
> This beauteous Island to the Beams of Day —
> Such as perennial charm the loit'ring Swain
> On Mat'vai's Banks, or sweet Poparra's Plain;
> Ah! blisful Seats of Innocence and Ease!
> Ere Pride-born Commerce taught it's Pow'r to please —
> Ere Wants created, kindled new Desires —
> Ere tend'rest Passions felt consuming Fires. . . .[54]

She calls on Wallis to hasten back to her from the land 'where Arts engender Strife,' and she ends with a prayer to the 'mighty Tané' in which she somewhat naïvely reserves to herself, out of the products of civilization, only Captain Wallis himself:

> Or far remove, if Vengeance be forgot,
> These Injur'd Isles to some sequester'd Spot,
> Some placid Corner of the boundless Main,
> Unmark'd by Science, unexplor'd by Gain,

[53] *The Injured Islanders; or the Influence of Art upon the Happiness of Nature*, London, 1779, ll. 251-80.
[54] Ll. 209-24.

> Where Nature still her Empire safe may hold
> From foreign Commerce, Confidence, and Gold,
> From foreign Arts — from all that's foreign free,
> Save Wallis only — if approv'd by Thee.[55]

I mention *Ouâbi; or, the Virtues of Nature*, a late eighteenth-century poem of the North American Indian by Mrs. S. W. A. Morton, of which Mr. Bissell has given a summary, only to show how it too fits into this same line of discussion. It is the familiar story of the European who seeks the relief of the virtue and justice of the savage after the corruption of a luxury-loving people. This situation, although somewhat weakened by the fact that Celario is a fugitive from justice in his own country, gives Mrs. Morton a chance to expand on the degeneracy of civilized man,

> Where soft luxuriance spreads her silken arms,
> Where gairish fancy leads the soul astray,
> And languid nature mourns her slighted charms.[56]

She enumerates the vices that spring from this luxurious life—revenge, malice, duplicity, slander, insolence, pride, envy, neglect, fear, jealousy, suspicion, fraud, reproach, meanness, affectation, passion.[57] The contrast with the Indians who ' tread the path, which INNATE LIGHT inspires ' [58] is inevitable:

> *Native reason's* piercing eye,
> *Melting pity's* tender sigh,
> *Changeless virtue's* living flame,
> *Meek contentment*, free from blame,
> *Open friendship's* gen'rous care,
> EV'RY BOON OF LIFE IS HERE! [59]

[55] Ll. 375-82.
[56] *Op. cit.*, Boston, 1790, p. 9.
[57] *Ibid.*, p. 17.
[58] *Ibid.*, p. 51.
[59] *Ibid.*, p. 27.

Mrs. Morton gives us in almost every detail just what one might have expected and predicted. It is in the stage adaptation of the poem by James Bacon in *The American Indian; or, Virtues of Nature*, that one finds the unexpected turns that make the pursuit of ideas through popular literature such an entertaining game. He follows Mrs. Morton's story and point of view fairly faithfully until he comes to the denunciation of luxury. At this point patriotism conquers moral indignation, and he substitutes for Mrs. Morton's description of the vices of civilization a panegyric of the English king and government! [60] He also gets somewhat confused on the philosophy of natural goodness, and lets the Indian maiden praise the European for *his* innate virtues. The fortunes of an idea are indeed precarious.[61]

IV

Perhaps a fitting conclusion to this section will be a brief survey of the work of a miscellaneous author who is an excellent example of the popularizer who appropriates as literary material any idea that happens at the

[60] *Op. cit.*, London, 1795, p. 6.

[61] For the sake of completeness I quote from Mackenzie's *The Man of the World*, 1773, a somewhat earlier treatment of the same theme of the European in America: 'When we consider the perfect freedom subsisting in this rude and simple state of society, where rule is only acknowledged for the purpose of immediate utility to those who obey, and ceases whenever that purpose of subordination is accomplished; where greatness cannot use oppression, nor wealth excite envy; where the desires are native to the heart, and the languor of satiety is unknown; where, if there is no refined sensation of delight, there is also no ideal source of calamity; we shall not less wonder at the inhabitants feeling no regret for the want of those delicate pleasures of which a more polished people is possessed. Certain it is that I am far from being a single instance, of one who had even attained maturity in Europe, and yet found his mind so accommodated, by the habit of a few years, to Indian manners, as to leave the country with regret.' London, 1773, II, 251.

moment to serve his purpose, from the slogans of early eighteenth-century optimism to revolutionary generalizations on liberty and equality. I refer to Samuel Jackson Pratt, 1749 to 1814, who wrote chiefly under the name of Courtney Melmoth. Starting his career with ordination in the Church of England, he abandoned the ministry for the stage in Dublin and London; failing there, he travelled about the country for a time telling fortunes, until he discovered that he could make more money telling the fortunes of humanity at large through the printed page. The title of his works, *Tears of Genius, or the Death of Doctor Goldsmith, The Pupil of Pleasure, The Tutor of Truth, Travels for the Heart, Shadows of Shakespeare, a Monody on the Death of Garrick,* are indicative of the way he did it. But he attained a considerable popularity in his time, his poem *Sympathy* going through many editions, and he was at least significant enough as a poet to be satirized by Byron in the first (manuscript) version of *English Bards and Scotch Reviewers.*[62]

The most interesting of Pratt's works for our purposes — it is hard to know how to classify it — is *Liberal Opinions, upon Animals, Man, and Providence. In Which are Introduced Anecdotes of a Gentleman,* 1775-77, but we shall also make use of the two poems, *Sympathy,* 1781, and *Humanity, or the Rights of Nature,* 1788. *Liberal Opinions,* through most of the six volumes of which runs the thread of the story of Benignus, is an informal, essay-like treatment of the problems of happiness and suffering, the origin of evil, and the principles of conduct. Benignus is a youth with a ' natural inclination to gentleness ' who has acquired a 'degree of primitive purity' in his ideas by reading the Bible and old numbers of the *Spectator.* Starting out at sixteen with a fortune of twenty thousand

[62] D. N. B.

pounds and the belief that to be good is to be happy, he gives away his fortune indiscriminately, hoping to win gratitude and fidelity in return. The results, alas, are quite different from what he had anticipated, and he retires to die, a complete misanthrope, finding only in ' the brute, the insect, and the reptile ' those ' endearing qualities ' that he had looked for in vain in man. But before he dies he writes his voluminous memoirs.

The idea in which Pratt is chiefly interested in *Liberal Opinions* is degeneration. It forms the starting point of his reasoning. He sums up as follows what the memoirs will serve to prove:

First,

To be good, would, to all intents and purposes, be to be happy, had not man degenerated in the extreme; and had not his worldly interest prevailed over the prospects and promises of futurity.

Secondly,

That the world is permitted to exist, for the same reasons it was spared in years which are far behind, when the Omnipotent declared with his own sacred voice that — if ten, or even five, just people could be found, the city (over which the almighty arm of vengeance, was raised in suspension) should be spared.

Thirdly,

That, the perversion of money, and the abuse of riches, has contributed more to the corruption of human nature, over every part of the habitable globe, than any other thing, since the invention of a commerce with it.

Fourthly,

That, this world (and more particularly the polished and voluptuous parts of it) would be intolerable, to a truly good mind, and, of all possible places of torment, the most severe, (to men engaged in society, but unengaged in its general aims) were it not for two reasons, which will not only be fully given in the promised histories — but may be briefly seen in the conclusive parts of these volumes.[63]

He gives us a picture of the early stages of society when ' the earth was a common property ' followed by the stage when ' indolence seized upon the comforts which had been acquired by industry ' and one human creature usurped dominion over another.[64] ' At length through the natural chain of consequences, we are arrived at the *crisis*. We are polished, populated, and refined in the extreme. Distinctions are so minute, property so tenacious, splendor so superior, and trade so jealous, that no distress you observe should surprise you.' [65]

Pratt expresses more emphatically the part that luxury plays in bringing about the degeneration of man in his poem, *Humanity*, where he gives a series of pictures of benevolence among the negroes, whom he frequently refers to as Indians, who were ' peaceful and blest where rich Bananas grew ' before they had been corrupted by the white man:

> Lo, as the Muse to Anticosta steers,
> Mid'st the wild waves Humanity appears!
> Escap'd the wreck, although their barks were lost,
> Whole crews were dash'd upon a savage coast;
> The coast, tho' savage, there the Christians find,
> Each God-like feeling in an Indian mind,
> For touch'd by cries that pierc'd the piny wood,
> The natives sought the margin of the flood,
> Then as th'expiring Christians caught their view,
> To human grief the generous Indians flew,
> The social passion glowing in his face,

[63] London, 1775-77, II, 101-3. The two reasons given in a later passage are faith and religion.
[64] *Ibid.*, pp. 58-59.
[65] *Ibid.*, p. 63.

> Thus spoke a Chieftain of the sable race:
> " Haste children haste, behold where brothers lie, —
> Rise strangers rise, the hand of help is nigh:
> Men like ourselves throughout the globe command,
> The shelt'ring bosom and the aiding hand,
> All, all are kinsmen of a different hue,
> Our faces vary, but our hearts are true;
> Ye poor white wanderers on our bounty thrown,
> Your griefs are sacred and your wants our own."
> This said, he gently to his Cottage led,
> Smil'd on his guests and yielded up his bed;
> Then watch'd till morn, a guardian at the door
> Bless'd and was bless'd — *could a Christian more?* [66]

Then follows the usual contrast between civilization and
primitive simplicity:

> In polish'd arts unnumber'd virtues lie,
> But ah! unnumber'd vices they supply;
> Here, if they bloom with ev'ry gentler good,
> There are they steep'd with more than savage blood;
> Here, with Refinement, if sweet Pity stands,
> There Luxury round them musters all her bands;
>
> .   .   .   .   .
>
> O Power of mercy, that suspends the rod!
> O shame to man, impiety to God!
> Thou polish'd Christian, in th'untutor'd see,
> The sacred rights of sweet Humanity. [67]

And the progress of corruption among the negroes:

> The work of Christians this, whose lawless rage
> Taught milder savages foul war to wage;
> Christians taught savages new modes of strife,
> And burst asunder all the ties of life;
> Christians taught savages to worship gold,
> Till, for their idol, sons and sires were sold. [68]

---

[66] *Op. cit.*, pp. 71-72.   [67] *Ibid.*, pp. 38-39.   [68] *Ibid.*, p. 22.

It is interesting to note that Pratt, like so many other authors, forgets his theory of degeneration when he comes to speak of England as a nation and describes its progress from ' Barbaric Ignorance ' to ' Justice and Law.' [69] This exception aside, however, luxury he considers to be the universal cause of progressive degeneration.

To turn back to *Liberal Opinions* again for the author's conclusions, one is surprised to find that having taken as his theme contemporary depravity, its causes and remedies, its relation to the problem of happiness, Pratt allows himself in the fifth volume the relief of a long soliloquy to establish the theory that ' Whatever is, is right! ' [70] And instead of giving us any solution to the problem with which he started, he ends his six volumes somewhat tamely with Golden Rules of Oeconomy: ' Liberty is independence, and slavery is a state of pecuniary obligation.'

Now for the other side of the picture. In the poem *Sympathy*, Pratt attempts a sketch, ' and only a sketch,' of the then fashionable ' Sympathetic Principle, or Social Principle ' derived quite clearly, whether directly or indirectly, from the ethics of Hume and Adam Smith. The poem is mainly descriptive of the outward signs of the sympathetic principle which he conceives not only to link together all humanity even in its primitive state —

Lo! the rude savage, naked and untaught,
Shares with his mate what arts and arms have caught; — [71]

but to pervade all nature as well.[72] To the reader's surprise, however, Pratt in this case works the ethics of sympathy, which in *Humanity* he was later to use for anti-slavery and anti-luxury propaganda, into a *defence*

[69] *Ibid.*, pp. 52-53.
[70] *Op. cit.*, V, 113 ff.
[71] *Op. cit.*, London, 1781, p. 17.
[72] *Ibid.*, pp. 5 ff.

of luxury by way of the principle of utility. After a
picture of commercial activity he writes:

> Gain, pleasure, passion, property, induce
> Each single man to study general use.
> Thus nature and necessity agree
> The social chain to stretch from land to sea.
> Thus e'en the miser; tho' his sordid soul,
> Loves but himself, befriends perforce the whole.[73]

The fact that this statement is a typical expression of the
theory of the natural identification of selfish and social
interests, more typical of the Mandevillian and Benthamite
type of utilitarianism which made almost no call on sympathy, than the Hume-Smith utilitarianism which depended on sympathy, is not so startling as the fact that
this new point of view brought Pratt into an explicit
contradiction of the position he had taken in regard to
luxury and degeneration in *Liberal Opinions* and was
again to take a few years later in *Humanity*. In contrast
to his other attitude he now defends luxury and gold
itself, the symbol of luxury:

> . . . tho' stigmatis'd with rage,
> Thro' many a rash, declamatory page,
> The gorgeous ruin by each bard decry'd
> In tuneful scorn or philosophic pride.[74]

Gold cannot be blamed, he now says, for the degeneration
of man. Before ever gold was discovered crime and
cruelty were abroad in the land:

> Ev'n in those times which raptur'd bards have sung,
> When nature triumph'd, and the world was young,
> Blest days! whose charms so many lays rehearse,
> Blest days, alas! which only bloom in verse — [75]

The only thing that distinguishes savage from social man

---

[73] *Ibid.*, p. 31.   [74] *Ibid.*, p. 33.   [75] *Ibid.*, p. 36.

is the *mode* of the crime and we must conclude that the vices are the same — ' Conclude that Man, not Gold, is still to blame.' [76] Fortunately for Pratt his readers and admirers, among whom he numbered, in the case of *Sympathy*, Gibbon, Lowthe, Beattie, Potter, Hayley, Sheridan, and Seward,[77] were more moved by the sentiments expressed than arrested by the line of reasoning.

It must be confessed that the defence of luxury exemplified in *Sympathy* is the exception and not the rule in popular literature at this time. Popular literature tends toward conservatism rather than radicalism. Novels, poetry, and pamphlets were used a little later, it is true, by revolutionary propagandists for the dissemination of radical ideas, but for every radical novel or poem of that period one can find at least three that either satirize the new or seek to re-express the old. In the case of the controversy over luxury the public found itself face to face with a new economic situation and new economic theories. The prudential maxims which had been held sacred by countless generations before were threatened. The alternative looked dangerous, not to say reckless. It violated the first principles of health, of morality, of private and public economy as the public had been taught them. Instinctively the writers who represented this public called on every sort of authority possible to combat the threatening relaxation of the moral fibre of the nation. Classical ethics, orthodox theology, the testimony of travellers among primitive tribes, all were called in to oppose the economic theory which admitted luxury as a necessary concomitant of national prosperity. Most useful of all to these writers was the way of thinking of the rationalists of the early part of the century which equated the idea of simplicity with ' what is right according to nature.'

[76] *Ibid.*, p. 37.   [77] *Ibid.*, p. v.

CHAPTER III

From the Light of Nature to Impulse

I

It may be observed by even a casual reader of primitivistic literature in the eighteenth century that there was a transition during the century from a rationalistic primitivism at the beginning, which tended to derive the qualities of goodness and sagacity in the savage from the unobstructed operation of the ' light of reason,' to a more emotional, sentimental, and antinomian primitivism which became increasingly the favored type as the century progressed. The former strain, so far as it had philosophical antecedents, was derived from the fundamental principles of the philosophy of the Enlightenment which we surveyed in the first chapter, and the latter either from the benevolence-principle of that philosophy, or from the ethics of the moral sense and of taste. In the period with which we are dealing, 1750 to 1815, the latter is the predominant type, but there is a lingering rationalistic tradition.

The early rationalistic type of primitivism is well illustrated by a letter from North Carolina quoted by Toland early in the eighteenth century. The emphasis, it will be seen, is on the irrationality of the life of Christians compared with the tranquillity of mind and happy quietude of spirit among the rational Indians. ' Yes, Sir, it is these very Indians that have made me blush for shame to be a Man, and yet so little reasonable; and to carry the name of a Christian, and yet so remote from the practice of an Evangelical life. We know our Saviour's precepts without observing them, and they observe them without knowing him: were they to have all the Gospel word by heart, they could not practice it with more exactness and strictness then they do it already.' [1] The Indians, writes this correspondent, on being urged to become Christian, replied, 'You would . . . have us become Christians? well, to what end and purpose? Is it to make us better than really we are, or is it not rather to make us as wicked and vicious as yourselves, to render us Adulterers, Whore-masters, Lyars, Murtherers, Robbers, without faith, honor, or honesty, minding nothing but how to deceive one another, and to destroy you upon pretence of Justice? Is this a party to choose, and to oblige us to renownce the simplicity of our manner of life, and the sweet tranquility of mind we now enjoy?' [2]

Examples of the praise of primitive man both for his knowledge of the law of nature and his willingness to follow it are numerous in the first half of the century, but as our present concern is with the second half, we shall look rather for the later and transitional expressions of this point of view. Thomas Amory, for example, as strong a believer in the ' *eternal law of reason* ' as his predecessors, drew, in *The Life and Opinions of John Buncle, Esq.*, the same primitivistic inferences that some of them had done, even though he was writing after the mid-century: ' . . . *moral truth*, right and wrong, good and evil, the doing as we would be done by, and acting towards all men as they really are, and stand related in society; these things are as evident to the understanding, as light and colors are to the eye, and may be called the intellectual, moral sense. Here needs no deep learning, or trouble and expence of education, but the same truths are as evident, and as much seen and felt by the learned and

---

[1] John Toland, *A Collection of Several Pieces*, London, 1726, II, 425.
[2] *Ibid.*, p. 427.

unlearned, the gentleman and the ploughman, the savage or wild *Indian*, as by the best instructed philosopher.' [3]

Very much the same line of reasoning is used at about the same time — somewhat humorously, it is true — by Bampfylde-Moore Carew in his popular book [4] best described by its own title-page: '*An Apology for the Life of Bampfylde-Moore Carew* . . . Commonly Known throughout the West of *England*, by the Title of King of the Beggars; and Dog Merchant-General. Containing, An Account of his Leaving *Tiverton* School, at the Age of Fifteen, and Entering into a Society of Gypsies; His Many and Comical Adventures, More Particularly, a Full and Faithful Relation of his Travels Twice through Great Part of *America*, his Manner of Living with the Wild *Indians*, his bold Attempt in Swimming the River *Delaware*, and many other Extraordinary Incidents; His Return Home, and Travels since in *England*, *Wales*, *Scotland*, and *Ireland*. The Whole Taken from his Own Mouth.' The King of the Beggars, on leaving the friendly Indians and crossing the river into Pennsylvania adopts the dress and demeanour of the Quakers. He thereupon makes the following reflection: ' Here Reader, it will be necessary to remark, that as our Hero is no longer among the simple and honest *Indians*, who are not enough polish'd to forget the Dictates of Nature, but follow her in all their Ways, who have not Art enough to deceive, but speak what they think, and act what they say; as he is no longer amongst such, but amongst a polish'd People, whose Knowledge has taught them to forget the ways of Nature, and to act everything in Disguise; whose

[3] London, 1756-66, II, 311-12.
[4] Cf. Bampfylde-Moore Carew, *The King of the Beggars,* ed. C. H. Wilkinson, Oxford, 1931, pp. vii-viii on the popularity of the book. (First published in one form in 1745; in the form of the *Apology* in c. 1750.)

Hearts and Tongues are almost as far distant from one another, as the North from the Southern Pole, and who daily over reach one another in the Occurrences of Life: We hope it will be no Disgrace to our Hero, if among such he appears as polish'd as the best, and puts on a fresh Disguise as often as it suits his Conveniency.' [5]

A treatment of the Indians, largely religious in character, retains many of the earmarks of rationalism even though it was written in the third quarter of the century. I refer to *The Female American; or, The Adventures of Unca Eliza Winkfield.* The opening episode of the story is reminiscent of the Pocahontas story, except that there is no such dramatic contrast between blood-thirsty and vengeful chieftians and benevolent princess as was to appear later in Davis's version of the story. Instead the Indian councillors after stating their claims against their prisoners with gravity and temperateness, dispassionately decree their death. They calmly and methodically cut off the heads of the first five of them before Unca, the Indian princess, touches Mr. William Winkfield with her wand and so saves him for herself. He finds her not only extremely beautiful, but, more important, in possession of an understanding ' uncommonly great, pleasantly lively, and wonderfully comprehensive, even of subjects unknown to her ' ! [6]

Most of the rest of the story deals with the adventures of Unca Eliza, the daughter of Unca and William Winkfield, among the Indians who come annually to worship at their shrine on an uninhabited island upon which she has been cast. She conceives the idea of converting them to Christianity and discourses to them first through the lips of a huge idol. In spite of this somewhat fantastic

[5] *Ibid.,* p. 58.   [6] London, 1767, I, 15.

and juvenile setting, the discourses themselves are purely rationalistic in nature. ' I remembered,' says Unca Eliza of her experiences with the Indians, ' when I was in England, that I used to look into some of the deistical writers in my uncle's study. These writers laboured to prove, that Christianity was repugnant to plain uncorrupted reason. Yet I found this assertion entirely false; for, here a people, who had no other guide but their reason, no sooner heard but they soon embraced it.' [7]

II

So far I have been giving a few examples of more or less consistent reasoning about primitive man on the basis of rationalism. Rather more interesting are the transitional examples that show the growing popularity of the idea that one's emotions and instincts are a better guide to action than one's reason. Of the transitional type is a passage in *Chrysal, or the Adventures of a Guinea,* 1760-65, attributed to Charles Johnstone. The most significant passage is a dialogue about the Indians between a British general and an officer in charge of Indian troops. The officer demurs at the policy of inaction which the general has ordered, saying that the Indians who judge things ' only by common sense' will interpret such a policy as cowardice. The general urges him to devise some reason for his action that will satisfy the Indians. ' " Really, Sir, not I! " ' replied the officer, ' " I never was good at devising reasons, destitute of truth, in my life; and have entirely forgot the practice since I have conversed with the Americans, who are far from being such fools as they are too generally thought to be. Though they have not the advantages of learning, they see by the

[7] *Ibid.*, II, 61-62.

light of natural reason through all the boasted wiles of policy; and as they never mean deceit themselves, detest it in others, however speciously disguised; nor ever place confidence a second time, where it has been once abused." ' [8] But as Johnstone is also inclined toward the more sentimental type of primitivism, we find in reading on a few lines: ' " Treat them with candour, probity, and tenderness; and they will return them tenfold, in all their intercourse with you; as on the other hand, they seldom fail to retort the contrary treatment with severe usury. Nor are they to be blamed. In all their dealings with the *Europeans,* they find themselves imposed upon in the grossest manner; in a manner not fit to be practised even with brutes. Their sensibility is quick, and their passions ungoverned; perhaps ungovernable: How then can it be wondered at, that they make returns in kind, when ever they find opportunity; and become the most dangerous enemies? Whereas if those passions were attach'd by good treatment, they would be the most affectionate, steady and careful friends." ' [9] But once more there is a shift in point of view. Reverting to the first, rationalistic, interpretation, the speaker now concludes that when he treats the Indians as rational creatures he finds no difficulty in dealing with them.[10] A further echo of rationalism is found in Johnstone's *Arsaces, Prince of Betlis* in which he speaks of the depraved Bedouins' having lost all traces of the ' rules of conduct, and mutual intercourse invariably imprinted by the hand of Nature.' [11] This blending of the two conceptions of primitive man in the works of a single writer is fairly typical of the more popu-

[8] London, 1771, III, 141-42.
[9] *Ibid.,* pp. 142-43.
[10] *Ibid.,* p. 143.
[11] London, 1774, I, 21. Cf. the description of the Byrsans, I, 105.

lar. handling of the material at this period. The characterization of the Indians from *Chrysal* above cited was used a few years later by Nicholas Creswell in his diary in which he purports to record his impressions during a journey to America in 1774-1777. It is probable that both Johnstone and Creswell were using the same source.[12]

The transition from a rationalistic primitivism to the more emotional and sentimental type may be interestingly seen in some of the Indian plays of the century, particularly in the adaptations of the popular *Arlequin Sauvage,* a French play by Louis François Delisle de la Drévetière, first produced in Paris in 1721.[13] The earliest of the adaptations, James Miller's *Art and Nature,* 1738, was followed by John Cleland's *Tombo-Chiqui,* 1758, and John Fenwick's *The Indian,* in 1800. Of the three, *Tombo-Chiqui* is the nearest to the original. Miller's version is a close translation of the fundamental parts of the play, but he has incorporated with these a farcical love intrigue in which Truemore, the hero, and Flaminia, the heroine, both employ as a go-between the parasite, Outside, who is really intriguing against both. I quote from Cleland's Advertisement in regard to the history of the play: ' The first plan of the following Dramatic Entertainment was taken from nature itself, by Monsieur Rodot, who, after having filled very eminent posts in Canada, died superintendant of the Marine Classes in France. It was from his dictating, and at his suggestion and intreaty, that his friend the Abbot Alainval threw the character of a young savage, that had belonged to Monsieur Rodot into a dramatic form; in a piece to which he gave the title of

---

[12] *The Journal of Nicholas Creswell, 1774-1777,* London, 1925, p. 120.
[13] *Receuil de Pièces de Théatre,* Dublin, 1749. See the discussion of the play in G. Chinard, *L'Amérique et le Rêve Exotique,* Paris, 1913, pp. 221 ff.

Harlequin Sauvage, and which was received in France
with the highest applause. A very ingenious gentleman
of our nation, in a play called Art and Nature, also ex-
hibited this character on our stage, but with unequal
success, perhaps because he had incorporated the subject
with a very indifferent piece of Rousseau's, entitled *Le
Flateur.'* [14]

The story so far as it concerns the Indians is very simple.
The hero brings an Indian (Julio in *Art and Nature,*
Tombo-Chiqui in Cleland's play, and simply Arlequin in
the original) back from the West Indies with him. As
Truemore, the hero of *Art and Nature,* explains, ' The
pure natural Wit, strong good Sense and Integrity of
Soul which appear'd in every thing he said, induc'd me
to bring him into *Europe.* I shall take great Pleasure in
seeing pure simple Nature in him oppos'd to Laws, Arts
and Sciences amongst us.' [15] The Indian is used as a
humorous means of satire on the customs of polite society,
the law, the unequal division of property. The emphasis
throughout—and here both of the early English versions
follow the French very closely—is on the rational quality
of the savage. He comes, he tells Sir Simon Dupe in
Art and Nature, ' from the Country of Woods and Forests, where there is not a Mortal of us that know one
Word of the Laws, but we are all naturally wise and
honest enough; we have no need of being forc'd to do our
Duty; we are so very ignorant, that mere natural Reason
is enough for us.' [16] He cannot understand why a people
endowed with reason to tell them what is right from what

[14] *Tombo-Chiqui,* London, 1758, Advertisement.
[15] London, 1738, p. 17.
[16] *Ibid.,* p. 25. Cf. Cleland, *op. cit.,* p. 14, and L. F. de Lisle de la
Drévetière, *Arlequin Sauvage,* ed. N. C. Goodyear, N. Y. and London
1928, p. 18.

is wrong should need laws to make them seek the good and shun evil.[17]   He is totally incapable of comprehending the advantages of riches: 'You are Fools because you eagerly pursue useless Trifles; you are Poor, because you place your sole Happiness in Money, instead of enjoying full Nature as we do, who in order to possess ev'ry thing without Restraint, monopolize nothing; you are Slaves to your Possessions, which you prefer to your Liberty, and your Brethren whom you'll hang for taking a trifle of that which is of no use to your selves; and you are Ignorant, because all your Wisdom consists in the knowledge of the Laws, whilst you neglect pure Reason which wou'd prevent your having any occasion for 'em.'[18]   There is one fine bit in *Art and Nature* suggestive of later educational discussion which does not appear in the other versions. The intriguer, Outside, is trying to win Julio to his side, and the Indian calls him a fool for his pains.

Outs.   Thou art the Fool to think me so; 'tis nothing but the Prejudice of thy poor Education.
Julio.   No, Friend, 'tis the Prejudice of Nature and Reason, yours is the Prejudice of Education: you must have tutor'd yourself with a Vengeance before you could break your Nature, and get rid of all Truth and Honesty thus—[19]

And again in *Art and Nature* alone the Indian is allowed all but the last word: 'Come along with me then, I'll take you to a Country where we shall have no need of Money to make us happy, nor Laws to make us wise; our Friendship shall be all our Riches, and Reason our only

[17] This section is somewhat reduced in *Art and Nature* where it is put in a dialogue between the Indian and Violetta instead of the hero and the Indian.   Cf. *Arlequin Sauvage*, p. 9 ff.
[18] *Art and Nature*, pp. 39-40.   *Arlequin Sauvage*, p. 52.
[19] *Art and Nature*, p. 72.

Guide; we may not say a great many fine things but
we'll take care to do 'em. . . . Let us hear no more then
of your Laws, your Arts, or your Sciences, for they are
good for nothing, by what I have seen yet, but to give
Knaves an Advantage over honest Men, and Fools Authority over wise ones—No, no, let us go, and enjoy
ourselves, and be as happy as Nature and Common-Sense
can make us.' [20]

Now let us turn to John Fenwick's *The Indian*, written
considerably later. Fenwick has taken various incidents
of the Arlequin story, combined them with a different
love story, and laid the scene in Spain. Itanoko, the Indian, is a nephew of Diego, the son of his sister and an
Indian. The striking thing about this later version is that
almost all the rationalistic philosophy has been dropped
out and Itanoko is now presented as a creature of feeling,
of instinctive benevolence. He is introduced on the scene,
bringing in a poor man to his uncle with the words,
' Thank him for the benefit he confers on you! He is in
distress, and has chosen you to relieve his wants,' while
his uncle exclaims ' Damme! but this ignorant Indian will
ruin me by his benefactions!' [21] Throughout the play the
Indian follows his benevolent impulses rather than the
light of reason. It is unnecessary to follow the episodes
in detail; the key-note of the treatment is sufficiently
indicated in the prologue where we are asked:

> Cannot a simple Indian. . . .
> With purest Flame acknowledge Love's sweet dart,
> And only speak the language of the heart? [22]

[20] *Ibid.*, p. 77.
[21] London, 1800, p. 7.
[22] Other Indian plays of the century are: *The Choice of Harlequin, or
the Indian Chief; a Pantomimical Entertainment*, London, 1782 (in
which the Indian Chief is conspicuous by his absence). *The Savages;*

We might in like manner contrast the seventeenth century Montezuma and Pizarro plays with eighteenth century
versions of the same stories, but here the contrast is not
so striking, for the demands of heroic tragedy called out
many of the same qualities of high emotional stress that
the later primitivist so loved to dwell on. As this group
of eighteenth-century plays and poems, derived largely
from Marmontel's *Les Incas* and Kotzebue's *Die Sonnenjungfrau,* and *Die Spanier in Peru,* has been somewhat
more fully discussed than the plays with which we have
just dealt, I shall make only a few observations in
passing.[23] In the first place, in spite of the fact that these
plays are usually cited in primitivistic discussions, there
is very little real primitivism in them. The Inca civiliza-
ton could hardly be regarded, even in the infancy of
archaeology, as primitive except by comparison with the
most advanced European civilization. That it was regarded even in the seventeenth century as far from primitive is evidenced by the lament of the priests of the sun
in Davenant's *Cruelty of the Spaniards of Peru* for their
former primitive innocence and freedom.[24] In spite of
the great display of sensibility, greatness of soul, and
heroic attitudinizing on the part of Peruvian heroes, the
writers who followed Kotzebue had very little of the
primitivistic point of view. In *The Virgin of the Sun,*
for instance (I am quoting from the Plumptre version)

or *Harlequin Wanderer,* London, 1792. James Bacon, *The American
Indian; or, Virtues of Nature,* London, 1795. George Coleman, the
Younger, *Inkle and Yarico,* London, 1787. Richard Cumberland, *The
West Indian,* London, 1771. Charles Dibden, *The New Serio-comic
Pantomime, Called Ko and Zoa, as Performed with Great Applause at
the New Theatre, Saddler's Wells,* 1803. John Gay, *Polly, an Opera,*
London, 1729. Robert Rogers, *Ponteach; or The Savages of America, a
Tragedy,* London, 1766.

[23] Cf. Bissell, *op. cit.,* pp. 118-27, 148-50, 154-62.

[24] London, 1658, p. 3.

Alonzo leaves the rapacious Spaniards for the mild and benevolent Peruvians—not to adopt the life of the Peruvians but to give them the civilization of the Spaniards: ' I will go, he said, among these mild and benevolent people, and by cultivating their minds, and instructing them in the arts of civilized life, become their friend and benefactor.' [25] Similarly in *Pizarro* (in the Sheridan version) Alonzo tells what he has accomplished among the Peruvians:

To him I should not need to urge the foul barbarities which drove me from your side; but I would gently lead him by the hand through all the lovely fields of Quito; there, in many a spot where late was barrenness and waste, I would show him how now the opening blossom, blade, or perfumed bud, sweet bashful pledges of delicious harvest, wafting their incense to the ripening sun, give chearful promise to the hope of industry. This, I would say, is my work! Next I should tell how hateful customs, and superstitions strange and sullen, would often scatter and dismay the credulous minds of these deluded innocents; and then would I point out to him where now, in clustered villages, they live like brethren, social and confiding, while through the burning day Content sits basking on the cheek of Toil, till laughing Pastime leads them to the hour of rest—this too is mine!—And prouder yet—at that still pause between exertion and repose, belonging not to pastime, labour, or to rest, but unto Him who sanctions and ordains them all, I would show him many an eye, and many a hand, by gentleness from error won, raised in pure devotion to the true and only God!—this too I could tell him is Alonzo's work! [26]

There is indeed in *The Virgin of the Sun* a hint of the ' beautiful soul ' in Cora, the priestess of the sun, who, uninstructed in the principles of right and wrong, pursues the path ' of nature and innocence ':

[25] Anne Plumptre, *The Virgin of the Sun*, London, 1799, p. 17.
[26] London, 1799, pp. 42-43.

Cora.   I swore to obey the ordinances of our temple.
Alonzo.   And what do they enjoin you?
Cora.   I know not. My father told me, that by whomsoever
            virtue was held sacred, its precepts would be fulfilled
            without particular instruction. To me virtue is sacred.
Alonzo.   And know you then what constitutes virtue?—Alas!
            your uncorrupted soul is ignorant of the terrible
            distinction between virtue as founded in the eternal
            principles of nature, and virtue as constituted by the
            distorted imaginations of fancies.[27]

And in the speech of the High Priest in defence of mercy
there is an interesting appeal to the doctrine of taste. The
cruelly severe laws, he explains, governing the virgins
of the sun may have been necessary in ' those rude times
when your illustrious ancestors first established the worship of the sun.' But a series of years ' has changed what
was then a forced obedience to the laws of order, into
an inward feeling of their beauty, and where this rules,
compulsive institutions are no longer necessary.'[28] Kotzebue in this passage has merely: ' Aber eine lange lange
Reihe von Jahren hat das Gesetz des Schicklichen in das
Gefühl des Schicklichen verwandelt.'[29]

Thomas Morton, in *Columbus; or a World Discovered,*
1792, which combines the discovery of America by Columbus with the Cora and Alonzo story of the City of the
Sun, makes use of this same episode to write a popular
diatribe against the force of custom.[30]

Perhaps the most typical anti-rationalistic passage occurs
in Helen Maria Williams' poem, *Peru,* which tells the
story of Pizarro and the conquest:

[27] *Op. cit.,* p. 25.
[28] *Ibid.;* p. 95.
[29] ' Die Sonnenjungfrau,' in *Deutsche Schaubühne,* Augsburg, 1788-
1802, XXIX, 318.
[30] London, 1792, p. 55.

Nor less for thee, blest Region, favour'd Clime!
The Virtues rose, unsullied, and sublime.
There, tender Charity, with ardor warm,
Spread her wide mantle o'er the shiv'ring form,
Chear'd with the festal Song her lib'ral toils,
While in the lap of Age she pour'd the spoils.
Simplicity in each low Vale was found.
The meek Nymph smil'd with Reeds and Rushes crown'd:
And Innocence in light, transparent Vest,
Mild Visitant! the gentle Region blest;
In her soft smile beam'd love, and artless grace,
And glow'd celestial beauty in her face:
Light as her snowy vesture sweeps the ground
Fresh flow'rets spring, and shed their odours round:
As from her lip enchanting accents part,
The sweet tones thrill thro' each responsive heart.[31]

Sotheby's *Siege of Cuzco,* in spite of the heroics among
the Peruvians, adds little that is new or important, and
Montezuma is only important for stressing sensibility
somewhat more than the other versions had done.[32]

III

There was one primitive quality which rationalistic
and sentimental primitivists could both logically hold.
It will be remembered that the one principle upon which
Cambridge Platonists, rationalists, and moral sense philosophers all insisted was the principle of benevolence,
whether this was regarded as a primary law of nature
or a natural affection. It is not surprising that from such
a universal belief in the benevolent character of human
nature, in opposition to the view of Hobbes and Mandeville, should have arisen a literature of primitivism that

[31] London, 1784, Canto I, ll. 47-62.
[32] Sometimes attributed to Henry Brooke but in reality only corrected
by him for an anonymous friend. Cf. *Poetical Works,* Dublin, 1792, I, ix.

dwelt upon the benevolence of primitive man, especially when it was so happily reinforced by the new accounts of the South Sea Islanders in the third quarter of the century.

Not only did the desire to believe in a doctrine of natural benevolence arise as a reaction to the egoistic hedonism of Hobbes and the even more irritating form of the same thing in Mandeville; it was further stimulated by the doctrine of the depravity and degeneration of man's nature called forth in response to the Mandevillian defence of luxury. But the Methodistic emphasis on the corrupt heart of man instigated just as vigorous a protest as that directed against either egoistic hedonism or against the cycle of thought about luxury and degeneration. George Whitefield, for instance, about the middle of the century seems to have left consternation in his wake by his attack on human nature. It is difficult to find out just which sermons caused the outcry, but we know that he was preaching in London in the winter of 1749-50 and making dramatic use of an earthquake to arouse the terrified inhabitants of that city to a sense of sin; and that he was preaching throughout Great Britain until August, 1751, when he again sailed for America.[33] Some time during that interval in England he must have made the remark that ' Man is by nature half-brute, and half-devil,' a ' doctrine made notorious by the press and rung through the streets and highways of G. B.' according to a contemporary statement.[34] The *Gentleman's Magazine* for 1751 is alive with defences of the natural goodness of man in reply.[35] One defender of Whitefield, it

[33] A. D. Belden, *George Whitefield, the Awakener,* London, 1930, pp. 184-87.
[34] *Gentleman's Magazine,* XXI (1751), 457.
[35] For the letters of controversy see *Gent. Mag.,* XXI (1751), 115, 152, 274, 304, 400, 446, and 457.

is true, says that men ought not so much to object to being called half-devil for the 'devil himself was a superior work of deity,'[36] but the reminder seems not to have lessened the indignation. If Whitefield's doctrine is true, writes Publicola, the soul of the child must come into the world corrupt either from its parents or from God. Proving the first supposition improbable and the second impossible, he reinforces his argument for the goodness of man's nature by an appeal to the tradition of the 'better notions' of even the heathens (Greeks) on this head.[37] Theophilus proposes inscribing on Mr. Wh-t-ld's door the following verses:

> Here lives one by *nature half-brute* and *half-devil*,
> Avoid him ye wise—tho' he speak kind and civil.
> The *devil* can seem like an *angel of light*,
> And *dogs* look *demure,* the better to bite.[38]

Thus, it may be noted in passing, the evangelical doctrine of corruption which directly encouraged a primitivism of universal degeneration gave rise indirectly, by the protest it evoked, to a primitivism based on the doctrine of natural benevolence.

But the layman of the eighteenth century had more to contend with than the aggressive evangelical pronouncement that his heart was desperately wicked. If he turned indignantly from that, feeling no such corruption, he was likely to encounter either a frigid rationalism which, while it did not arouse his anger, satisfied him even less, or the survival of seventeenth-century Puritanism, which taught him the unpalatable doctrine of self-suppression. No wonder that he turned in relief to an ethics that let him believe that his natural feelings were right and good, and even more to the corollary that if he fol-

[36] *Ibid.,* p. 152.   [37] *Ibid.,* pp. 446-47.   [38] *Ibid.,* p. 115.

lowed his natural instincts he could not go wrong. How much simpler than finding out the laws of nature by the light of reason! To support the pleasant view that his salvation depended on following his natural instincts, he went about finding seeds of compassion in even the most depraved, and natural rectitude of feeling in the child of nature. The semi-savage people of the Piedmont were used by a correspondent in the *Edinburgh Magazine* to prove the ' Natural Benevolence of Mankind.' ' I return to my text: *Man is naturally good.* And he who relies fully upon this, is right twenty times to one against him who distrusts it; provided he is just and tolerant.' [39] ' Many an untutored mind,' wrote the author of ' Thoughts on Disinterested Virtue' in the *London Magazine,* ' throbs with the love of goodness, when the profound enquirer is insensible . . . Among the rudest nations, and in the rudest ages, the great lines of morality are accurately delineated.' [40] Lawrence Sterne, not a layman it is true, roused some of his contemporaries by his defence of human nature from ' the rough usage she has met with from the satirical pens of so many of the French writers, as well as of our own country, who, with more wit than well-meaning, have desperately fallen foul upon the whole species, as a set of creatures incapable either of private friendship or public spirit, but just as the case suited their own interest and advantage.' [41] He tells the story of the wicked and profligate Alexander, tyrant of Pheres, who burst into tears at a performance of the story of Hecuba and Andromache: ' . . . then Nature

[39] *Edinburgh Magazine,* I (1785), 499.

[40] *London Magazine* enlarged, II (1784), 222.

[41] *The Sermons of Mr. Yorick,* London, 1766, I, 112. Cf. Macmahon's attack on Sterne, *Essay on the Depravity and Corruption of Human Nature,* London, 1774, pp. 167-69.

awoke in triumph, and shewed how deeply she had sown
the seeds of compassion in every man's breast; when
tyrants, with vices the most at enmity with it, were not
able entirely to root it out.' [42] All of which was taken
by the popular writers to prove that the benevolent affections ' proceed from a principle, which is simple, original,
interwoven in the human constitution.' [43] ' Nor is there
any more difficulty or impropriety,' writes Charles Bulk-
ley, another apologist for human nature, ' in supposing
that man should be made naturally benevolent, than there
is in supposing that he should be made naturally rational
or intelligent. Accordingly we find that a principle of
universal benevolence makes an essential part of his
internal frame.' [44] Man, and man alone among created
beings, has done violence to his nature in not recognizing
it for what it is: ' Such then is MAN, thus venerable in his
frame, thus godlike in his nature! How glorious would
have been his history; how exalted his attainments; how
exquisite and permanent would have been the felicity
of this lower world, had man been duly conscious of
himself! But alas! whilst other creatures around us remain inviolably true to the original order of their being,
it is MAN, and MAN alone, revolts! ' [45]

The quality of benevolence is so universally attributed
to primitive man in primitivistic literature of the second
half of the century that illustration cannot be inclusive.
Perhaps the anonymous novel called *The School for
Fathers; or the Victim of a Curse. A Novel, Containing
Authentic Memoirs and Anecdotes, with Historical Facts,*

[42] *Ibid.,* p. 87.
[43] ' Remarks on the Benevolent Affections,' *Edin. Mag.,* N. S. XX
(1802), 9.
[44] *Apology for Human Nature,* London, 1797, pp. 22-23.
[45] *Ibid.,* pp. 33-34.

1788, will picture the benevolent Indian as well as any.
Matilda's husband, a royalist, has been imprisoned during
the course of the revolutionary war in America and is
left with her children undefended and starving. In this
condition she and the children are found by the ' Gentle-
minded' Indian chief, Logan. '" I ask not," said he,
" what country you are of. Whether you belong to our
brother on the other side of the lake; or whether you are
an enemy to us and to him. I see you are in distress;
that is country enough for an Indian to pour the balm
of consolation into the wounds of adversity. The great
Spirit suffers his creatures to be afflicted, to teach them
wisdom, and to inspire man with compassion one toward
another." [46] The Indian hero is undoubtedly intended
to represent the Logan of the famous speech preserved
by Jefferson in his *Notes on Virginia,* 1784, and popular
as a recitation speech for school boys for a dozen years
before that.[47] The first sentence of the speech had furnished the clue to the character: ' I appeal to any white
man to say, if ever he entered Logan's cabin hungry, and
he gave him not meat; if ever he came cold and naked,
and he clothed him not.' [48] Logan, in the fictional version of the story, takes Matilda to his home where she is
' charitably sustained by the humanity of these so im-
properly styled savages.' [49] During the course of her stay,
Logan, whose wife and children had been murdered by
the white men, conceives a deep love for Matilda and
tries to persuade her to stay with him—in a strictly Platonic relation: '" Child of affliction, thy husband, thy
loved partner, though separated from thee, is still living.
I ask thee not to supply the place of my beloved Atilla.

[46] London, 1788, I, 226.
[47] *Writings of Thomas Jefferson,* Washington, 1904, II, 88-92.
[48] *Ibid.,* p. 89.   [49] *School for Fathers,* p. 227.

Yet my eyes have never looked on woman since her death,
till I beheld thee. But thy children may supply to me
the loss of my own; and the hand of Logan shall defend
their mother from evil. I will respect thee; and if thou
canst not love me like thy husband, call me thy brother;
and Logan shall suffer death before his beloved sister
shall be injured: is not the wampum still in thy
hand?" ' [50] Matilda pleads the necessity of a return to
her friends at Albany, at which Logan nobly offers to
sacrifice his love and accompany her thither. But the
sacrifice was too much for his noble heart. Taking his
leave of her, ' with a fearful solemnity of countenance,
he said, " I have brought you to a place of safety; and
Logan has no more to do with life. May the great Spirit
protect you, and re-unite you to the happiest of men!
Logan has drank of the bitter cup of affliction; but this
is the last draught. Farewell!" Saying which, he struck
a dagger into his breast, and falling at her feet, expired
without a groan.' [51]

A very simple episode of benevolence on the part of a
negro is to be found in *A Brother's Advice to His
Sisters:* ' I saw an honest negro, not long since, as he
was walking toward Deptford, at the rate of about five
miles an hour, stop short, in passing an old sailor, of a
different complexion, with but one arm and two wooden
legs—It was my fortune, I say, to have the luxury to watch
this worthy savage take three halfpence and a farthing,
his little all, out of the side pocket of his tattered trow-
sers; and wrap them up in a bit of an old hand-bill, which
held his tobacco, when he was so rich as to have any;
force them into the weeping sailor's retiring hand; wipe
his eyes with the corner of his blue-patched jacket; and
walk away so happy, and so fast—that I was obliged to

    [50] *Ibid.,* pp. 231-32.   [51] *Ibid.,* p. 237.

put your friend Sport into a Canterbury gallop, to get up to the dog, in order to shake him by the hand.' [52]

IV

Episodes of benevolence such as the above abound in eighteenth-century popular literature. The reading public loved to drop an inexpensive tear with the giver of alms and the comforter of misery.[53] But the enthusiasm for benevolence in the eighteenth century actually issued in more than the words of sentimental literature: it played its part in the launching of various humanitarian movements and was especially prominent in anti-slavery propaganda. The study of the anti-slavery movement might very properly have a place in this book, but it is such a large and far-reaching subject in itself that I prefer to reserve it for a separate study to follow. To illustrate, however, the extent to which the idea of benevolence enters into the literature of propaganda, I shall cite Mrs. Anna Marcia Mackenzie's *Slavery; or the Times*—an *Uncle Tom's Cabin* of the eighteenth century.

As a device to win the hearts of Englishmen to the cause of the negro and make them feel ashamed of their own brutality, Mrs. Mackenzie makes benevolence the dominating characteristic of the hero, Adolphus, a handsome young African prince. He is brought to England, is fêted and courted, and finally honored with the hand of a charming English heiress—or rather, it is the English girl who is honored by his condescension. His father, Zimza, a negro of feeling who had spent his youth in England and had a truly primitivistic conception of the

---

[52] Sir Herbert Croft, *A Brother's Advice to his Sisters*, London, 1776, pp. 121-22. First ed. 1775.

[53] Cf. J. M. S. Tompkins, *The Popular Novel in England, 1770-1800*, London, 1932, pp. 92-115.

corruptions of civilization, relinquishes him into the hands of his friend, Mr. Hamilton, with the greatest trepidation, lest his savage virtues become tarnished by European vices. ' Oh! let him not sink, with the noble name of Zimza, those qualities which, I am honest to own, are resident in my bosom. And may the sacrifice I have made, in permitting my son to take the title of a European, never burn indignantly on Zimza's conscious cheek!' [54] His son, Adolphus, writes reassuringly and patronizingly from England: ' Indeed, the Europeans are not all bad. Who . . . but must own that, when the savage perfections of Africa are tempered by the soft polish of refined manners, the lustre becomes hardly supportable to an eye unused, like mine, to their brilliancy.' [55] But the prince becomes the victim of his own best quality, his benevolence. So susceptible is he to any appeal to his sympathies that he falls an easy prey to a gambler and his mistress, and is involved in a series of deceptions. Unable to face the consequences of his mistaken benevolence, he sails with a Frenchman to Martinico. The Martinico episode gives the writer the opportunity that she wants to picture the cruelties of slavery and the sympathetic horror of Adolphus. The episode reaches a climax in Adolphus's rescue of his own father, who had been sold into slavery by his subjects. Here, it will be seen, the author's sentimental primitivism breaks down, for Zimza is forced to conclude by the treachery of his own tribe that human nature is primarily selfish. But this incidental counter-current is scarcely perceptible in the sultry gulf stream of benevolent feeling that sweeps the reader to the concluding reconciliation of Adolphus with his English friends.

[54] Dublin, 1793, p. 2.
[55] *Ibid.*, p. 99.

CHAPTER IV

POPULAR PRIMITIVISTIC INFERENCES FROM THE ETHICS
OF TASTE AND OF SENTIMENT

I

Let us turn now to the primitivism that was directly
influenced by the moral sense school. Here we shall find
the transition from philosophical premises to popular
inference an interesting one to follow. The relation between primitivistic theory and the rationalistic philosophy
of the late seventeenth century and early eighteenth century
had been clear-cut and decisive. Many of the rationalists,
as we have seen, made the transition themselves from their
moral philosophy to primitivism. The relationship is not
so clear in the case of the later moral sense school.
Shaftesbury, as we have seen, leans toward theories of
primitive goodness in some passages, but the general implications of his theory of proportion and harmony in
the moral life have a quite opposite tendency. The more
democratic aspect of Hutcheson's philosophy finds its
primitivistic implications within his own writings, but
one would look in vain for any real acceptance of primitivism either in his work or in that of Hume. Yet far as
most of these men and other thinkers of their school are
from any real primitivism, one can clearly discern the
transition from their philosophical premises in the hands
of more popular writers to a primitivism of a sentimental
and anti-intellectualistic type.

Let us consider first the inferences from the theories of
taste and the moral sense. In general in the literature of
the time the theory of taste led directly away from primitivism to aesthetic and moral exclusiveness and sophistica-

tion. Even Hume had written in 1741 that delicacy of taste gives a man ' little enjoyment but in the company of a few select companions. He [the man of taste] feels too sensibly, how much all the rest of mankind falls short of the notions he has entertained.' [1] Samuel Hall, writing in the *Edinburgh Magazine* in 1786, mentions the ' excessive and sickly kind of delicacy' which the doctrine of taste had made prevalent.[2] That even this phase, however, of the philosophy of the mid-eighteenth century, sophisticated as it was in its tendencies, was manipulated into primitivism by popular writers I shall try to show.

One step in the transition followed the path marked out by Hutcheson in his insistence on the non-rational character of the moral sense and its universality. J. G. Cooper, a follower of Shaftesbury and Hutcheson and author of the poem, *The Power of Harmony*, 1745, and the prose work, *Letters concerning Taste*, 1755, emphasizes the immediacy, without the operation of reason, of the perception of what is beautiful and harmonious in morals. The earlier work, *The Power of Harmony*, is a poetical amplification of the idea that contemplation of what is perfect and beautiful in nature will gradually harmonize the soul to a corresponding regularity and order. He proposes to rescue his readers from ' mists of forced belief' through which they only dimly see their Maker, and show them God

> . . . through each object of proportion fair,
> The source of virtue, harmony, and bliss! [3]

This is to be accomplished directly ' through untainted

---

[1] ' Of the Delicacy of Taste and Passion,' *Essays Moral, Political and Literary*, London, 1882, I, 94.

[2] *Edinburgh Magazine*, III (1786), 7.

[3] *Poems*, The British Poets, LXXII, 62.

sense'[4] by 'an instantaneous glow of joy'[5] which teaches man to recognize beauty both moral and natural

> . . . ere Reason with her tardy eye
> Can view the form divine.[6]

It is precisely this thesis of the immediacy of moral perception, purely non-rational in its nature, that paves the way for primitivistic inferences. Cooper emphasizes the point even more strongly in *Letters concerning Taste*. 'The effect of *good* Taste,' he here writes, ' is that instantaneous Glow of Pleasure which thrills thro' our whole Frame, and seizes upon the Applause of the Heart, before the intellectual Power, Reason, can descend from the Throne of the Mind to ratify it's Approbation, either when we receive into the Soul beautiful Images thro' the Organs of bodily Senses; or the Decorum of an amiable Character thro' the Faculties of moral Perception; or when we recall, by the imitative Arts, both of them thro' the intermediate Power of the Imagination.'[7] And again: ' Never the less that *internal Sense* we call Taste . . . has as quick a Feeling of this secondary Excellence of the Arts, as for the primary Graces; and seizes the Heart with Rapture long before the Senses, and Reason in Conjunction, can *prove* this Beauty by collating the Imitations with their Originals.'[8]

Although Cooper does not himself draw the inference that if the mind is universally so naturally ' attuned' to truth that all beauty makes a ' responsive Harmony vibrate within' without the cultivation of any rational process, the mind of primitive man must be capable of

---

[4] *Ibid.*, p. 73.
[5] *Ibid.*, p. 76. Cf. note.
[6] *Ibid.*, p. 76.

[7] *Op. cit.*, London, 1757, pp. 2-3.
[8] *Ibid.*, pp. 6-7.

a high quality of morality,[9] yet there are two other aspects of his philosophy of taste that make such an inference not only natural but almost inevitable.   In the first place he adopts the doctrine of progressive degeneration through the influence of wealth and luxury, quoting Longinus on the effect of luxury on morals, and links with the corruption which accompanies luxury a corresponding ' Depravity of Taste for Arts and Sciences and natural Beauty.'[10]

To see how Cooper might have combined this idea with his other premises and so arrived at primitivism one only needs to turn to Thomas Finch's *Essays on Man Delineating his Intellectual and Moral Qualities,* where one finds in the third essay, ' On the Symptoms of Intellectual Degeneracy,' an example of the actual coupling of a similar theory of degeneration with a Hutchesonian conception of the beauty of moral excellence. This excellence, writes Finch, is found in primitive man, for man was created perfect, having a ' noble conformity of character to the moral excellence of the supreme Beauty.'[11] In the beginning all of the elements of his character worked in harmony; all his faculties cheerfully cooperated in the pursuit of good. 'His mind was dignified, his temper virtuous, and his character upright. But to say that mankind in general are still beautified with these perfections, would discover the grossest perversion, or manifest the most pitiable ignorance of the human race. . . . Wherever the eye directs its glance, it perceives some disgusting feature of this miserably debilitated child of nature.'[12]

---

[9] In fact in his   Essay on Solitude and Society,' *ibid.,* p. 207, he repudiates the enthusiasm of the ' Retrogrades in Perfection' for primitive man.

[10] Letter XII, *ibid.,* pp. 78-80. Cf. Letter VIII, *ibid.,* p. 49.

[11] *Op. cit.,* London, 1811, p. 122.

[12] *Ibid.,* pp. 130-32.

Everywhere now one sees ' the pitiable symptoms of intellectual degeneracy and moral corruption.' [13]

The second aspect of Cooper's thought that favored primitivism is the familiar appeal to nature as a norm or standard. In his ' Essay on Good and Beauty,' he makes nature the final criterion of conduct by this reasoning: ' Whatever then is proportionable and harmonious, is good; everything that is so, is *natural* . . . every Being that obeys *her* Dictates partakes of the general Good, and the Deviation alone from them constitutes particular Evil; so that Vice in Morals is destructive to Pleasure, and Disorder in Matter cancels Beauty. *Nature* therefore, in the Enquiry concerning *Good* and *Beauty,* which I shall prove to be the same, must be the Criterion to go by.' [14] The inference of course is ' natural goodness' which Cooper further sanctions by his suggestion in another essay that education often serves to pervert rather than foster his natural goodness: ' When I consider the natural Propensity of human Nature to Good, I am often greatly surprized how the Power of Education is able to subvert it.' [15] Thus Cooper carries the philosophy of taste one step nearer to primitivism of the sentimental type.

Interestingly enough the transition to primitivism that Cooper does not quite make, Henry Home, Lord Kames, actually does come to in the course of his work. The name of Kames was often linked in the eigtheenth century with that of Shaftesbury, Hutcheson, and Hume in discussions of the moral sense and taste.[16] ' Ingenious' was

[13] *Ibid.,* p. 127.
[14] *Letters concerning Taste,* p. 161.
[15] Essay IV, ' On Self-Love,' p. 169.
[16] Cf. Samuel Hall, *op. cit.,* and John Bonar, *An Analysis of the Moral and Religious Sentiments contained in the Writings of Sopho* [*Kames*] *and David Hume,* Edinburgh, 1755.

the epithet applied to Lord Kames in the eighteenth century, and ingenious he certainly was in his manipulation
of current thought; so much so that he might easily be
claimed by several schools of thought at once. We will
have occasion to discuss some of his compromises in
another connection; here we shall look merely at his
version of the doctrine of the moral sense and taste.
Both in his early *Essays on the Principles of Morality and
Natural Religion,* 1751, and his later *Sketches of the
History of Man,* 1774, he takes issue with Shaftesbury.
In the former—and here he includes Hutcheson in his
criticism—he attacks him for taking no account of duty
and obligation in his system of morality. He approves of
Butler's re-establishment of the principle of conscience
as the guide and director of the principles of action. He
conceives that conscience functions, not through an act
of reflection, but through ' direct feeling . . . without
the intervention of any sort of reflection.' [17] In *Sketches
of the History of Man* he criticizes Shaftesbury—having
read him somewhat carelessly—for holding that ' man is
a benevolent being, and that ev'ry man ought to direct
his conduct for the good of all, without regarding himself
but as one of the number.' [18] On the contrary, man's
nature, he says—following Shaftesbury without knowing
it—is made up of both the benevolent and selfish principles.[19] In spite of his criticism of Shaftesbury and
Hutcheson, however, Kames's system of morality, in his
earliest work especially, is, with the modification of the
Butlerian note, essentially that of Shaftesbury and Hutcheson. Here is a typical passage from the *Elements of*

[17] *Essays on the Principles of Morality and Religion,* Edinburgh, 1751,
p. 63. Cf. *Sketches of the History of Man,* Edinburgh, 1774, II, 268.
[18] *Ibid.,* p. 256.
[19] *Ibid.,* p. 257.

Criticism, 1762: '. . . a taste in the fine arts goes hand
in hand with the moral sense, to which indeed it is nearly
allied. Both of them discover what is right and what is
wrong. Fashion, temper, and education, have an influence
on both, to vitiate them, or to preserve them pure and
untainted. Neither of them are arbitrary or local. They
are rooted in human nature, and are governed by principles common to all men.' [20] Now in the *Principles of
Morality*, Kames is chiefly concerned to prove that this
moral sense and taste for beauty are innate and universal.
He holds to this view in spite of, rather than because of,
what he then considered to be the nature of primitive man.
In 1751 Kames could find nothing too bad to say of primitive man: ' If we can trust history,' he writes, ' the original
inhabitants of this earth were a brutish and a savage
race. And we have little reason to doubt of this fact,
when, even at this day, we find the same sort of people
in distant corners, who have no communication with the
rest of mankind. The state of nature is accordingly represented by all writers, as a state of war; nothing going
on but rapine and bloodshed.' [21] If this be true, one might
ask, what is to become of the theory that a sense of
beauty and deformity in morals is natural and innate?
' We cannot help being in some pain for the principles
above laid down,' says Kames in distress. ' Brutish manners imply brutish principles of action; and, from this
view of the original state of mankind, it may seem that
moral virtues are not natural, but acquired by means of
education and example in a well regulated society. In a
word, that the whole moral part of our system is artificial. . . .' [22] But Kames satisfies himself of the fallacy

[20] *Op. cit.,* Edinburgh, 1762, I, 7.
[21] *Op. cit.,* p. 136.
[22] *Ibid.,* pp. 136-37.

of that conclusion by a simple reiteration of his foundation principles: ' If the feeling of beauty and deformity in external existence be natural to man, the feeling of beauty and deformity, and of *right* and *wrong* in actions, is equally so. And indeed, whatever be the influence of education and example, 'tis an evident truth, that they can never have the power of creating any one sense or feeling. They may well have the effect of cherishing and improving the plants of nature's formation, but they cannot introduce any new or original plant whatever.' [23] Looking for another explanation for the deceptive appearances in primitive life he finds it in the peculiar circumstances of savage life, such as the need of self-defence, lack of established rules, the natural shyness and timorousness of man which are sufficient to ' over-balance ' the natural operation of the moral sense. He feels moreover that the moral sense, innate and universal though it is, needs cultivation. But nevertheless ' The most polished nations differ only from savages in refinement of taste, which being productive of nice and delicate feelings, is the source of pleasure and pain, more exquisite than savages are susceptible of.' [24]

It is clear that a simple change in the description of primitive man such as might be justified by many contemporary travel books would turn all this into a thorough-going primitivism, and indeed Kames himself makes this shift in 1774 in the *Sketches*. In the earliest stages of society, he there writes, when the earth was still thinly populated and there was no contest over food or land, men lived ' innocently and cordially together: they had no irregular appetites, nor any ground of strife. In that state, moral principles joined their influence with that of

[23] *Ibid.*, p. 137.   [24] *Ibid.*, p. 144.

national affection, to secure individuals from harm. Savages accordingly, who have plenty of food, and are simple in habitation and cloathing, seldom trasgress [sic] the rules of morality within their own tribe.' [25] He gives a long list of examples to reinforce this view.[26] It is only after increase in population creates rivalry between tribes that the anti-social passions prevail. Thus Kames actually evolves a primitivistic theory from the premise of an innate moral sense and taste for moral beauty. Along with this primitivistic strain, however, as we shall see later, he maintains, in defiance of consistency, his original theory of the necessity of the cultivation of the moral sense and works out a theory of progress on that basis.

II

The problem becomes complicated at this point by the development during the century of a somewhat specialized off-shoot from the ethics of sentiment in the doctrine of sensibility. I am here using sensibility in its somewhat restricted eighteenth-century sense of extreme delicacy and keenness of feeling and ultra-refinement of sensitiveness to beauty both natural and moral. While the origins of the vogue of sensibility, in common with the ethics of sentiment in general, go back, as we saw in the first chapter, to the anti-Stoical and anti-Hobbesian development of the principle of benevolence and the reassertion of the importance of the passions, sensibility in the narrower sense defined above, the notion of sensibility that one meets in eighteenth-century popular novels *ad nauseam,* was given its characteristic form by Shaftesbury and Hutcheson and the ethics of taste. Shaftesbury's eloquent

[25] *Sketches of the History of Man*, II, 315.
[26] *Ibid.*, pp. 315-18.

passages on the cultivation of a taste for beauty to the point of virtuosity laid the foundation of the popular vogue which followed for a delicacy of feeling and of manners so extreme as to be unhealthy and morbid; and it added at the same time a distinct flavor of aristocratic exclusiveness. Sensibility, it was thought, could only be achieved by a mind already highly refined which gave assiduous attention to all that was beautiful and lovely and excluded all that was ugly. This exclusiveness is well illustrated by Hannah More's poem, ' Sensibility ' :

> Let not the vulgar read this pensive strain,
> Their jests the tender anguish wou'd profane:
>
> .   .   .   .   .
>
> For tender Sorrow has her pleasures too;
> Pleasures, which prosp'rous Dulness never knew,
> She never knew, in all her coarser bliss,
> The sacred rapture of a pain like this!
>
> .   .   .   .
>
> Then take, ye happy vulgar! take your part
> Of sordid joy, which never touch'd the heart.[27]

While Hannah More in this passage probably intended to include more than the ' common people ' in her term ' vulgar ' (although she uses the terms ' vulgar classes ' and ' common people ' interchangeably in her writings), it is worthy of notice that in her *Tales for the Common People* and in her *Stories for Persons in the Middle Ranks* she never once treats the theme of sensibility. In her *Strictures on the Modern System of Female Education with a View of the Principles and Conduct Prevalent among Women of Rank and Fortune*, however, she deals at length with sensibility, its beauties and its dangers. And one recalls in this connection Lady Booby's admoni-

[27] *Sacred Dramas . . . To which is added Sensibility, a Poem,* London, 1782, pp. 277-78.

tion to her maid, Mrs. Slipslop: 'I believe indeed thou dost not understand me. Those are delicacies which exist only in superior minds; thy coarse ideas cannot comprehend them. Thou art a low creature, of the Andrews breed, a reptile of a lower order, a weed that grows in the common garden of the creation.'

The possessor of sensibility was likely to consider himself a rare exception among men, and to deplore—and treasure—his special affliction. One frequently meets such exclamations as the following: 'Sensibility, thou source of human woes, thou aggrandiser of evils, had I not been possessed of thee, how calmly might my days have passed! Yet would I not part with thee for worlds. . . .' [28] Mary Wollstonecraft's definition of sensibility—not, so far as I can tell, intended to be ironical—is typical: 'To give the shortest definition of sensibility, replied the sage, I should say that it is the result of acute senses, finely fashioned nerves, which vibrate at the slightest touch, and convey such clear intelligence to the brain, that it does not require to be arranged by the judgment. Such persons instantly enter into the characters of others, and instinctively discern what will give pain to every human being; their own feelings are so varied that they seem to contain in themselves, not only all the passions of the species, but their various modifications. Exquisite pain and pleasure is their portion; nature wears for them a different aspect than is displayed to common mortals.' [29]

But the popularity of sensibility was its undoing. The idea caught fire and spread from the hall to the kitchen. 'Sensibility, or the characteristic of a susceptible mind,' writes the fictional representative of Lord Lyttleton in *The Correspondents*, 'is a fashionable and almost thread-

---

[28] 'Descant on Sensibility,' *London Magazine*, XLV (1776), 263-64.
[29] 'The Cave of Fancy,' *Posthumous Works*, London, 1798, II, 135-36.

bare topic. Much has been written, much is every day
said about it, and numbers affect to possess it, who have
no other claim than thinking it a recommendation.' [30]
Few heroines of popular fiction from the time of Richardson to the close of the century are without sensibility.
The outward signs of it (in fictitious characters) are a
capacity for strong emotional reaction, especially on slight
provocation, an unaccountable alternation of strong ' sallies of the spirit ' and moods of depression, a pronounced
inclination toward tears and fainting fits on occasions of
joy as well as sorrow, and even, toward the end of the
century especially, a tendency to die, not necessarily of
a broken heart but of wounded feelings.

The reign of sensibility lasted in spite of frequent
challenge [31] well toward the end of the century when,
among other influences, the growing popularity of utilitarianism called forth a different temper. ' Utility is now
commonly understood to be the only characteristic of
virtue;' writes the Enquirer in 1796, 'that course of
action which is most productive of good, is admitted to
be most virtuous; and he is esteemed the best man, who,
with the greatest integrity of principle, ardour of spirit,
and energy of action, endeavours to promote the general
welfare.' [32] And later in the year he writes, 'As everything in fashionable life hastens to extremes, the affectation of refinement produced a degree of softness, which

[30] *The Correspondents, an Original Novel*; . . . *in a Series of
Letters*, London, 1775, pp. 198-99.
[31] Cf. among other attacks, Fielding's implied criticism of Clarissa
Harlowe in Sophia; Mrs. Radcliffe's criticism of sensibility in *The
Mysteries of Udolpho*, and Jane Austen's delicious satire on heroines of
sensibility in *Love and Freindship*. Also 'Enquirer No. IX: Ought
Sensibility to be Cherished, or Repressed?' *Monthly Magazine*, II
(1796), 706-9.
[32] 'Enquirer No. IV. Question: Is Private Affection Inconsistent with
Universal Benevolence?' *Monthly Magazine*, I (1796), 273.

soon became ridiculous: by a sudden stroke of caprice, the polite world passed over to the contrary extreme of affected insensibility; and now it is become the mode, to consider every expression of tenderness as a mark of vulgarity; in the most interesting situations, a freezing air of indifference is assumed; . . . in short nature is banished, to introduce, in its stead, a rude and vulgar kind of stoicism, of which Zeno would have been ashamed.' [33]

It is not surprising that any fashion so popular as was sensibility at its height should gradually win for itself a much more universal application than, by its relations to the doctrine of taste, it had any right to, and by winning this universal application should lose much of its original character. The popular writer, attempting to cater to two vogues at once, that of sensibility and the equally prevalent vogue of Indians, negroes, and South Sea Islanders, must needs give the latter the same fashionable ultra-refinement of spirit that the most aristocratic heroine suffered under, however far the savage might actually be from Shaftesbury's original virtuoso. By this transference of characteristics, the idea of sensibility was enlarged and modified by the other primitivistic presuppositions that it found itself in company with and it modified them in turn.

The attribution of sensibility to the savage was probably made by many writers without the least sense of incongruity. It is possible to find in popular literature of various dates examples of the transitional forms of the conception of sensibility, although it is now impossible to trace out chronologically the stages by which it was sufficiently modified to make it possible to apply it without

[33] ' Enquirer No. IX,' *Monthly Magazine,* II (1796), 706.

too much violation of logic to primitive man. Hannah More, for instance, in the very poem in which she so patronizingly spurned the 'vulgar mind,' makes sensibility entirely non-rational and stresses the immediacy of the feeling of the beautiful and good. She thus makes it logically possible for the 'vulgar' to be possessed of sensibility although she herself does not perceive this implication.

> Sweet Sensibility! thou soothing pow'r,
> Who shedd'st thy blessings on the natal hour,
> Like fairy favours! Art can never sieze,
> Nor Affectation catch thy pow'r to please:
> Thy subtile essence still eludes the chains
> Of Definition, and defeats her pains.
> Sweet Sensibility! thou keen delight!
> Thou hasty moral! sudden sense of right!
> Thou untaught goodness! Virtue's precious seed!
> Thou sweet precursor of the gen'rous deed!
> Beauty's quick relish! Reason's radiant morn,
> Which dawns soft light before Reflexion's born.[34]

It is a delightful bit of irony that it was Hannah More's protégée, Mrs. Anne Yearsley, the 'poetical milk woman,' who took advantage of this line of reasoning to claim that she felt sensibility more potently than the people whose intellects were trained to withstand its pains. In fact she felt that intellectual refinement was a real hindrance to the feelings of sensibility:

>   My rough soul,
> O Sensibility! defenceless hails,
> Thy feelings most acute. Yet, ye who boast
> Of bliss *I* ne'er must reach, ye, who can fix
> A rule for sentiment, if rules there are,

[34] *Op. cit.*, p. 282.

(For much I doubt, my friends, if rule e'er held
Capacious sentiment) ye sure can point
My mind to joys that never touch'd the heart.
What is this joy? Where does its essence rest?
Ah! self-confounding sophists, will ye dare
Pronounce *that* joy which never touch'd the heart?
Does Education give the transport keen,
Or swell your vaunted grief? No, Nature feels
Most poignant, undefended; hails with me
The Pow'rs of Sensibility untaught.[35]

Likewise John Armstrong, in other respects no worshiper of ' the people' and certainly not a primitivist, is ready to agree that refinement of taste may be found among the illiterate: ' In the most stupid ages there is more good taste than one would at first sight imagine. . . . An honest farmer, or shepherd, who is acquainted with no language but what is spoken in his own country, may have a much truer relish of the *English* writers than the most dogmatical pedant. . . . '[36] Beattie, again, says of the ' ancient dame' in *The Minstrel:*

> . . . Nor let it faith exceed,
> That Nature forms a rustic taste so nice.
> Ah! had they been of court or city breed,
> Such delicacy were right marvellous indeed.[37]

Yet Beattie himself is clearly no primitivist. The glowing picture of the golden age offered by Edwin is definitely labeled as the work of fancy and repudiated for that reason.[38] I merely quote the passage to illustrate one

---

[35] *Poems on Several Occasions,* London, 1785, p. 6.

[36] *Miscellanies,* London, 1770, II, 136-37. But cf. ' Vox Populi, Vox Dei,' *ibid.,* pp. 210-11.

[37] Bk. I, st. LII.

[38] Bk. II, Sts. XXXVIII-XXXIX. I cannot agree with Professor R. D. Havens, ' Primitivism and the Idea of Progress in Thomson,' *Studies in*

direction of development of the idea of sensibility which tended to make it more congenial to primitivism.

Further, the tendency to identify sensibility with what is ' natural ' and the dictates of sensibility with ' what is right by nature ' helped to swing it over into the category of primitive qualities. The two illustrations that I am using are relatively late but they help us to see nevertheless how primitive man who—in the person of the North American Indian at least — had usually been characterized as stoical and laconic came to burst into fictional tears of rapture, or to faint or even die from too much sensibility.

Percival, a man of sensibility, in *Percival, or Nature Vindicated,* is also a man of nature. ' I must assure you,' writes Philip Towers of Percival, ' that what you think like art in the character of my friend, is either pure Nature or Nature's faithful substitute, honest habit.' [39] And his correspondent agrees with him on reading the description of Percival's transports of love: ' . . . "my heart is Julia's; ' tis Julia's, Julia's, Julia's." How delicious, my dear Lord Digby, are the pure effusions of nature! . . . In pronouncing "'tis Julia's," his appearance would have been a great treat to you, as it was to me. His attitude was firm, his right hand pressed his heart, his left was raised towards heaven; his cheeks glowed with his trans-

Philology, XXIX (1932), 52, that there is no denial of the golden age in *The Minstrel.* The lines of the Sage in regard to Edwin's ' fancy ' are:

> Fancy enervates, while it soothes, the heart,
> And, while it dazzles, wounds the mental sight.

Bk. II, st. XL.

And the final conclusion is that

> . . . The mind untaught
> Is a dark waste, where fiends and tempests howl;
> As Phoebus to the world, is science to the soul.

Bk. II, st. XLV.

[39] R. C. Dallas, *op. cit.,* London, 1801, I, 1-2.

ported blood; his eyes overflowed with life, and his words gave a passage to his soul.' [40] ' I am satisfied,' replies his correspondent, ' that your friend is an amiable man. His passion for Julia, his conduct at the lodge, his letters, are all nature, and nature delightfully refined.' [41] This identification of sensibility with what is natural is generalized toward the end of the novel into the complete identification of ' nature ' and virtue. [42]

In Mary Robinson's *Walsingham, or the Pupil of Nature,* again, not only the ' pupil of nature ' but the pupil's mother are creatures of sensibility. The mind of Walsingham's mother was ' formed in nature's most perfect mould; it was composed of the purest passions, the most exquisite sensibility; she harmonized the ills of life by the affections of the heart; she could bear the humiliations of fortune, but not the neglect which is too often their attendant.' [43] As for Walsingham himself, he traces all his anguish of over-sensitive feelings—an anguish on which he prides himself—to the fact that he was taught from his earliest days to ' explore the page of nature ' [44] and follow his natural impulses. [45] ' I am the child of sorrow, the victim of deception. . . . Mine have been the errors of a too vivid imagination; the miseries of sensibility, acute, but not indiscriminate. It is not from the multitude that I derive my anguish; the senseless throng,

[40] *Ibid.*, pp. 69-70.
[41] *Ibid.*, p. 171.
[42] *Ibid.*, III, 182. Dallas, it should be noted, did not discard education as a means of drawing forth the genius of man. He advocated more education of the masses. While he was too conservative to think possible a system of universal education on earth he thought that there might be such a system among the spirits in heaven! I, 179.
[43] *Op. cit.*, London, 1805, I, 41. The first edition was published in 1797.
[44] *Ibid.*, p. 91.
[45] *Ibid.*, p. 232.

and the gaudy ephemera of prosperous days, never had
power, to sting me—for they could not interest my
heart! Cold and cheerless neglect has been my destroyer;
and the shaft which pierced my bosom was winged by a
resistless hand—*the hand of nature.*' [46] The novel is the
story of his persecutions by the 'demons of art' who
'lift the empty brow of arrogance and pride above the
illustrious pupil of Genius, Truth, and Nature!' [47]

III

That the language of sensibility passed very early into
the literature of primitivism is evidenced by two novels
that came out in the fifties. The first, *The History of the
Life and Adventures of Mr. Anderson,* 1754, need not
keep us long.[48] The most important section for our purposes is the story of Calcathony, an Indian remarkable
for 'greatness of soul' both in prosperity and adversity,
for a sense of justice and honesty, and for an 'inflexible
disposition to preserve that jewel, liberty.' [49] He has an
equally noble wife, Taloufa,[50] who is stolen from him
by a French captive whom Calcathony had rescued. His
reaction to the tragic culmination is that of the typical
hero of sensibility: 'the *Indian* stoicism was not proof
against so home a stroke—he fainted, and, when recovered, made the saddest and most moving complaints,
till rage and fury broke in upon his soul, and the thoughts
of vengeance, occupied in its turn, his breast.' [51] And he
never smiled again.

[46] *Ibid.,* p. 7.
[47] *Ibid.,* IV, 368.
[48] Cf. the summary of the story in Bissell, *op. cit.,* pp. 87-89.
[49] *Op. cit.,* Dublin, 1754, p. 96.
[50] Not Talousa, as in Bissell, *op. cit.,* p. 88.
[51] *Ibid.,* p. 109.

More important is Shebbeare's *Lydia, or Filial Piety,*
which was written in the full flush of enthusiasm for
the ' softer emotions,' the ' seraphic Sensations, dwelling
in the Human Heart.' [52] This book is a long, disjointed
story of the fortunes and misfortunes of Lydia, with countless secondary narratives introduced more or less after
the manner of Smollett. But such a vogue had Indian
material attained at this time that Shebbeare actually
starts with an Indian scene and uses an Indian love story
as one of the threads of his narrative. The Indian story
deals with the noble Cannassatego who tears himself
away from his beloved Yarico to make a pilgrimage to
England in an endeavor to interest the English ' Sachems '
in the cause of the Indians and if possible to right some
of their wrongs. ' Long have my eyes beheld our situation
with afflicted heart,' says Cannassatego, ' the autumnal
blast has not scattered more leaves than I have uttered
sighs, the rushing cataracts of the Catarakui poured more
drops of water, than I have shed tears in surveying our
abject state.' [53] As is evident from the foregoing quotation the quality that is emphasized in the Indians is sensibility. Cannassatego's face was ' animated with features
that spoke sensibility of soul, high and open was his
forehead, from his eyes flashed forth the beams of courage
and compassion, as each passion at different moments
animated his bosom, within which his heart beat with
honest throbbing for his country's service.' [54] The Indians
are animated by only the most noble feelings of love,
friendship, and patriotism, for in this country ' the primae-
val laws of nature still hold their native sway over human
hearts; the views of heaven have not yet been violated

[52] *Op. cit.,* Dublin, 1756, I, 17.
[53] *Ibid.,* p. 7.
[54] *Ibid.,* p. 2.

by the pernicious and impious schemes of corrupted men.' [55] On the other hand the civilization of England is a bitter disappointment to the Indian hero. Treated with contempt and neglect, he is appalled at the havoc wrought by luxury on the natural feelings of the heart: ' Oh! Bane of every Virtue, Bane of all our *Indian* Peace and Happiness; Oceans roll between, Rocks, Woods and Mountains in vain seclude us from the ravenous Thirst of Gold; Sensation dies, the Feelings of Humanity expire before its baneful Breath, frozen is the Heart, the Eye refuses that Tear which Nature gave to wait upon Compassion; we die unpitied like the stricken Deer.' [56] He returns to America and the solace of Yarico's love. ' "Art thou return'd?" she cried, "Do I hold thee to my Heart?" "I am, and thine, my Soul, my very Bliss," replied the Prince.' [57]

The passing of the conception of sensibility into primitivistic literature is further illustrated in the work of John Davis. [58] There is a typical primitivistic passage in his *Travels of Four Years and a Half in the United States of America during 1798, 1799, 1800, 1801, and 1802.* [59] He begins with the usual observation that the Indians afford us valuable material for the study of primitive man, whereas before we have always been dependent on descriptions of the Scythians and the Germans in classical sources. We can now revise our notions of primitive man. ' The *Indians* of *America* want only an historian who would measure them by the standard of *Roman* ideals, to equal in bravery and magnanimity the proud masters of the

[55] *Ibid.*, p. 11.   [56] *Ibid.*, III, 172.   [57] *Ibid.*, IV, 75.
[58] For biographical details see Thelma Louise Kellog, *The Life and Works of John Davis, 1774-1853,* Orono, Maine, U. Press, 1924, University of Maine Studies, 2nd series, No. 1.
[59] First edition, London, 1803.

world.' [60] In fact he compares the Indians and the early Romans to the advantage of the former, for the Indians are more benevolent and peaceful than the Romans. ' Let us compare with these dignified butchers,' he writes, ' the depreciated *Indians* of *America*; and if a love of peace be the criterion of a great character, how will a *Roman* shrink at the side of an *Indian*. The *Romans* were ever found to sheathe the sword with reluctance; the *Indians* have been always ready to lay down the hatchet.' [61] But it is for their sensibility that they seem especially praiseworthy to Davis: ' That in humanity and all the softer emotions the *Indians* of *America* will rival the most polished nations of the world let facts establish. When, after a sanguinary war between the whites and the *Indians,* a treaty of peace was concluded, no scene could be more affecting than the sensibility with which the *Indians* restored their captives to the *British* . . . of the captives that were restored, many had been taken when children by the *Indians.* These had been accustomed to consider the *Indians* as their only relations; they spoke no other language but that of the *Shawanese*; and beholding their new state in the light of captivity, they separated from their savage benefactors with mournful reluctance. On the parting of the *Indians* from the *British,* a *Shawanese* Chief addressed the white men in a short but humane speech. "Fathers, said the *Indian* warrior, we have brought your flesh and blood to you; they are our children by adoption and yours by natural right. Inmates with us from their tender years, they are wholly unacquainted with your customs and manners, and therefore we beseech you to treat them with kindness, that at length they may become reconciled to you." ' [62]

[60] *Op. cit.,* p. 298.
[61] *Ibid.,* pp. 298-99.   [62] *Ibid.,* pp. 299-301.

In his novel, *The First Settlers of Virginia, an Historical Novel,* which retells the Pocahontas story that Davis had already briefly related in his *Travels,* he had an excellent opportunity for the display of primitive sensibility. It would be a pity to give the scene in any but the author's own words:

The women now became more bitter in their lamentations over the victim; but the savage monarch was inexorable, and the executioners were lifting their clubs to perform the office of death, when Pokahontas ran with mournful distraction to the stone, and getting the victim's head in her arms, laid her own upon it to receive the blow. Fair Spirit! thou ministering Angel at the throne of grace! if souls disengaged from their earthly bondage can witness from the bosom of eternal light what is passing here below, accept, sweet seraph, this tribute to thy humanity.

Powhatan was not wanting in paternal feeling; his soul was devoted to his daughter Pokahontas; and so much did his ferocity relent at this display of her innocent softness, that he pronounced the prisoner's pardon, and dismissed the executioners.[63]

But the crowning touch comes in the reaction of Nantaquas, the brother of Pocahontas: ' It was then the emotions of the young red warrior discovered themselves in all the ebullition of native greatness. He first tenderly embraced his sister for her sensibility, and running to captain Smith, fell on his neck with mingled rapture and admiration.' [64]

It is an interesting fact that in *Walter Kennedy: an American Tale,* written between 1802 and 1804,[65] several years before *The First Settlers,* Davis, in spite of the fact that he is here more thoroughly primitivistic than

[63] Second edition, N. Y., 1806, pp. 40-41.
[64] *Ibid.,* p. 43.
[65] Cf. *The First Settlers,* pp. 283-84.

he is in the latter story in which Pokahontas and her brother are in a sense exceptions to the rest of the tribe, adopts a definitely humorous tone antagonistic to any implications of sensibility.[66]

Not the most philosophical but the most extravagant of the late eighteenth century emotional outbursts were inspired by the South Sea islanders. While the greatest impetus to the enthusiasm for these carefree and happy 'children of nature' came, as Professor Tinker has remarked,[67] from the French voyages of the sixties and those of Captain Cook immediately following, and from the bringing of Omiah—and later, Lee Boo—to England, it is possible to over-emphasize the influence of the *Journals* of Captain Cook and Keate's *Account of the Pelew Islands* to the exclusion of other sources and influences. Our survey of the progress of thought up to the appearance of Omiah and Lee Boo in England should have shown us, if nothing else, that those ill-fated princes were at most handy illustrations of theories already well established and that they in no sense initiated a vogue for their type of child of nature. I have already pointed out in an article entitled 'Thomas Blackwell, a Disciple of Shaftesbury' a clear case of sentimental primitivism as early as 1735 in Blackwell's *Enquiry into the Life and Writings of Homer,*[68] and it was Edmund Gosse who first pointed out similar passages in Joseph Warton's *The Enthusiast*, written in 1740, published in 1744.[69] Further,

---

[66] Much of the geographical lore of this tale was probably derived, as Professor Chinard has pointed out, from Bartram and Carver, and the sentimental Indian love story at the end seems to derive from Chateaubriand's *Atala*. Cf. Gilbert Chinard, 'Un Frère Cadet de René en Amérique' (Extrait des *Mélanges Baldensperger*), Paris, 1930, pp. 11-19.

[67] *Op. cit.*, pp. 5-9.

[68] *Phil. Quart.*, V (1926), 200-201.

[69] 'Two Pioneers of Romanticism: Joseph and Thomas Warton, *Proc. Brit. Acad.* (1905), p. 151.

as we have just seen, the anti-rationalistic primitivists
were quite capable of turning the stoical and taciturn
North American Indian into a perfect illustration of their
theories of sensibility, benevolence, and the sacredness of
the natural instincts; and if they tired of using the Indian
for all purposes, there was material on the South Seas
already available before Captain Cook, and plenty of
'happy African' material. Indeed Monboddo himself,
whom Professor Tinker cites in this connection, expressly
tells us that 'What I shall here set down of the wild
people found in those countries is taken from a French
collection of voyages to the South sea, printed at *Paris*
in the year 1756, in two volumes 4to. The author's name,
as I am informed, is *Labrosse*.'[70] But the enthusiasm for
Omiah and the idyllic life of Otaheite is indeed amazing.
Professor Tinker has quoted from the Poem called
Otaheite, 1774. Even more striking, in spite of the dull
passages of conventional satire on English life, are the
primitivistic passages in *An Historical Epistle from Omiah
to the Queen of Otaheite; being his Remarks on the
English Nation,* 1775, for it is wholly laudatory whereas
the author of *Otaheite* recites the crimes of a land of
love as well as the delights. I quote representative lines
from the *Epistle:*

> Sick of these motley scenes, might I once more,
> In peace return to *Otaheite's* shore,
> How might I there with rational delight,
> Their faults and merits, unreserv'd recite;
> Well pleas'd to hear our aged sires debate,
> On the vile morals of a polisht state.
> How vain is learning, and how senseless art,
> United tending to pervert the heart.

[70] *Origin and Progress of Language,* Edinburgh, 1773-92, I, 232.

Callous to all the finer strokes which Heav'n,
To undeprav'd, untutor'd man has giv'n;
Whose honest heart no sordid interest fires,
No fashion sways, no prejudice inspires;
Where nature only rules the lib'ral mind,
Unspoil'd by art, by falsehood unrefin'd.
She feels his wants, and taught by her to live,
He feels that comfort, riches cannot give.

. . . .

Thus might we long indulge extatic flames,
And leave chill virtue to *European* dames.[71]

Prince Lee Boo was introduced to English readers
through Keate's *Account of the Pelew Islands,* 1788, and
immediately became a great favorite with the popular
writers.[72] The literary adaptation that I have chosen to
quote from is the anonymous prose *Interesting and Affecting History of Prince Lee Boo,* which was published
the year after Keate's *Account,* and draws on it largely for
quotation. Written for young people, the benevolent and
prudential traits are greatly stressed. The author dwells
on the simplicity of manners and the delicacy of the
sentiments of the natives of the Pelew Islands, and gets
the full value out of the pathetic parting of the English
and Prince Lee Boo from the islanders: 'As the canoes
drew together, surrounding that of the king, the natives
all eagerly looked up as if to bid adieu, while their
countenances imparted the feelings of their benevolent

[71] Ll. 707-722; 735-36. See also *Omiah's Farewell; Inscribed to the
Ladies of London,* London, 1776. For a discussion of Cowper's lines
on Omai, see Fairchild, *op. cit.,* pp. 71-75. See also Anna Seward,
' Elegy on Captain Cook,' *Poetical Works,* Edinburgh, 1810, II, 43 ff.;
and ' Remonstrance Addressed to William Cowper, Esq., in 1788, on
the Sarcasm Levelled at Natural Gratitude in the Task,' *op. cit.,* III, 5 ff.
[72] Cf. Mr. Fairchild's discussion of the *Account, op. cit.,* pp. 112-17,
and also of the Lee Boo poems by Bowles, Coleridge, and Cottle, *ibid.,*
pp. 272-73, 276-77, 458.

hearts in looks far more expressive than language. The English might truly say that they left a whole people in tears. . . .'[73] But the best opportunity for delineating the quality of sensibility comes in the episode where Lee Boo acts as peacemaker between Captain Wilson and his son: '. . . he took his young friend by the hand, and, entering the parlour, went up to his father, laid hold of his hand, joined it with that of his son, and, pressing them together, dropped over both those tears of sensibility which his affectionate heart could not on the occasion suppress.—Would to God that those who have been taught from Heaven that " Blessed are the peace-makers " would *go and do like* this unenlightened child of Nature!'[74] Keate, it may be noted in passing, is not himself a true primitivist, however many benevolent qualities he gives to the South Sea islanders. Primitive tribes, according to him, which like those of the Pelew Islands, are gentle and honorable in their dealings, have attained to that degree of refinement only after a long process of development, while other primitive tribes have retained ' that darkness and absolute barbarism, from the sight of which humanity gladly turns away.'[75]

One of the most unexpected appearances of Prince Lee Boo occurs in a book by Miss Charlotte Palmer entitled *Letters on Several Subjects from a Preceptress to Her Pupils Who Have Left School* (London, 1797). At the end of a slim volume of letters ' To Miss S—— On the Subject of Complimentary Cards' in which the use of the third person in complimentary messages is vindicated, ' To Eliza—On Dress,' and so forth, Miss Palmer some-

[73] *Op. cit.,* London, 1789, pp. 84-85. Cf. Keate, *op. cit.,* London, 1788, pp. 260-64.
[74] *Ibid.,* p. 149. Cf. Keate, *op. cit.,* p. 352.
[75] Keate, *op. cit.,* p. vii.

what unexpectedly brings into this genteel company the famous Prince Lee Boo in the setting of Mrs. West's Poem, ' Pelew,' based on Keate. ' *Nature* had been the tutor of the deservedly-lamented prince (Lee-Boo),' writes Miss Palmer in comment on the poem, ' and had so highly cultivated his understanding, that he possessed the powers of discrimination in a far greater degree than most of our *civilised* people of fashion.' [76] Forgetting that her whole book—and apparently her school—had been devoted to the cultivation of the niceties of etiquette, she commends Lee Boo's criticism of the over-elaborateness of Chinese manners, and remarks: ' This passage ought to be considered as an instructive reproof by those who pay more attention to *form* than *propriety*.' [77] She cites as an example of over-attention to form, not the usage controlling complimentary cards, for which she apparently had a blind spot, but the affectation of using the fork instead of the knife to carry food to one's mouth!

This introduction of Prince Lee Boo into a fashionable boarding school may be taken as a symbol of what had been accomplished by the force of popularity: it had brought together again two divergent lines of thought, and that after each had developed so far in its own direction that the union by logical means would have seemed impossible. On the one hand we have a primitivism developed from the idea that man is naturally good and benevolent and that he is universally and uniformly moved by a moral sense which is independent of the exercise of reason. On the other hand there is the ideal of extreme delicacy and refinement in the appreciation of moral beauty. As I have suggested, the union of the two brought about a modification of both. The savage devel-

[76] *Op. cit.*, p. 127.　　　　[77] *Ibid.*, pp. 127-28.

oped a quite unexpected refinement of feeling and manners, and the idea of sensibility took over some of the primitivistic enthusiasm for what is natural, instinctive, and emotionally free. As a result we find at the end of the century a distinct tendency to consider praiseworthy, not the refinements of intellect, but almost any expression of emotion and instinct for its own sake.

IV

This tendency to exalt emotion and instinct is well illustrated by the author of *The Indians,* 1790. The play is attributed to William Richardson, who was professor of the humanities at Glasgow University and defender of *Ossian.* He has a prose version of the same story [78] which is even more significant than the play. The keynote of the play is struck by the Prologue:

> The children of the wild, the froward brood
> Of Nature, ere by reason's law subdu'd,
> She rein'd her reckless will; for as they range
> The dreary wilderness, their passions change
> Various and rapid as the gales that sweep
> The bending forest, and convulse the deep.[79]

It is characteristic of this type of primitivistic literature that the range of passion attributed to the savage should be much greater than before. Gone are the classic tranquillity and self-control of the rational savage; vehemence of emotion is now the ideal. The sentimental primitivist no longer fears to give his savage many of the fiercer passions, for he counts on offsetting them with the greater intensity of the benevolent affections; he counts on show-

---

[78] *Poems, chiefly Rural, with The Indians, a Tale,* Glasgow, 1781, fourth edition.
[79] *The Indians, a Tragedy,* London, 1790, Prologue I, pp. ii-iii.

ing that the fiercer passions are a necessary but harmless characteristic of a people capable of true nobility of soul. Thus Ononthio, the venerable chieftain in *The Indians,* says of the younger warriors who want revenge on the Englishman, Sidney, for the death of Onaiyo:

> They are indeed too vehement. They feel
> Too ardently: too ardently resent
> The suff'rings of their brethren. Yet their wrath
> Is like the rushing of a mountain blast,
> Sudden but soon appeas'd. I trust they know not
> The hate that rankles in a vengeful breast.[80]

In the prose version the point is brought out even more strikingly. Ononthio at first consents to the torture and death of Sidney, but on finding that he is the brother of Maraino, his adopted daughter and the wife of his son, Oneyo,[81] he not only releases Sidney but adopts him as his son in place of Oneyo. At Sidney's surprise at the sudden transition, Ononthio explains to him that he is surprised only because he is reasoning like Europeans, who, ' Conscious of the bitterness of their own souls' impute ' a corresponding temper to their adversaries. . . . But the resentment of generous souls is liberal, and leaves room for reconciliation and future friendship. Men of mild and benevolent dispositions, unpolluted by covetous or ambitious desires, and therefore unimbittered by their unhappy effects, by envy, rancour, and malice, are magnanimous without any effort, even desirous of being forgiven, and ever apt to forgive. . . . Our reason may be obscured, but our principles are innocent. Our passions may be excessive, but they are not corrupt.' [82] He goes on to explain that they had not been instigated to decree

[80] Act III, pp. 39-40.
[81] The spelling of the names in the prose version is different.
[82] *The Indians, a Tale,* pp. 189-91.

Sidney's torture and death by any personal animosity against him, but had merely wanted to honor their dead warrior! Still Sidney wonders how a person of such different background as his could become a member of their nation. Ononthio's reply has deistical echoes: ' " It is the language of prejudice," replied Ononthio, " the simple, unaffected Indian, the child of nature, unwarped by servile prepossessions, is a stranger to your distinctions. Is not the great Spirit the father of us all? are we not all children of the same family? and have we not in the structure both of body and mind, undoubted evidence of the same original?" ' [83] When Sidney wonders further whether he could find the uncivilized life of the Indian preferable to the culture and refinement of Europe, Ononthio rises to the full height of his eloquence: 'Away with your culture and refinement. . . . Do they invigorate the soul and render you intrepid? Do they enable you to despise pain and acquiesce in the will of heaven? No! They unnerve the soul. They render you feeble, plaintive, and unhappy. Do they give health and firmness? Do they enable you to restrain and subdue your appetites? No! they promote intemperance and mental anarchy. They give loose reins to disorder. The parents of discontent and disease! Away with your culture and refinement! Do they better the heart or improve the affections? The heart despises them. Her affections arise spontaneous. They require no culture. They bloom unbidden. They are essential to our existence, and nature hath not abandoned them to our caprice. All our affections as we receive them from nature are lively and full of vigour. By refinement they are enfeebled. How exquisite the sensations of youth! In the early seasons of life ye are

[83] *Ibid.,* pp. 132-33.

moved with every tale of distress, and mingle tears of sympathy with every sufferer. Ye are then incapable of perfidy, and hold vice in abhorrence. In time ye grow callous; ye become refined; your feelings are extinguished: ye scoff at benevolence, and reckon friendship a dream. Ye become unjust and perfidious; the slaves of avarice and ambition; the prey of envy, of malice, and revenge. Away with your refinement! enjoy the freedom and simplicity of nature. Be guiltless—Be an Indian.' [84]

The contrast between the natural religion of the sentimental and the rationalistic primitivist is more clearly brought out in the essay which Richardson contributed to Patrick Graham's defense of Ossian. It is entitled ' The Origin of Superstition, illustrated in the Mythology of the Poems of Ossian.' Here Richardson contends that mankind in the very earliest periods of society has a knowledge of the doctrines of true religion. Primitive men ' believe in the existence, in the power, wisdom, goodness, and superintending providence of one Supreme Being; who, as the Creator, and the Preserver, of all things, was the object of religious worship.' [85] Primitive men, however, did not arrive at this knowledge either through revelation or the ' deductions of a well-informed understanding.' The principles of religion were derived ' solely from the impulses of passion and sensibility, cooperating with those associations of thought which proceed from the influences of a prompt and ungoverned imagination.' [86] He illustrates by showing how the idea of immortality could arise from pleasure in the companion-

[84] *Ibid.*, pp. 133-35. Cf. the golden age passage in Richardson's poem, *Ambition and Luxury*, Edinburgh, 1778, pp. 22-25.

[85] In Patrick Graham, *Essay on the Authenticity of the Poems of Ossiam*, Edinburgh, 1807, pp. 411-12.

[86] *Ibid.*, p. 413.

ship of someone who is the object of affection and admiration and pain at separation from him, through death,
so great that it forms a ' predisposition in the mind to
think of the dead, as if he still existed.' [87]

William Richardson might well be taken as the pattern
of the complete anti-rationalistic primitivist.[88]

V

Before we leave the phase of primitivistic literature
that selected for admiration not the rational but the emotional qualities of the savage, and substituted native instincts for natural law, let us consider a few of the books
in which this set of generalizations about human nature
was carried over into educational theory. To sum up
William Richardson's typical statement, the characteristic
assumptions are that the affections of the heart as they
come from nature before the refinements of civilization
are not only vigorous but benevolent and good; that the
base passions of envy, malice, and revenge, come only
with the perversions of a false culture; finally that the
affections furnish us with all the principles of morality
and knowledge of religion that we need. The obvious
educational corollary to theories of this nature one finds
in such novels as Frances Brooke's *Julia Mandeville* and
Emily Montague. I imply no direct influence; Mrs.
Brooke's novels, as a matter of fact, came out a few years
earlier than Richardson's *The Indians.* They are merely
a parallel expression of the same trend of thought. Mrs.

[87] *Ibid.,* p. 417.
[88] It is interesting to note that even Richardson could write, however,
in his *Essays on Some of Shakespeare's Dramatic Characters,* that ' to
follow nature ' cannot mean ' the original unimproved appearance of
things,' for then the ' wild American savage is more according to
nature than the civilized European.' London, 1798, pp. 386-87.

Brooke's line of reasoning is as follows: Virtue and not vice is natural to man.[89] The benevolent passions predominate, and only man fails to understand his real nature: 'When I see the dumb creation, my dear Harry, pursuing steadily the purposes of their being, their own private happiness, and the good of their peculiar species, I am astonished at the folly and degeneracy of man, who acts in general so directly contrary to both; for both are invariably united. The wise and benevolent Creator has placed the supreme felicity of every individual in those kind, domestic, social affections, which tend to the well being of the whole. Whoever presumes to deviate from this plan, the plan of God and nature, shall find satiety, regret, or disappointment, his reward.' [90] It therefore follows that in education we should seek to nourish the natural impulses of the human heart: 'it has always appeared to me, that our understandings are fettered by systems, and our hearts corrupted by example: and that there needs no more to minds well disposed than to recover their native freedom, and think and act for themselves. . . . Convinced that the seeds of virtue are innate, I have only watched to cherish the rising shoot, and prune, but with a trembling hand, the too luxuriant branches.' [91] 'I

---

[89] This she seeks to establish in a delightfully contradictory passage: 'Good people . . . are generally too retired and abstracted to let their example be of much service to the world: whereas the bad, on the contrary, are conspicuous to all; they stand forth, they appear on the fore ground of the picture, and force themselves into observation. 'Tis to that circumstance, I am persuaded, we may attribute that dangerous and too common mistake, that vice is natural to the human heart, and virtuous characters the creatures of fancy; a mistake of the most fatal tendency, as it tends to harden our hearts, and to destroy that mutual confidence so necessary to keep the bonds of society from loosening, and without which man is the most ferocious of all beasts of prey.' *The History of Emily Montague*, London, 1769, II, 140.

[90] *The History of Lady Julia Mandeville*, London [1763], I, 151-52. Cf. *Emily Montague*, III, 47.   [91] *Julia Mandeville*, I, 146-47.

cannot help observing here, that the great aim of modern education seems to be, to eradicate the best impulses of the human heart, love, friendship, compassion, benevolence; to destroy the social, and encrease the selfish principle. . . . If my ideas of things are right, the human mind is naturally virtuous; the business of education is therefore less to give us good impressions, which we have from nature, than to guard us against bad ones, which are generally acquired.' [92] 'If moralists would indeed improve human nature, they should endeavor to expand, not to contract the heart; they should build their system on the passions and affections, the only foundations of the nobler virtues.' [93]

The question that inevitably arises is, how much of this reasoning about education comes from English tradition and how much of it comes straight out of Rousseau? There is good external evidence that Mrs. Brooke was an admirer, if a none too careful reader, of Rousseau. The evidence occurs in *Emily Montague,* part of the scene of which is laid in Quebec. Mrs. Brooke, although she came directly in contact with the Indians when she and her husband were posted among them in Canada, gives a somewhat conventionalized description of the Hurons under the familiar heads of liberty and equality, religion, organization of the tribe, and so forth. Praise and blame are mingled, with the former predominating. But later comes this somewhat contradictory passage which would seem to indicate at one and the same time a first hand acquaintance with the writings of Rousseau and a pretty thorough misunderstanding of the *Discours sur l'inégalité*: 'Rousseau has taken great pains to prove that the most uncultivated nations are the most virtuous: I have all due

<hr>

[92] *Emily Montague,* III, 32-33.   [93] *Ibid.,* p. 47.

respect for this philosopher, of whose writings I am an enthusiastic admirer; but I have a still greater respect for truth, which I believe is not in this instance on his side. . . . From all that I have observed, and heard of these people, it appears to me an undoubted fact, that the most civilized Indian nations are the most virtuous; a fact which makes directly against Rousseau's ideal system.' [94]

There seems to be little doubt that Mrs. Brooke was familiar with *Emile*. The resemblances are obvious—but the differences are even more interesting and instructive than the similarities. The first two of the above quotations on education inevitably suggest Rousseau's negative system. But the idea, implied in all three of the quotations from Mrs. Brooke on education, but most emphatically expressed in the third, that education should be founded on the passions and affections which should be allowed almost spontaneous development, although often attributed to Rousseau, is much less characteristic of Rousseau himself than of a line of philosophy that had developed in England and France independently of him. In *Emile* there is no such glorification of the affections and passions as one finds in the pages of Mrs. Brooke. The whole aim is the development of the rational man. While Rousseau makes it clear that the reason is not the first faculty to develop and should not be forced into a premature ripeness,[95] he is far from advocating a cultivation of the affections to the neglect of the reason. On the contrary he expressly advises against allowing a child to have sensations in advance of a power of judgment to evaluate them: ' For

---

[94] *Ibid.*, III, 107-9. See A. O. Lovejoy, ' The Supposed Primitivism of Rousseau's *Discourse on Inequality,*' *Modern Philology*, XXI (1923), 165-86.

[95] *Emile*, Paris, 1851, L. II, p. 74 ff.

the good is not real unless enlightened by reason.' [96] Here
we have the heart of the difference between Rousseau and
this group of English primitivists that we are considering.
Far from identifying virtue with a pre-intellectual state,
whether a state of childhood or of primitive society, Rousseau makes it clear that there is no moral character in
actions performed before reason teaches us to distinguish
between good and evil: 'Reason alone teaches us to know
good and evil. . . . Before reaching years of reason, we
do good and evil unconsciously. There is no moral character in our actions.' [97] There is, it is true, a somewhat
contradictory passage in *La Profession de Foi du Vicaire
Savoyard*: 'The decrees of conscience are not judgments
but feelings. . . . To exist is to feel; our feeling is undoubtedly earlier than our intelligence, and we had feelings before we had ideas.' [98] Rousseau himself partially
reconciles this contradiction by saying that though conscience exists independently of reason it cannot develop
without the aid of reason: 'La conscience qui nous fait
aimer l'un et haïr l'autre, quoique indépendante de la
raison, ne peut donc se développer sans elle.' [99] And even
in the passage quoted from the *Profession de Foi* the
'sentimens' that Rousseau lists are no such ideal ones as

[96] 'Car il [le bien] n'est jamais tel que quand la raison l'éclaire.'
Ibid., p. 80.
[97] 'La Raison seule nous apprend à connaitre le bien et le mal. . . .
Avant l'âge de raison, nous faisons le bien et le mal sans le connaître,
et il n'y a point de moralité dans nos actions.' *Ibid.*, p. 47.
[98] 'Les actes de la conscience ne sont pas des jugemens, mais des
sentimens. . . . Exister pour nous, c'est sentir; notre sensibilité est incon-
testablement antérieure à notre intelligence, et nous avons eu des sentimens
avant des idées.' *Édition Critique . . .* par Pierre-Maurice Masson,
Paris, 1914, pp. 265-66. See the editor's excellent note, p. 269, on this
paragraph, in which he shows that Rousseau is here trying to reconcile
the theory of conscience, spontaneous and instinctive, with the theory
that there are no innate ideas.
[99] *Emile*, p. 47.

Mrs. Brooke's. Compare Rousseau's ' L'amour de soi, la crainte de la douleur, l'horreur de la mort, le désir du bien-être,' [100] with Mrs. Brooke's ' love, friendship, compassion, benevolence.' Similarly in Rousseau's description of the first pre-political state of man in the *Discours sur l'inégalité* the passions are by no means raised to the position they occupy in the works of the English writers: ' The passions, again, originate in our wants, and their progress depends on that of our knowledge; for we cannot desire or fear anything, except from the idea we have of it, or from the simple impulse of nature. Now savage man, being destitute of every species of intelligence, can have no passions save those of the latter kind: his desires never go beyond his physical wants. The only goods he recognizes in the universe are food, a female, and sleep: the only evils he fears are pain and hunger.' [101] Rousseau is nearer the pure Lockean tradition than the English writers of the second half of the century. Clearly there had been other influences at work in England than that of Rousseau. How far Mrs. Brooke had gone from the tradition of Locke may be seen from a single sentence of his *Thoughts concerning Education*: 'And the great Principle and Foundation of all Virtue and Worth, is placed in this, That a Man is able to *deny himself* his own Desires, cross his

---

[100] *Edition Critique*, p. 267.

[101] ' Les passions à leur tour tirent leur origine de nos besoins, et leur progrès de nos connaissances. Car on ne peut désirer ou craindre les choses que sur les idées qu'on en peut avoir, ou par la simple impulsion de la nature; et l'homme sauvage, privé de toute sorte de lumière, n'éprouve que les passions de cette dernière espèce. Ses désirs ne passent pas ses besoins physiques; les seuls biens qu'il connaisse dans l'univers sont la nourriture, une femelle et le repos; les seul maux qu'il craigne sont la douleur et la faim.' ' Discours sur l'inégalité,' *The Political Writings of Jean Jacques Rousseau*, ed. C. E. Vaughan, Cambridge, 1915, I, 150-1.

own Inclinations, and purely follow what Reason directs as best, tho' the appetite lean the other way.' [102]

One finds a similar emphasis on the feelings as opposed to the understanding in Kames's *Loose Hints upon Education, chiefly concerning the Culture of the Heart* (Edinburgh, 1781), and Elizabeth Hamilton's *Letters on the Elementary Principles of Education* (Boston, 1825). Neither author, it is true, goes quite so far as to say,, with Mrs. Brooke, that the natural feelings are always good and just and need only be left to develop as nature intended them without interference from man. On the contrary both of them are too devoted to the principle of associationism to leave early impressions determining the desires and affections to chance. 'Rousseau advances a strange opinion,' writes Kames, 'that children are incapable of instruction before the age of twelve. This opinion, confined to the understanding, is perhaps not far from the truth. But was it his opinion, that children before twelve are incapable of being instructed in matters of right and wrong, of love and hatred, or of other feelings that have an original seat in the heart? If it was, gross must have been his ignorance of human nature.' [103] Both feel that the affections and the desires need cultivation, that 'few arts are more complicated or more profound' than that of the cultivation of the heart, but both agree as to the superior importance of the feelings as springs of action. 'In planning the present work, I had chiefly in view the culture of the heart; prompted by two motives, first, its superior importance in the conduct of life; next, its being in a great measure over-looked by writers upon education.' [104] Our opinions and belief, he feels, depend principally upon passion and prepossession,

[102] London, 1695, p. 42.   [103] *Op. cit.*, pp. 5-6.   [104] *Ibid.*, p. 232.

little on reason, and not at all upon the will.[105] As to opinion founded on reasoning, he writes elsewhere, ' it is obvious, that the conviction produced by reasoning, can never rise above what is produced by the intuitive proposition upon which the reasoning is founded.' [106] Similarly Elizabeth Hamilton writes that ' the highest cultivation of the intellectual powers will not be sufficient, unless these powers be properly directed; this direction they must receive from the bias that has been given to the desires and affections of the heart. If these desires and affections have been corrupted by improper indulgence, or perverted and depraved by means of powerful impressions made upon the tender mind, we may give our children knowledge, we may give them learning, we may give them accomplishments, but we shall never be able to teach them to apply these acquirements to just or noble purposes.' [107] Elizabeth Hamilton was no doubt considerably influenced by Kames as well as by Locke and Hartley.[108] Kames in turn, for all his criticisms of Rousseau throughout his book, had a considerable respect for him.[109] But it is clear that he is even farther than Mrs. Brooke from any essential harmony with his point of view.

VI

Somewhat nearer to one phase of Rousseau's thought is Mrs. Inchbald's *Nature and Art*. It tells the story of two cousins, William, brought up by his learned father, the dean, who required him to pass his time ' from morning till night, with persons who taught him to walk, to ride, to talk, to think like a man—a foolish man, instead of a wise

[105] *Ibid.*, p. 270.
[106] *Sketches*, III, 209-10.
[107] *Op. cit.*, Boston, 1825, II, 12.
[108] *Ibid.*, I, 21.
[109] *Op. cit.*, pp. 26-27.

child, as nature designed him to be,' [110] and Henry, brought up by his father among the natives of Zocotora Island. It goes without saying that the former turns out to be proud, selfish, and profligate—though successful, while the other, educated among the savages, is humane, generous, just—and unsuccessful. By making an island of savages the scene of the education of the young Henry, Mrs. Inchbald gives her novel the air of embracing the popular primitivistic theories of the day, but in reality there is no genuine primitivism here, only a confusion of several points of view. Henry, in the first place, is educated by his father not by the savages, and the example of the savages is used apparently only as a demonstration of how not to behave.[111] The island was chosen by Mrs. Inchbald as a place where the ideal conditions of a social vacuum free from the corrupting prejudices of polite society could best be realized. In this she is of course following the advice of Rousseau, but one is moved to wonder why, if Henry had the innate qualities necessary to develop into a youth of sensibility and gentleness [112] under the negative régime in which he had been brought up, the natives, who shared his humanity and were brought up in the same social vacuum, should have become so ferocious? The social-vacuum idea had however taken hold of the imagination of theorists at this time. Mrs. Inchbald may very well have been further influenced in this point of view by a play by the Countess de Genlis which she had translated. She calls the play *The Child of Nature* in her version. In this case the child of nature is reared by the Marquis Amanza, not in an uncivilized country, but in total seclusion in his own castle in Spain with one old duenna. So uncontaminated by the world has her mind

[110] London, 1796, I, 44-45.   [111] *Ibid.*, p. 55.   [112] *Ibid.*, p. 75.

been kept that she has not even been allowed any books except those of the Marquis's own writing. ' Hear me, Amanthes,' he says to her at the end of his labors, ' I have hitherto secluded you from the tumult and dissipation of the world, in order to form your heart and mind; and to give you leisure to attain every useful science, and every accomplished talent—you have surpassed my utmost expectations—and I would now enjoy the pride of what I have completed—I must show you to the world—we were born for society, and you will be the ornament and delight of that which you shall make your choice.' [113] The interesting thing about this educational experiment from our point of view is that Amanza has brought his ward up in isolation in order to give her the virtues of the original *primitive* child of nature. Witness the Epilogue:

> The Child of Nature was, in days of yore,
> What, much I fear, we shall behold no more,
> The simple dress, the bloom that art wou'd shame,
> The frank avowal, and the gen'rous flame;
> The native note, which sweetly warbling wild,
> Told the soft sorrows of the charming child—
> Turn to a modern Miss, whose feather'd brow
> Speaks the light surface of the soil below
>
> .   .   .   .
>
> Thus are the feelings of the youthful day,
> By fashion's raging tempest whirl'd away:—
> May I, but with no wish to under-rate her,
> Entreat you to prefer our Child of Nature.

Another French experiment in the use of the social vacuum for educational purposes, an experiment which was popular enough to go through many editions in France and appear in at least two English versions, is

[113] Brulart de Sillery, Countess de Genlis, *The Child of Nature*, trans. E. Inchbald, London, 1788, p. 13.

Beaurieu's *L'Élève de la Nature*.[114] I mention this book in passing with only a comment or two since it has already been discussed by M. Emile Legouis.[115] As M. Legouis has pointed out, the present author goes Rousseau one better: instead of secluding the pupil with his paragon of a tutor from corrupting social contacts, he isolates the pupil entirely by shutting him in a wooden cage until he is fifteen and then placing him ' in the hands of Nature ' on an uninhabited island. He turns into a complete deist upon his first view of the beauties of nature,[116] and becomes a creature of such exquisite sensibility that he even shed tears for the falling of the leaves. ' If the reader is surprised that I should shed so many tears for the falling leaves,' writes the Man of Nature in explanation, ' remember that *Nature* only began her work upon you, and that *Art* unfortunately finished you: . . . It is possible that you might behold nature afflicted without emotion; but I, whom she alone formed; I, who was entirely the work of her hands, could I avoid sighing when I saw my mother expiring, and did not know that she would shortly be born again.' [117] We find here the same emphasis on the rightness of the natural feelings that we found in Mrs. Brooke's novels: the Man of Nature is never vindictive; he remembers the benefits conferred on him and forgets the injuries; his feelings are tender and intense, his impulses generous. He is finally recalled to his native

---

[114] Gaspard Guillard de Beaurieu, *L'Élève de la Nature*, La Haye et Paris, 1763; other editions in 1764, 1766, 1771, 1777, 1778, 1783, 1790, 1794. Translated, fairly faithfully, by James Burne, as *The Man of Nature*, London, 1773, and adapted in shorter form as ' Imerice, or The Child of Nature,' by the Abbe Laurent, in *Favourite Tales; Translated from the French*, London, 1787.

[115] *G. G. de Beaurieu et son Élève de la Nature*, 1763, Oxford, 1925.

[116] *Man of Nature*, I, 206.   [117] *Ibid.*, p. 228.

country to demonstrate by his example that men ' are born humane, affectionate, virtuous: that the most perfect education is not that which gives them those virtues and talents which excite admiration, but that which prevents their acquiring the vices of society, that brings them nearest to *Nature,* and trusts them in her hands, as I have done thee.' [118] But he returns eventually to the Island of Peace to become an educator, forgetting apparently how successfully nature had functioned unaided in his own case.

Among the writers interested in educational theory in England, Thomas Day was in his time perhaps the most notorious disciple of Rousseau. The story of his experimental attempt to rear himself a wife upon Rousseau's principles has been so well told that I will not here repeat it, tempting as the details are.[119] And *Sandford and Merton,* that delectable story of naughtiness and goodness —or perhaps I should say in the language of the book, pusillanimity and intrepidity—to its culmination in the seven year old Tommy's final resolution, ' from this time I shall apply myself to the study of nothing but reason and philosophy; and therefore I have bid adieu to dress and finery for ever,' [120] has likewise been delightfully reviewed. All that is left for us is the less grateful task of looking a little more carefully at some of the underlying ideas, to see just where Day fits into the scheme of thought of his time.

There is an interesting combination of ideas in *Sand-*

[118] *Ibid.,* II, 120.
[119] Cf. Dowden, *The French Revolution and English Poetry,* N. Y., 1901; Michael Sadler, *Thomas Day, an English Disciple of Rousseau,* Cambridge, 1928; and Hesketh Pearson, *Doctor Darwin,* London, 1930, Ch. V.
[120] London, 1783-89, III, 256.

ford and Merton. Thomas Day is nearer to Rousseau in putting less emphasis than does Mrs. Brooke on the ' cultivation of the Heart.' He does indeed believe apparently in a certain fund of natural goodness in the child. After Tommy's great relapse, Mr. Barlow says to his father: ' the seeds of different qualities frequently lie concealed in the character, and only wait for an opportunity of exerting themselves; and it is the great business of education to apply such motives to the imagination, as may stimulate it to laudable exertions.' [121] ' He has always appeared to me generous and humane, and to have a fund of natural goodness amid all the faults which spring too luxuriously in his character.' [122] Day, it may be observed in passing, forgets here that he had remarked at the time of the relapse that ' Tommy himself had now completely resumed his natural character, and thrown aside all that he had learned during his residence with Mr. Barlow.' [123] However this may be, Day, it is clear, has rather more in common with the rationalists of the beginning of the century than with the later moral sense school. That many of the principles he professes are also those of the revolutionists is only to be expected, for the revolutionists, as we shall see in a later chapter, clung to much that was old in defiance of the logic of their position. Mr. Barlow, when questioned by Tommy's father, denies strenuously that he is one of the perfectionists who look for the speedy reform of society; he advocates, rather, a program of expediency to avoid ' disgusting weak and luxurious minds ' by the rigour and ' primitive simplicity ' of the doctrines of social equality that are the ideal of religion.[124] The fundamental principles of Mr. Barlow's

[121] *Ibid.,* p. 22. Cf. III, 12.
[122] *Ibid.,* p. 23.
[123] *Ibid.,* II, 263.
[124] *Ibid.,* I, 30.

(and Thomas Day's) social and educational creed are simplicity, the equality of men, the wholesomeness of poverty and honest labor, and the unwholesomeness of luxury. There is more than a hint that Day looks on these principles in very much the same light as the earlier rationalists had looked on the laws of nature. This rationalistic strain is very much reinforced in a passage from his *Letters of Marius*: ' I have often thought it a wonderful fallacy of some divines to depreciate human reason in order to exalt religion: for, unless that religion be imported by particular inspiration to every individual, what other method is there of establishing it, than proofs adapted to his reason? . . . But this fallacy does not seem to be confined to the venerable order of the clergy. Politicians practice it at least with equal success, when they descant upon the blindness and ignorance of, what they call, the multitude.' [125] In the emphasis on simplicity, anti-luxury, equalitarianism, Day's primitivism had undoubtedly more in common with the rationalistic than the sentimental primitivism which followed. The ' natural ' state of man, for Day, is either the pre-political state or the pre-cultural state characterized by freedom, simplicity, and equality. ' Poverty,' he writes, ' that is to say, a state of labour and frequent self-denial, is the state of man—it is the state of all in the happiest and most equal governments, the state of nearly all in every country:—it is a state in which all the faculties both of body and mind are always found to develop themselves with the most advantage, and in which the moral feelings have generally the greatest influence.' [126] The virtues of the primitive state he is never tired of illustrating—with em-

[125] *Letters of Marius: or Reflections upon the Peace and the East-India Bill, and the Present Crisis,* London, 1784 (3rd edition), pp. 13-14.
[126] *Ibid.,* I, 21-22.

phasis on the absence of corrupting luxury—in the High-landers of Scotland,[127] the Scythians,[128] the Kamtschat-kans,[129] and the Arabians.[130]

With this rationalistic primitivism is combined a typical late-eighteenth-century belief in the power of education and the importance of early impressions in moulding the mind and the character. ' May not all human characters,' he writes, ' frequently be traced back to impressions made at so early a period, that none but discerning eyes would ever suspect their existence? Yet nothing is more certain; what we are at twenty depends upon what we were at fifteen; what we are at fifteen, upon what we were at ten: where shall we then place the beginning of the series? ' [131] Whether Day got his sense of the importance of early impressions from Locke by way of Rousseau, or more directly from the associationists and utilitarians, it is impossible to say.

We have now made the complete round from rationalism to an ethics of feeling and back to the dawning of a new rationalism. In the next chapters we shall trace the course of this new rationalism in popular literature.

[127] *Ibid.*, III, 105.
[128] *Ibid.*, III, 214 ff
[129] *Ibid.*, II, 187 ff.
[130] *Ibid.*, III, 70 ff.
[131] *Ibid.*, I, 33.

CHAPTER V

CHAIN OF BEING, EVOLUTION, AND PROGRESS

I

While a host of popular writers were thus deploring the loss of a natural, primitive simplicity, whether it was the simplicity of an uncorrupted reason that followed the dictates of the law of nature, or the simplicity of the natural affections uncontaminated by the refinements of civilization, and were advocating reform by a return to that primitive simplicity, another host of writers, for whom the adjectives 'eternal' and 'immutable' had lost their former fascination, were concentrating on the idea of change, of becoming, of *progress* from the simple to the complex instead of *degeneration* from the simple. They were headed toward the future instead of toward the past, were interested in what life might become in new terms instead of what it might become if it imitated the past. That either group, primitivists or progressivists, should ever have thought that they could look, Janus-like, both directions at once, hold both their primitive simplicity and evolutionary diversity within the same system, cling to permanence and change at the same time, would seem to be an impossibility outside of a logician's nightmare. But popular thought has a hardy digestion and does not recoil from a diet of mutual incompatibles that would send an epicure of fine philosophical distinctions to his grave. That popular writers did try to reconcile these two divergent points of view I shall try to show before we have done; but first let us pick up the thread of the various popular forms of the theory of progress.

One version of the idea of progress in the eighteenth

century was that which grew out of the development of the theory of evolution. But as the theory of evolution got itself confused in popular literature with the principle of continuity, or the chain of being, which looks on the surface like an evolutionary theory but really has a quite different metaphysical foundation, it will be necessary to deal with the two ideas together.

The history of the idea of the chain of being and its confusion in the eighteenth century with incipient evolutionary theories is a full story in itself, a story which has recently been exhaustively treated by Professor A. O. Lovejoy in his William James Lectures, (1932-33). For the complete history of the idea, therefore, I refer the reader to his forthcoming book, *The Great Chain of Being: a Study in the History of an Idea,* and I shall content myself with a brief summary of the philosophical concepts which lay behind the popular eighteenth century development of the idea of continuity and the theory of evolution.[1] Without attempting, thereafter, a full illustration of the history of these ideas in the eighteenth century, such as is to be found in Professor Lovejoy's book, I shall merely show, first, by an analysis of several works not used by him, how the idea of continuity led to theories of progress, and, second, by reference to Erasmus Darwin, how the doctrine of evolution afforded further sanction for the more extravagant theories of infinite perfectibility.

There had been two doctrines from classical philosophy that, almost unchallenged, had held their ground through the medieval period well into the seventeenth century and had formed the background of scientific thought until

---

[1] The conception has been briefly summarized by the same writer in his ' Optimism and Romanticism,' *Pub. of the Mod. Lang. Assoc. of America,* XVII (1927), 930-933.

then. They were the doctrine of final causes and that of the immutability of species, both Aristotelian in their traditional form. In regard to final causality the traditional pattern of thought as it came down through the church fathers was something like this: nature was created for the use and convenience of man; there is a gradation in created beings from the lowest forms up to man; man, the nearest to God of earthly creatures, was created for the glorification of God and a final mystical absorption into his spirit. God, in other words, is the end or final cause of all creation as he is also the first cause. If man could only comprehend the whole scheme of things—and there were many theologians who apparently felt that they could qualify for the trial—he would see that even the most inconspicuous object in the universe has its appropriate place in the design of the whole for which it was uniquely and admirably adapted, and all parts of the whole work together toward a single end or final cause. In other words, the design of the whole preceded the parts and was their final cause. The doctrine of immutable species was almost inseparable from that of final causality, for the perpetuation of the species was taken as one of the clearest proofs of an informing purpose in nature.

Now both the idea of final causality and that of immutable species were quite compatible with, in fact necessary to, the principle of continuity which, as Professor Lovejoy has pointed out, came into great popularity as part of the philosophy of optimism of the late seventeenth and early eighteenth century. But it is evident on the other hand that these premises were incompatible with any evolutionary theory of the transformation of species. Clearly something had to happen to the dominant metaphysics before biologists would be so oriented in relation to their material as to see it from an evolutionary perspective. Fortunately something did happen to change this dominant metaphysics—perhaps only too thoroughly for the advancement of the science of biology.

It is unnecessary to trace the steps whereby Galileo, Descartes, Boyle, and Newton developed their mechanical hypotheses for the explanation of physical phenomena. It is sufficient to remind ourselves that by the reduction of physical phenomena to a harmonious, geometrical system governed by natural law, the scientific tendency was to concentrate on what was measurable by mathematical law: matter (resolved into its constituent atoms) and motion, operating in space and time. From these ingredients seventeenth-century science rebuilt the universe. It was clear—or should have been clear very early in the scientific development—that the new universe created by the physicists no longer fitted the old metaphysics of final causality. That seventeenth-century physicists, however, were no more impeccable in the logic of their metaphysics than certain contemporary physicists need not surprise us. There seems to have been considerable apprehension on the part of the scientists of the possible materialistic implications of their mechanical hypothesis. Indeed they had, in the philosophy of Hobbes, an unpalatable example of what would happen were the natural laws which they were investigating extended to the realm of metaphysics. Consequently every attempt was made to keep God in the picture not only as the first creator but as a kind of officiating mechanic and trouble-man. Not a few scientists clung to the doctrine of final causes and saw in the wonders of the new harmonies of a mechanical universe only a more fertile ground for the argument from design.[2] There was indeed a great burst of popular enthusiasm in the eighteenth century for the argument from design either in attack on mechanism, or in the attempt to reconcile a mechanical physical universe with final causality. Philosophers and scientists set to work with more diligence than ever to find illustrations of the inscrutable perfection with which God had fashioned even the minutest part of every creature to the end for which it was supposed to have been designed—and descriptive biology and geology progressed as never before.[3]

Anything like a pure mechanistic metaphysics was very slow in getting under way, especially in England, but even without a clear-cut recognition in the early eighteenth century of the metaphysical implications of the new physics, the work of the scientists went on, and the Newtonian principles were extended to other fields of investigation. Most important for us at the present moment was the extension to the field of biology. The attempt to reduce the operations of the body to a purely mechanistic basis had started very early with Harvey's work on the circulation of the blood and had grown in favor in the seventeenth century through the influence of such works as Borelli's analysis of the mechanism of animal motion (*De motu animalium*, 1679), and Perrault's *Méchanique des animaux*, (Volume III of his *Essais de la physique*, 1680), and in the eighteenth century through the work of

[2] See M. E. Prior, ' Joseph Glanvill and Seventeenth Century Science,' *Mod. Phil.*, XXX (1932), 170-77, for a discussion of the use of the new physics in the argument from design.

[3] References to English and German examples will be found in Ernst Krause, *Life of Erasmus Darwin*, London, 1887, pp. 149-51, and French references will be found in D. Mornet, *Les sciences de la nature en France, au XVIIIᵉ siècle*, Paris, 1911, pp. 148 ff., and in P. M. Masson's review of this book in *RHL*, XIX (1912), 944-51.

Boerhaave in Holland and La Mettrie in France. This mechanistic line of development inspired by the physical sciences was both a help and a hindrance to biology— perhaps for the time being more of a help than a hindrance. By tending to free men's minds from the incubus of final causes which directed attention to the finished product rather than to the problem of origins, by demonstrating the adequacy of natural causation to explain almost everything in the existing universe, and, most of all, by throwing the emphasis on change rather than permanence, on the process of becoming rather than immutability, the new physics and metaphysics did the biological sciences an immense service. They raised the question why, if the physical world has conceivably been evolved from the interaction of motion and matter, may not life in its present complex forms have arisen from equally simple components by equally natural processes. They freed the ground for an explanation of evolution by a theory of the survival of the fittest incompatible with the former doctrine of design as ordinarily conceived.[4]

Such was the metaphysical battleground in the early eighteenth century. It will be seen from the above that there was a double reason for the popularity at this time of the doctrine of final causality: it had the sanction of long tradition, and it was the chief weapon against the materialistic implications of the mechanistic hypothesis. The doctrine of continuity, or the chain of being, as I have said, presupposed this very metaphysics. Summarized briefly, the most typical form of the doctrine of continuity is as follows: this universal system, which is the best of all possible systems that God might have created, is the manifest product of design in its symmetrical and har-

[4] Cf. A. O. Lovejoy, ' Some Eighteenth Century Evolutionists,' *Pop. Sc. Monthly*, LXV (1904), 240-51, 323-27.

monious pattern. One of the chief excellences of the system is the fecundity of nature in the creation of life forms. When all the forms of life are graded from the highest to the lowest, there is seen to be no gap in creation anywhere; every possible form has been created. Whatever apparent evil there may be in the system is due merely to the fact that one cannot have a complete chain at all without having a gradation from the most excellent to the least excellent forms of life. The evil for any species is incident to its place in the chain. Though members of the chain may strive to perfect themselves in their appointed sphere, the happiness of each member depends on knowing and keeping his proper place in the chain. If any species of being in the scale were to invade the province of the species just above, the whole system would be destroyed.

It will easily be seen that in versions of this doctrine which put emphasis on the minuteness of the gradation between species and upon the upward striving of each member of the chain, the whole scheme had an evolutionary air, if one overlooked the fact that it was irrevocably coupled with the ideas of fixed species and design. But as a matter of fact there was no implication in the chain of being in its original form that one species had been ' evolved ' from the one below it. As Baker says in *The Universe,*

> 'Tis Nature's constant Law that ev'ry Thing
> From Parents like itself, in order, spring.[5]

Although each member of the species was conceived as striving to perfect itself in its place in the scale, there was no expectation that it would actually invade the precinct

[5] London [1727], p. 22.

of its next higher neighbor; in other words there was no room for mutation of species in the chain of being. In fact it was a logically necessary corollary of the idea of the *plenum formarum* that all the members of the scale should exist simultaneously rather than consecutively.

What then are the inferences from the doctrine of continuity that one might expect to find in popular litera- ture? In the first place, it was perfectly possible for a writer to head in the opposite direction from either progress or evolution and, by emphasizing the perfection of the original creation as it issued from the hand of God and by dwelling on the imperfections only too ap- parent in the scheme of things at present, to adapt the chain to a doctrine of primitivism and the theory of progressive degeneration. The following quotation from the *Sentimental Magazine* illustrates the point: ' We shall find an infinite subordination of beings, all ultimately dependent on the great Creator for life and breath and all things. . . . Surely then, if man is the highest order of beings in this terrestrial chain, the two links which unite heaven and earth together must be angel and man; and therefore man was made a little, a very little lower than the angels; though some are so depraved as scarcely to retain the least vestiges of their glorious origin, besides their external appearance. God certainly made man up- right . . . although they have sought out many inven- tions, and now fall short of that primitive rectitude, innate purity, and exalted talents, with which man was originally created.' [6] Monboddo, as we shall see in a later chapter, likewise dwells upon the perfection of the creature as it issued from the hands of its maker, and its subsequent degeneration.

[6] II (1774), 62. There is a very amusing parody of this point of view in *Poetry of the Anti-Jacobin,* ed. Charles Edmonds, London, 1852, p. 69.

When, however, the chief emphasis was thrown, as was frequently the case, on the idea of movement upward within each species toward the greater perfection of the next species, the doctrine provided a favorable environment for a theory of progress in man apart from any evolutionary idea. Finally, in spite of the fact that the conception of the chain is logically antagonistic to the larger doctrine of evolution by virtue of its allegiance to immutable species and design, it provided a fertile soil for that doctrine by its very work of classification and gradation which called attention to the smallness of the difference between one species and another and especially between the highest animals and man. As the century progressed the tendency in regard to the chain of being was to drop out the anti-intellectualist implications of Pope's *Essay on Man* and the ' know thy place ' admonition, to stress less the beauty of ' th'amazing whole ' *in statu quo,* and to throw the emphasis on the endless striving of the whole chain toward the perfection next above each member, until in some cases the idea of the chain actually merged into an evolutionary theory.

II

One of the most important and fully formulated theories of progress based on the idea of progressive change in organic life, almost reaching a species of evolutionism, but clinging nevertheless to the chain of being, is that of Adam Ferguson, an eighteenth-century thinker who has received less attention than he deserves. Ferguson arrived at much the same idea of limitless progress that Godwin came to, but by a totally different channel. One gets some conception of the complexity of the history of the idea of progress from an analysis of Ferguson's premises and a comparison with those of Godwin.

Godwin's theory of progress was largely based, as we shall see in more detail in Chapter VII, on the rationalism and mechanism of the late eighteenth century; the theory of Ferguson, on the other hand, of which part was formulated at least as early as 1766 and part was published in 1792, almost contemporaneously with *Political Justice,* was based chiefly on the psychology and ethics of the opposite school—that of the moral sense and benevolence. The recent publication of an elaborate analysis of the sociological thought of Ferguson [7] makes it unnecessary to give more than a brief and highly selective account of his thought. On the other hand, the presence in Professor Lehmann's book of such dubious and inaccurate statements in regard to the thought-background of Ferguson's work as ' the romantic Rousseauan idealism of a savage paradise,' [8] ' Even the intellectualist Hobbes does not deny the operation of the passions,' [9] ' " the law of nature," a rational principle derived, essentially from a Newtonian conception of the universe,' [10] and so forth, are justification enough for a further orientation of Ferguson's ideas, in spite of the really valuable work Professor Lehmann has done in the analysis of his sociological thought.

In method Ferguson allies himself definitely with men like Burke, Hume, and Priestley who insisted on the importance of historical fact, rather than with the speculators like Godwin. 'Human knowledge,' he wrote, 'begins

[7] W. C. Lehmann, *Adam Ferguson and the Beginnings of Modern Sociology,* New York, 1930.

[8] *Ibid.,* p. 59. Prof. Lehmann says that in Ferguson's day ' careful accounts ' of the life of the savages were available. He cites—to mention only one name—Lafitau. The merest glance at the plates in *Mœurs des Sauvages* even without a reading of the text would have saved Prof. Lehmann from this error.

[9] *Ibid.,* p. 191.

[10] *Ibid.,* p. 190.

and ends with particulars.' [11]   Just as ' Men advance in
real science by tracing facts to their general laws, and by
applying these laws to phenomena, which of themselves
never would have suggested the law,' [12] so the historian
of man should collect facts and ' endeavour to conceive
his nature as it actually is, or has actually been, apart from
any notion of ideal perfection, or defect.' [13]   Allying himself thus with the method of inductive science, he deplores
speculations on the nature of man based on mere conjecture: ' in framing our account of what man was in some
imaginary state of nature, we overlook what he has always
appeared within the reach of our own observation, and in
the records of history.' [14]   Close as Ferguson is, however,
to the method of science, he sees a danger of superficiality
in that method when applied to moral science. In this
matter, as in many others, he takes issue with Hume.
Lehmann has made much of Ferguson's dependence on
Hume,[15] but we shall see in the course of our discussion
that he diverges from Hume almost oftener than he follows him. Certainly the following criticism refers (among
other things) too clearly to Hume's professed attempt to
found a science of morals to be neglected: ' Physical science,
they [certain writers unnamed] suppose to be a knowledge
of subjects natural; moral science, a knowledge of mind
or subjects intellectual. . . . In their apprehension, moral
approbation and disapprobation are mere phenomena to
be explained; and, in such explanation their science of
morals actually terminates. The phenomena of moral

[11] *Principles of Moral and Political Science,* Edinburgh, 1792, I, 279.
[12] *Ibid.*
[13] *Ibid.*, p. 1.
[14] *Essay on the History of Civil Society,* Dublin, 1762, p. 3. See also
pp. 4, 7, 111.
[15] *Op. cit.,* p. 197 ff.

approbation have been supposed no more than a diversified appearance of the consideration that is paid to private
interest, to public utility, to the reason of things; or they
have been supposed to result from the sympathy of one
man with another. But if moral sentiment could be thus
explained into any thing different from itself, whether
interest, utility, reason or sympathy, this could amount to
no more than theory. And it were difficult to say to what
effect knowledge is improved, by resolving a first act of
the mind into a second, no way better than the first.' [16]

Thus Ferguson, who might have been led by his interest
in the method of science into an attempt similar to that of
Godwin and the utilitarians to found a moral science that
would have the same objective validity as physical science,
was diverted from that direction by his sense of the inadequacy of such an ethics. In like manner he keeps clear
of the mechanistic premises of Godwin and his group.
'The subject from which physical laws are collected,' he
writes in his *Institutes of Moral Philosophy*, ' may be
classed under four principal heads: Mechanism, vegetation, animal life, and intelligence. It has not hitherto
been made appear, although sometimes attempted, that
the operations of any of these different natures are comprehended under the same laws to which the others are
subjected. The phenomena of vegetation are not comprehended under any known law of mechanism, much less
animal life or intelligence.' [17] Denying the application of
mechanism to organic life, he also repudiates moral necessity and proclaims the freedom of the will. [18] It followed
almost as a matter of course that he would see the fallacies

---

[16] *Principles*, I, 161. Cf. Ferguson's defence of objective reality in
opposition to Berkeley and Hume, *ibid.*, pp. 75-76.

[17] Edinburgh, 1769, pp. 5-6.

[18] *Principles*, I, 153 ff.

of the extreme rationalism of Godwin and his group. In fact one recognizes in Ferguson's work both early and late many of the clichés of the Platonists and of Shaftesbury, with a considerable flavor of Stoicism.[19] Many of his principles are identical with those which with other writers had formed a basis for primitivism. To rehearse them briefly, he, like the thinkers of the late seventeenth century, takes as axiomatic the principle that man is a social being.[20] That this social tendency comes from a real regard for our fellow beings and no mere instinct of self-preservation, he argues from the fact that this ' affection operates with the greatest force where it meets with the greatest difficulties. . . . In the breast of a man, its flame redoubles where the wrongs or sufferings of his friend, or his country, require his aid.' [21] Ferguson, it is true, is no mere sentimentalist. He sees the dissensions in society as well as the harmony. He repudiates the sentimental conjectures relative to the ' state of nature,' concluding that that state was one exclusively neither of war nor peace.[22] But, agreeing with Shaftesbury and others that man is moved by both the selfish and benevolent affections,[23] he also agrees with Shaftesbury and Hutcheson that the social affections are the dominating ones.[24] This principle is combined with a conception of an almost instinctive moral sense.[25] This gives Ferguson a much less rationalistic basis

. [19] See *Principles*, I, 7, for his acknowledgment of a Stoic preference.

[20] *Ibid.*, p. 21 and *Essay*, p. 24.

[21] *Essay*, p. 27.

[22] *Ibid.*, p. 23.

[23] *Essay*, p. 15 ff.; see also *Institutes*, pp. 90-91, 114-15, where he repeats the idea with a footnote reference to ' Shaftesbury's *Inquiry into Virtue*.'

[24] See the summary of his discussion in *Essay*, pp. 50-51.

[25] *Principles*, I, 300: ' The distinction of right and wrong is coeval with human nature: It is perceived without instruction, in acts of fidelity and benevolence, or of perfidy and malice.'

for his ethics than Godwin had. Ferguson, however, did not go to the opposite extreme of Hume. He was too much of a Stoic to agree with Hutcheson and Hume that the pleasure-pain test of right could be the basis of moral behaviour. 'The love of what is excellent,' he writes in the *Institutes,* ' is a sure guide to what is pleasant; but the desire of pleasure is not a sure guide to what is excellent.' [26] Somewhat vaguely—like Shaftesbury—he believes in a sensibility, or moral sense, which ' joined to the powers of deliberation and reason . . . constitutes the basis of a moral nature.' [27] There is, he admits, a ' felicity of conduct in human affairs, in which it is difficult to distinguish the promptitude of the head from the ardour and sensibility of the heart. Where both are united, they constitute superiority of mind. . . .' [28] The understanding it is which enables man intelligently to relate his actions to the good of society as a whole.[29]

Whence, then, is derived Ferguson's theory of progress? So far his premises are, as we have said, such as might easily have led to primitivism and are quite different from the usual bases of the theory of progress. When we consider further that Ferguson still kept the argument from design and at least the terminology of the chain of being, even in his latest work, it seems even more puzzling to find a well formulated theory of progress even in his earliest book, published in 1767, when ' progress ' had not yet become a catchword.

Ferguson seems to have arrived at the belief in progress partly through his historical view of the rise of civilization

[26] P. 161.
[27] *Essay*, p. 48.
[28] *Ibid.*, p. 42.
[29] *Principles*, I, 35, 313; *Essay*, pp. 55, 79-80; *Institutes*, pp. 171-72, 173-74.

but chiefly through his observation of the principle of change in all life processes. I have said that he kept something of the conception of the chain of being. ' In the variety of being,' he writes, ' we observe the gradation of excellence displayed on a scale of great extent. The parts rise above one another by slow and almost insensible steps. That man is placed at the top of this visible scale has never been questioned.' [30] Within this chain, however, there is the principle of change and progression. ' Parts that constitute the system of nature, like the stones of an arch, support and are supported; but their beauty is not of the quiescent kind. The principles of agitation and of life combine their effects in constituting an order of things, which is at once fleeting and permanent. The powers of vegetation and animal life come in aid of mechanical principles; the whole is alive and in action: The scene is perpetually changing; but, in its changes, exhibits an order more striking than could be made to arise from the mere position or description of any forms entirely at rest. Man, with his intellectual powers, placed at the top of this terrestrial scale, like the key-stone of the arch, completes the system.' [31] Unlike the earlier believers in the chain of being again, Ferguson conceives that creation was not simultaneous but is a continuous process: ' In this wonderful scene, the power that works was originally creative, and is equally so in every successive period of time.' [32] In fact in this principle of change Ferguson comes very near to a theory of evolution of species: ' The genius of variation, which is so eminent in comparing different species of being together, is carried into the economy with which the same species, in respect to the individuals that compose it, is continually changing; and the genera-

[30] *Principles*, I, 329.   [31] *Principles*, p. 174.   [32] *Ibid.*, p. 175.

tions that *were* and *are,* hasten to make way for those
which are to come.' [33] But Ferguson does not get nearer
than this to a conception of evolution. In other passages
he seems to indicate a belief in immutable species.[34] In
regard to man he points out his physical relation to the
animals below him but considers that his intelligence constitutes him a distinct species.[35]

Nevertheless, in spite of the fact that he does not go
all the way with the evolutionists, Ferguson has found in
this principle of change an adequate basis for a theory of
progress for man. The ' law of nature ' has become for
him the law of progress. That member of the scale of
being has the highest place ' which is destined to grow in
perfection, and may grow without end: its good is advancement, and its evil, decline.' [36] The primitive state
can no longer be regarded as the sole state of nature: ' If
we admit that man is susceptible of improvement, and has
in himself a principle of progression, and a desire of perfection, it appears improper to say, that he has quitted the
state of his nature, when he has begun to proceed; or that
he finds a station for which he was not intended, while,
like other animals, he only follows the disposition, and
employs the powers that nature has given him.' [37] Further-
more art is not at war with nature in man for art is in a
sense natural to man. [38]

It is through the accumulated inheritance of generations
that the progress of man is achieved.[39] But while the
progress of man is so achieved, it is in no sense a man-

[33] *Ibid.,* p. 174.
[34] *Ibid.,* pp. 167-68.
[35] *Principles,* I, 48; *Essay,* p. 8.
[36] *Principles,* I, 191.
[37] *Essay,* p. 12.
[38] *Ibid.,* p. 9.
[39] *Principles,* I, 175, 194, and *Essay,* p. 7.

controlled progress, as Godwin and the other speculators would make it. It is brought about unconsciously, almost through a necessity of his nature, instead of through his own volition. ' Like the winds, that come one knows not whence, and blow whithersoever they list, the forms of society are derived from an obscure and distant origin; they arise, long before the date of philosophy, from the instinct, not from the speculations, of men. . . . Every step and every movement of the multitude, even in what are termed enlightened ages, are made with equal blindness to the future; and nations stumble upon establishments, which are indeed the result of human actions, but not the execution of any design.' [40] Like Burke he believes that this progress is necessarily slow, cannot indeed be hurried,[41] and like Burke he faces the fact that this progress leads inevitably to increasing complexity.[42] In this he is more consistent than Godwin who clung to the principle of simplicity.

There is an interesting change in Ferguson's thought to be observed in the *Principles* which was published twenty-five years after the *Essay on Civil Society*. In the earlier book, while he defines all the principles of progress in man, he puts considerable emphasis also on the possibility of retrogression and devotes a long section to the familiar contemporary theme of the dangers of luxury.[43] In the later book, however, the discussion of luxury has dropped out, he has much less to say about the possibility of retrogression, and in the spirit of the time is more extravagant in his prophecies of an unlimited progress for the species. The progress of man, he there writes, ' in its continual approach to the infinite perfection of what is eternal . . .

---

[40] *Essay*, pp. 182-83. [42] *Ibid.*, p. 272; *Principles*, I, 324.
[41] *Ibid.*, p. 10. [43] *Essay*, p. 353 ff.

may be compared to that curve, described by geometers, as in continual approach to a straight line, which it never can reach.' [44]

Thus Ferguson, by a totally different path, arrives at practically the same point as Godwin.

Another treatment of the chain of being of considerable importance is that of Mrs. Macaulay, because it is a clear example of another line of reasoning whereby the chain of being was made the basis of the theory of progress, and also because it is such an excellent example of what happens constantly in popular literature. In her *Treatise on the Immutability of Moral Truth,* Mrs. Macaulay, without giving up the chain of being, endeavors to refute William King's very premises in the *Origin of Evil,* or what she supposes are his premises. King's motive in supporting the idea of the chain was, as Leibniz's had been, to substitute a more satisfactory solution of the problem of the origin of evil for Bayle's dualism of good and evil principles. As we have seen, the solution was the doctrine of the evil of imperfection incident to the gradation of created life forms in the scale. This doctrine Mrs. Macaulay objects to for three reasons. The second of her reasons, which alone concerns us, is that the theory is derogatory to God because, as she interprets King, it makes creation an act of self-gratification instead of one of benevolence. Mrs. Macaulay finds herself unable to accept a divine motivation for the creation of the scale of being that to her mind could so easily be interpreted as the mere aesthetic satisfaction that God was to receive from the eternal, self-complacent contemplation of the harmony of the system. If evil is admitted for the sake of the harmony of the whole, she seems to reason, then that

[44] *Principles,* I, 184.

harmony takes precedence over benevolence as the motive for the creation of this type of world rather than some other.[45] She offers, therefore, the alternative solution that God had bestowed with benevolent intention all the happiness on his creatures that their natures were capable of receiving at the moment of creation, and had purposely refrained from making man, for instance, as perfect as possible, so that he could have the pleasure of becoming more perfect: he is to have ' a continued series of fresh satisfaction and new delights, whilst he is continually approaching nearer and nearer to that perfection, the excellence of which he has been taught to prize.' [46] Mrs. Macaulay here gives expression to an idea that was later to become one of the leading ideas of early nineteenth-century romanticism: the preferability of endless striving to actual achievement. Now if she had read William King's *Origin of Evil* more carefully she would have seen that he himself specifically refutes the idea that creation was an act of self-gratification with God. ' I know 'tis commonly said,' he writes, ' that the World was made for the *Glory of God*: But this is *after the manner of Men.* . . . Infinite knows no Bounds, nor has the Goodness of God any other Bounds beside his *Wisdom* and *Power,* which are also infinite, and in reality this makes most *for the Glory of God viz.* to have created a World with the greatest *Goodness.*' [47] And King's commentator, Edmund Law, in a note in the edition which Mrs. Macaulay evidently used,[48] reinforces the point of view. So far as Law can interpret the mind of God in the creation of life—and

---

[45] London, 1783, pp. 37, 41.

[46] *Ibid.*, p. 42. Cf. *Letters on Education, with Observations on Religious and Metaphysical Subjects*, London, 1790, pp. 348-49.

[47] *An Essay on the Origin of Evil*, Cambridge, 1739, pp. 60-61.

[48] See her reference on p. 27 which tallies with the 1739 edition.

he does not hesitate to speak with considerable authority
on the subject—the motive is one of as pure benevolence
as Mrs. Macaulay herself could desire. ' In order to confirm this belief,' he writes, '. . . it is necessary to consider (with reverence) what this Mind of God might be
in framing the World, and what was the most proper
Method of answering it. Now it appear'd from the
Conclusion of the first Chapter and Note 13. that the sole
Design of Almighty God in creating the Universe, was to
impart Felicity to other Beings: and in the beginning of
this Chapter it was proved that any Happiness thus com-
municated could not be *infinite*. His Design then is completely answer'd, if the greatest Degree of Happiness be
imparted of which created Beings are capable.' [49]   Further-
more the alternative suggestion made by Mrs. Macaulay,
that beings were created imperfect so that they might have
the pleasure of becoming more perfect, Law makes with
great eloquence. The infinite wisdom and goodness of
God, he reasons, would not produce beings in such a state
as to prohibit development toward perfection, for ' changes
from worse to better must be attended even with greater
degrees of Pleasure than a settled permanence in any the
highest State conceivable of Glory or Perfection, and consequently become necessary to the completion of all finite
Happiness.' [50]   The idea was not an uncommon one at the
time. Of it Mrs. Macaulay says, ' The blessing of a growing happiness is a notion which has been embraced both
by the divine and the philosopher, and is described in
glowing colours by Mr. Addison, in his Spectator, No.
III.' [51]   Thus Mrs. Macaulay, with rare economy though

[49] *Ibid.*, pp. 121-22 note.
[50] *Ibid.*, p. 124 note.
[51] *Op. cit.*, pp. 42-43. She apparently took her quotation from the very
note of Edmund Law referred to for she mistakes his No. 111 for No. III.
Cf. *Origin of Evil*, pp. 123-34, note 19.

probably complete unawareness, finds the grounds for her attack on King in what she supposes he said and the material for her reply in what he and his editor really did say.[52]

Mrs. Macaulay admits, in *Letters on Education,* that, so far, Man's use of his gift of reason, his tool for progression to a more perfect state, has brought rather more misery than happiness to him. He is not really so well off from the point of view of happiness as the animals below him in the scale who follow their natural instincts. In this attitude the author verges on anti-intellectualism and primitivism, but she goes on to say that ' this phenomenon does not prove that reason and the enlarged powers of imagination will finally and absolutely produce more misery than good to any being who has possessed them. It is far from a necessary consequence, that those gifts should ever produce evil; and when misery attends them, it always proceeds from incidental causes. The human faculties rise, by practice and education, from mere capacity to an excellence and an energy which enables man to become the carver of his own happiness.' [53]

As time went on this tendency to emphasize in the discussion of the scale of being the faculty of reason which forms the distinction between man and the animals beneath him in the scale threw into relief even more strikingly the idea of perfectibility in man.

III

It was perhaps inevitable that anything that looked on the surface so much like an evolutionary theory as the

[52] For a complete exposition of the thought of Edmund Law on this subject, see R. S. Crane, ' Anglican Apologetics and the Idea of Progress, 1699-1745,' *loc. cit.*

[53] *Letters on Education,* p. 10.

chain of being should get itself confused in popular literature with such a theory. And perhaps it is well that the evolutionary hypothesis made its début into eighteenth-century popular literature under the respectable chaperonage of the time-honored metaphysics of the chain of being. If that hypothesis had been first presented to the eighteenth-century public in such a way as to demand a preliminary relinquishing of inherited morality and religion—if it had demanded of the public that it cast away the anchor and ballast of permanence and immutability, of eternal and unchanging truth, of a belief in a beneficent design in the mind of God, if it had asked the public to trust the ship to such fearsome forces as change, mutability, and necessity—then evolutionary theory would have made small headway. But a generation that could not have been brought even to consider the idea of evolution if it had been obliged first to repudiate the very foundations of its morality and religion was quite easily induced to entertain that idea when combined, with whatever defiance of logic, with a traditional metaphysics. Thus disguised and protected did the hypothesis of evolution have, as it were, a happy seed-time, a period in which to germinate and take root, before the orthodox world scented the danger.

Without, however, going into the various literary documents which show the confusion between the two ideologies and the gradual emergence of an evolutionary hypothesis, all of which are analyzed by Professor Lovejoy, I pass at once to a brief resumé of the theory as developed by Erasmus Darwin into a doctrine of the infinite perfectibility of man.

Although even Darwin uses the terminology of the chain of being at times, [54] he has had the courage to drop

[54] *Zoonomia*, London, 1794-96, I, 533.

for all practical purposes the doctrine of final causes. I find only one passage which refers to final causality, but it is admitted there more to complete the historical list of different kinds of causes than as part of Darwin's system of thought.[55] Indeed the anthropocentric character of the doctrine of design would be quite out of place in the realms of the natural world that Darwin delighted to explore. The doctrine of design tends to establish usefulness to man as the criterion on which nature proceeded when she created the rest of the world; but usefulness to man could hardly be assumed to be her purpose in the creation of the useless appendages and odd experiments in form that Darwin never tired of describing. He points out the rudimentary filaments of flowers without antlers, the styles without stigmas, the rudimentary wings of insects, but instead of trying to find a final cause for them he makes the pregnant suggestion that ' Perhaps all the supposed monstrous births of Nature are remains of their habits of production in their former less perfect state, or attempts towards greater perfection.' [56] In another passage he couples this suggestion with a significant analogy with the processes of the physical world: ' Perhaps all the productions of nature are in their progress toward greater perfection? an idea countenanced by the modern discoveries and deductions concerning the progressive formation of the solid parts of the terraqueous globe, and consonant to the dignity of the Creator of all things.' [57] But the reasons for Darwin's shift in philosophical premises go much deeper than this. His repudiation of the doctrine of design is an outcome of his conception of the

[55] *Ibid.*, p. 532.
[56] *Botanic Garden*, London, 1791, Pt. I, Canto I, l. 101, note. Cf. *Phytologia*, Dublin, 1800, p. 515.
[57] *Ibid.*, Pt. II, c. I, l. 65, note.

nature of life itself. He conceives that all life forms can
be traced back ultimately to a single life ' filament' which
of its own vitality had, and still has, the power not only
of self-reproduction but of self-adaptation and diversification to meet changing environments. Following is his
brief summing up of this idea: ' From thus meditating on
the great similarity of the structure of the warm-blooded
animals, and at the same time of the great changes they
undergo both before and after their nativity; and by
considering in how minute a portion of time many of the
changes of animals above described have been produced;
would it be too bold to imagine, that in the great length
of time, since the earth began to exist, perhaps millions
of ages before the commencement of the history of mankind, would it be too bold to imagine, that all warm-
blooded animals have arisen from one living filament,
which THE GREAT FIRST CAUSE endued with animality,
with the power of acquiring new parts, attended with
new propensities, directed by irritations, sensations, voli-
tions, and associations; and thus possessing the faculty
of continuing to improve by its own inherent activity, and
of delivering down those improvements by generation to
its posterity, world without end!' [58] The spontaneous
activity of the organism is stimulated by certain wants—
sexual desire, hunger, desire for security. After the initial
communication of vital force to matter the whole organic
system of nature has been built up by a natural succession
of cause and effect. Hence the elimination of final causes
from the organic as from the inorganic world, but hence
also the greater glorification of the first cause: ' This perpetual chain of causes and effects, whose first link is riveted
to the throne of God, divides itself into innumerable
diverging branches, which, like the nerves arising from the

[58] *Zoonomia*, I, 505.

brain, permeate the most minute and most remote extremities of the system, diffusing motion and sensation to the whole. As every cause is superior in power to the effect, which it has produced, so our idea of the power of the Almighty Creator becomes more elevated and sublime, as we trace the operations of nature from cause to cause, climbing up the links of these chains of being, till we ascend to the Great Source of all things.' [59] ' For if we may compare infinities, it would seem to require a greater infinity of power to cause the causes of effects, than to cause the effects themselves. This idea is analogous to the improving excellence observable in every part of the creation; such as in the progressive increase of the solid or habitable parts of the earth from water; and in the progressive increase of the wisdom and happiness of its inhabitants; and is consonant to the idea of our present situation being a state of probation, which by our exertions we may improve, and are consequently responsible for our actions.' [60]

The details of the actual story of evolution as one meets it in Darwin need not detain us. Darwin raises the question whether there may not have been a separate filament for the plant and animal kingdoms or for individual species, but rejects the hypothesis in favor of the single original filament.[61] Forgetting for a moment, in the face of what seemed like good scientific evidence, his religious enthusiasm for a first cause, he acknowledges the possibility of the spontaneous generation of microscopic animals.[62] He supposes that life began in microscopic form

[59] *Ibid.*, pp. 532-33.
[60] *Ibid.*, p. 509.
[61] *Ibid.*, p. 507.
[62] *Temple of Nature*, London, 1803, Additional Note I. Cf. *Zoonomia* Sect. XXXIX, xi, 5.

in the sea, gradually became more complex, and, with the formation of land, became first amphibious and then terrestrial.[63]   Darwin follows Buffon and Helvétius in supposing that when animal life reached highly developed forms the transition between the four-footed animals of the monkey species and man came about by the growth of the sense of touch in the accidental development of the thumb muscle—' that strong muscle which constitutes the ball of the thumb, and draws the point of it to meet the points of the fingers.' He thinks that ' this muscle gradually increased in size, strength, and activity, in successive generations; and by this improved use of the sense of touch, that monkeys acquired clear ideas, and gradually became men. Perhaps all the productions of nature are in their progress to greater perfection!' [64]   The progress of the mind follows naturally, according to Darwin, on the development of the sense of touch, and the mind is capable, like the rest of nature, of unlimited perfectibility: ' Thus it would appear, that all nature exists in a state of perpetual improvement by laws impressed on the atoms of matter by the great CAUSE OF CAUSES; and that the world may still be in its infancy, and continue to improve FOR EVER AND EVER.' [65]

Darwin prepares the way for his grandson's theory of the survival of the fittest by his vivid description of the struggle for existence in both the plant and animal world. Erasmus Darwin himself is however less interested in this inference from the spectacle of the struggle for existence than in the evidence which it offers of the fecundity of nature, her striving through reproduction to vanquish

[63] *Temple of Nature*, C. I, ll. 295 ff.
[64] *Temple of Nature*, C. II, note to l. 122.
[65] *Zoonomia*, I, Sect. XXXIX, xi, 4. Cf. *Temple of Nature*, C. III, passim.

death and conquer time.[66] He includes in his system an interesting revival of the classical idea of world cycles. The earth, he argues on the basis of geologic evidence, is now in its youth, as humanity is in its youth; both will progress until they ' dissolve in a general conflagration, and be again reduced to their elements. Thus all the suns, and the planets, which circle round them, may again sink into an eternal chaos; and may again by explosions produce a new world; which in process of time may resemble the present one and at length again undergo the same catastrophe! these great events may be the result of the immutable laws impressed on matter by the Great Cause of Causes, Parent of Parents, Ens Entium! ' [67] Or if one prefers to give Darwin, the poet, the last word:

> Roll on, ye STARS! exult in youthful prime,
> Mark with bright curves the printless steps of Time;
> Near and more near your beamy cars approach,
> And lessening orbs on lessening orbs encroach;—
> Flowers of the sky! ye too to age must yield,
> Frail as your silken sisters of the field!
> Star after star from Heaven's high arch shall rush,
> Suns sink on suns, and systems systems crush,
> Headlong, extinct to one dark centre fall,
> And Death and Night and Chaos mingle all!
> —Till o'er the wreck, emerging from the storm,
> Immortal Nature lifts her changeful form,
> Mounts from her funeral pyre on wings of flame,
> And soars and shines, another and the same.[68]

Such, in outline, are the theories of Erasmus Darwin concerning the evolution of species and the progressive nature of all life, theories in which he has anticipated most

[66] *Temple of Nature*, C. IV, ll. 447 ff.
[67] *Ibid.*, C. IV, l. 453, note.
[68] *Botanic Garden*, Pt. I, C. IV, ll. 367-81.

of the characteristic features of the Lamarckian system.[69] It has not been pointed out before, I believe, that Darwin seems to have read Hume's *Dialogues concerning Natural Religion* to good advantage before writing the three works which we have just been reviewing, and that perhaps we ought to give Hume a place in the genesis of English evolutionary theory. In the *Zoonomia*, in the midst of his discussion of the derivation of all life from a single life filament, Darwin writes: ' The late Mr. David Hume, in his posthumous works, places the powers of generation much above those of our boasted reason; and adds, that reason can only make a machine, as a clock or a ship, but the power of generation makes the maker of the machine; and probably from having observed, that the greatest part of the earth has been formed out of organic recrements; as the immense beds of limestone, chalk, marble, from the shells of fish; and the extensive provinces of clay, sandstone, ironstone, coals, from decomposed vegetables; all which have been first produced by generation, or by the secretions of organic life; he concludes that the world itself might have been generated, rather than created; that is, it might have been gradually produced from very small beginnings, increasing by the activity of its inherent principles, rather than by a sudden evolution of the whole Almighty fiat.—What a magnificent idea of the GREAT ARCHITECT! THE CAUSE OF CAUSES! PARENT OF PARENTS! ENS ENTIUM! ' [70]

In Hume's *Dialogues,* it will be remembered, Philo in his criticism of Cleanthes' argument from design based on the familiar analogy of the house and its builder, the machine and its intelligent creator, and the universe and the Intelligence or Mind that created it, makes this point

[69] Krause, *op. cit.*, pp. 189-90.   [70] *Op. cit.*, I, 509.

among others, that thought, or design, or intelligence is
but one of the springs and principles of the universe;
' It is an active cause, by which some particular parts of
nature, we find, produce alterations on other parts '; [71] but
as there are four such principles, reason, instinct, generation, vegetation, why, asks Philo, should we pick out
reason alone to give us our theory by which to judge of
the origin of the world. In many ways the world seems
much more like an organic whole analogous to a vegetable
or animal than it does a mechanical structure analogous
to human contrivances. Why not then, half playfully and
half seriously proposes Philo, suppose that the creation
of the present world has been a process similar to generation, that it started with something analogous to a seed
that contained its own principle of organization and power
of growth. [72] The principle of generation is, as far as we
can judge, Philo goes on to say, superior to that of reason
' for we see every day the latter arise from the former,
never the former from the latter.' [73] Darwin takes what
was intended as an alternative theory of the evolution of
the world and applies it with more plausibility to the evolution of life. [74] It is improbable that Darwin found his
first hint for his idea of the living filament in Hume. The
passage in Hume was probably only an interesting corroboration of a hypothesis which he was already working on;
yet it is interesting to note how many of the other ideas
that one meets in Darwin's work occur at least in embryo
in the *Dialogues*. In the passage on the perpetual chain of

[71] *Philosophical Works*, Edinburgh, 1826, II, 446.

[72] *Dialogues*, Pt. VII, *passim*. In a former passage Hume had suggested
that ' For ought we know *a priori*, matter may contain the source or
spring of order originally within itself.' *Ibid.*, p. 444.

[73] *Ibid.*, p. 486. Cf. p. 487.

[74] It is interesting to note however, that Darwin's heading for this
section is ' The World Itself Generated.'

causes and effects already quoted Darwin echoes the
phraseology of Demea's argument for a first cause from
the ' infinite chain or succession of causes and effects ' [75]
without paying any attention to Cleanthes' and Philo's
prompt criticism of the idea—or perhaps Darwin relied
on Philo's final conclusion that ' all the sciences almost
lead us insensibly to acknowledge a first intelligent
Author.' [76] More interesting is the parallel emphasis on
the struggle for existence, the war of individual on individual, and species on species so that ' on each hand, before
and behind, above and below, every animal is surrounded
with enemies which incessantly seek his misery and
destruction.' [77] Here too the picture of the struggle is
combined with the conception of the enormous fecundity
of nature that insures the continuance of the species:
' Look round this universe. What an immense profusion
of beings, animated and organized, sensible and active!
You admire this prodigious variety and fecundity. But
inspect a little more narrowly these living existences, the
only beings worth regarding. How hostile and destructive
to each other! How insufficient all of them for their own
happiness! How contemptible or odious to the spectator!
The whole presents nothing but the idea of a blind
Nature, impregnated by a great vivifying principle, and
pouring forth from her lap, without discernment or
parental care, her maimed and abortive children!' [78]
Finally there is even, in one of Philo's suggestions, a
parallel to the theory of cycles: ' This world, therefore,
with all its events, even the most minute has before been
produced and destroyed, and will again be produced and
destroyed, without any bounds or limitations. No one,
who has a conception of the powers of infinite, in com-

[75] *Ibid.*, p. 497.
[76] *Ibid.*, p. 531.
[77] *Ibid.*, p. 504.
[78] *Ibid.*, p. 526. Cf. pp. 509-10.

parison of finite, will ever scruple this determination.' [79] It would be absurd of course to suppose that Darwin would need to go to Hume for any one of these ideas, yet the coincidence of the combination makes one feel that he must have been considerably stimulated in the formation of his theories by his reading of the *Dialogues concerning Natural Religion.*

[79] *Ibid.*, pp. 489-90. See also pp. 479-80.

CHAPTER VI

THE RELATION OF ASSOCIATIONISM AND UTILITARIANISM
TO THE IDEA OF PROGRESS [1]

I

While the physical sciences based on mechanistic principles were sweeping everything before them in the eighteenth century, another stream of thought which flowed on quietly beside the scientific, gathering force as it went, would have effectually undermined the whole scientific method had the scientists paid any attention to it. Whether fortunately or unfortunately for the future of science, they did not. I refer to the course of epistemology following on the revolutionary work of Locke, which in Hume reached a radical criticism of induction and scientific generalization.

Locke's criticism of the theory of innate ideas and his conception of the *tabula rasa* are too familiar to need elaboration here. The *tabula rasa* theory bears an interesting relation to our problem. In reality it cleared the ground for either primitivism or a theory of progress. One inference that might be drawn from the theory was that while the infant whose mind is a blank page at birth is not so well off from the primitivistic point of view as the one who comes into the world already equipped with a complete set of the laws of nature and a predisposition to obey them, he is infinitely better off than the infant whose poor little mind had been loaded with original sin

---

[1] Perhaps I ought to say at the outset that in sketching in the *immediate* background of the popular theories of progress of the later eighteenth century I am in no sense attempting to write a *history* of the idea of progress in England. Any such undertaking would of course have to begin very much farther back than I am beginning.

by his remote ancestors. For the orthodox baby, born in sin, there is almost no hope, except in supernatural aid; but if we suppose that man's ideas are all derived, as Locke postulated, from sense-impressions, then we may conclude that all men, rich and poor, primitive and civilized, are on an equal footing intellectually at birth. Although the primitive child does not have the help of civilization in the development of his mind, neither does he have its superstitions, prejudices, and corrupting influences; and he might actually be better off than the product of civilization—at least so many a primitivist argued. But one might draw another inference from the *tabula rasa* theory. Men, however corrupt they are now, may still have a chance of regeneration if their mind is really like blank paper at birth. This inference led to the theory that there had been an initial period of degeneration from the type, but that, with the development of the science of mind and morals, one might look forward to an ultimate period of progress. If, finally, one turned one's mind from exclusive attention to the blank-paper aspect of the epistemology to a consideration of the actual process of individual development the possibility of progress of the race was suggested by a natural analogy.

That the development of epistemology through Berkeley to Hume's scepticism concerning the ability of the mind to deal with the world of experience and arrive at any scientific laws that involved the principle of causation, a scepticism which might have shaken scientific belief in knowable laws of nature, did not affect the advance of scientific thought in the eighteenth century was due merely to the fact, as I have said, that the scientists paid no attention to it. What the scepticism of Hume did do was, on the one hand, to encourage, by the general doubt which it cast on the ability of the mind to arrive at truth, either moral or metaphysical, the anti-rationalistic ethics which we have already surveyed, and on the other hand to stimulate further inquiry into the processes of mental development, an inquiry, already going on before Hume, which issued ultimately, ironically enough, in the theories of the perfectibility of man through the agency of his reason.

II

Let us follow the story of the science of mind in the eighteenth century. When Hume in 1739 published his *Treatise of Human Nature* he called it 'An Attempt to introduce the experimental Method of Reasoning into Moral Subjects.' His desire was to establish as exact a science of mind as ' careful and exact experiments ' and observation could yield. 'And tho' we must endeavour to render all our principles as universal as possible, by tracing up our experiments to the utmost, and explaining all effects from the simplest and fewest causes, 'tis still certain we cannot go beyond experience; and any hypothesis, that pretends to discover the ultimate original qualities of human nature, ought at first to be rejected as presumptuous and chimerical.' [2] It was in the same spirit that David Hartley, ten years later, undertook his *Observations on Man, His Frame, His Duty, and His Expectations*. Repudiating the deductive methods of some of his philosophical predecessors, he writes, ' The proper Method of Philosophizing seems to be, to discover and establish the general Laws of Action, affecting the Subject under Consideration, from certain select, well-defined, and well-attested Phaenomena, and then to explain and predict the other Phaenomena by these Laws. This is the Method of Analysis and Synthesis recommended and

[2] *A Treatise of Human Nature*, Selby-Bigge ed., Oxford, 1896, p. xxi.

followed by Sir *Isaac Newton.'* [3] Accordingly Hartley, following certain hints of Newton, generalized from physical science that since it seemed to be the general tenor of nature that many of its phenomena are carried on by attractions and repulsions, it was possible that attraction and repulsion and the attendant vibration might take place in the 'medullary substance' of the sensory nerves and brain and explain the phenomenon of the registering of sensation. The details of the mechanism of vibration as Hartley works them out are not important for our purposes except as they indicate the tendency to reduce all natural phenomena to a measurable mechanism, a tendency which played such an important part in the genesis of the typical eighteenth-century theory of progress, and led Monboddo to characterize its advocates as mathematical politicians.[4] Just as Newton had suggested the mechanism for the operation of the nervous system under the stimulus of sensation, so Locke suggested in the principle of association the mechanism for the building up of the complex thought-fabric of the mind from its beginning in simple sensation; or perhaps we should say Locke reinforced by Gay in his 'Preliminary Dissertation concerning the Fundamental Principle of Virtue or Morality,' prefixed to Law's translation of William King's *Origin of Evil* (1731), for Gay does sketch out briefly there the way in which 'mixed modes' may be derived from simple ones by a process of association.[5] Locke, as we have said, laid a foundation for a theory of

[3] London, 1749, I, 6.
[4] Wm. Knight, *Lord Monboddo and Some of His Contemporaries*, London, 1900, p. 109.
[5] Cf. *Observations on Man*, London, 1791, I, 5, and Preface. For a discussion of the genesis of the *Observations on Man* see Benjamin Rand, 'The Early Development of Hartley's Doctrine of Association,' *Psychological Review*, XXX (1923), 306 ff.

progress by his premise that all our ideas are to be derived
ultimately from sense impressions; Hartley, by working
out much more elaborately and concretely than Locke had
done the mechanism of the thought-building process,
seemed to put the operations of the mind on such a
manipulable basis as to make progress through its control
not only possible but well-nigh inevitable. The process
was simple and almost mathematically calculable, for he
assumed that ' the simple ideas of sensation must run
into clusters and combinations, by association; and that
each of these will, at last coalesce into one complex
idea by the approach and commixture of the several compounding parts. It appears also from observation, that
many of our intellectual ideas, such as those that belong
to the heads of beauty, honour, moral qualities, etc. are,
in fact, thus composed of parts, which, by degrees, coalesce into one complex idea. . . . One may hope, therefore, that, by pursuing and perfecting the doctrine of
association, we may some time or other be enabled to
analyse all that vast variety of complex ideas . . . into
their simple compounding parts. . . . ' [6] The fabric of the
mind is thus built up by a process of increasing complexity, complex ideas even running into ' decomplex ' ones
The obvious conclusion, which Hartley himself did not
hesitate to draw, is that since the thought product is
ultimately dependent on the nature of the simple ideas
of sensation, control of the simple impressions would
mean control of the resulting abstract idea: ' If beings of
the same nature, but whose affections and passions are,
at present, in different proportions to each other, be exposed for an indefinite time to the same impressions and
associations, all their particular differences will, at last,

[6] *Op. cit.*, I, 74-76.

be over-ruled, and they will become perfectly similar, or even equal. They may also be made perfectly similar in a finite time by a proper adjustment of the impressions and associations. . . . This proposition and its corollaries, afford some pleasing presumptions; such are, that we have a power of suiting our frame of mind to our circumstances, of correcting what is amiss, and improving what is right: that our ultimate happiness seems to be of a spiritual, not a corporeal nature; and therefore that death, or the shaking off the gross body, may not stop our progress, but rather render us more expedite in the pursuit of our true end: That association tends to make us all ultimately similar; so that if one be happy, all must: and, lastly, that the same association may also be shewn to contribute to introduce pure ultimate spiritual happiness, in all, by a direct argument, as well as by the just mentioned indirect one.' [7]

But it is not only the process of thought-building that fits into Hartley's mechanistic scheme. If it were only that, the incalculable realm of the passions and affections might be conceived to threaten the validity of one's estimate of the net results of educational control of sense impressions. But according to Hartley the affections and passions themselves ' can be no more than aggregates of simple ideas united by association.' [8] The passions, since they are states of pleasure or pain, must be ' aggregates of the ideas, or traces of the sensible pleasures and pains.' The intellectual affections, likewise, which Hartley designates as six in number, imagination, ambition, self-interest, sympathy, theopathy, and the moral sense, have sensation as their common foundation. Not only that, but each in turn is an ingredient of all the affections

[7] *Ibid.*, pp. 82, 84.   [8] *Ibid.*, p. 368.

above it. Thus ' Let sensation generate imagination; then will sensation and imagination together generate ambi tion '—until finally ' sensation, imagination, ambition self-interest, sympathy, and theopathy ' go to the making of the moral sense.[9] Thus not only does Hartley put the passions and affections on an ultimately sensational basis but he follows Gay in taking the moral sense out of the realm of the instincts where Hutcheson had almost put it and his readers conceived that he had put it, and makes it the highest product of the process of association. The Hartleian interpretation of the moral sense, therefore made it quite useless for the purposes of the primitivists for whom the Hutchesonian variety had furnished excel lent backing. The Hartleian variety, on the other hand put as it was on a calculable basis, fitted admirably into a theory of progress.

With the intellect, the passions, and the affections all conceived as products of association, all that was necessary to make this system completely mechanistic was to banish freedom of the will. This Hartley—somewhat reluct antly—did, finding himself forced into determinism by the logic of his position.[10] The will becomes simply ' that desire or aversion, which is strongest for the present time For if any other desire was stronger, the muscular motion connected with it by association would take place, and not that which proceeds from the will, or the voluntary one, which is contrary to the supposition. Since therefore all love and hatred, all desire and aversion, are factitious and generated by association; i. e. mechanically; it fol lows that the will is mechanical also.' [11] Having taken this step, Hartley finds all sorts of beauties in the doctrine

[9] *Ibid.*, pp. 368-69.
[10] Cf. the Preface to *Observations on Man.*
[11] *Ibid.*, p. 371.

of necessity, the chief of which is the sureness of its operation. 'It has a tendency to make us labour more earnestly with ourselves and others, particularly children, from the greater certainty attending all endeavours that operate in a mechanical way.' [12] If a man is convinced that certain things have a ' necessary influence ' to change his mind for better or worse, if he is convinced that out of certain ingredients the moral sense is generated ' necessarily and mechanically ' he will be encouraged to make a larger investment of his capital on the basis of this moral guarantee than he would otherwise risk. Hence the progress of virtue is assured. It is not to be supposed, however, that Hartley's is a materialistic determinism. He keeps God well in control of the whole mechanism. In fact one of the beauties of necessity is to his mind that it is more easily reconcilable with the prescience of God than is the doctrine of free will.[13] And it was largely in the interests of Christian optimism that he built up his system of thought. He even echoes Aristotle in recommending the doctrine of final causes as ' the best clue for guiding us through the labyrinths of natural phaenomena.' [14]

Finally, in the realm of social ethics, Hartley, by anticipating the later utilitarian position, seeks a certainty similar to the certainty he had found in the psychological processes. Proposition LXX which deduces ' practical Rules for the Conduct of Men towards each other in Society' designates benevolence towards others as the primary rule of life, and considers that benevolence dictates ' that we are to direct every action so as to produce the greatest happiness, and the least misery in our power.' [15] As it is often difficult to calculate what is going

[12] *Ibid.*, p. 510.
[13] *Ibid.*

[14] *Ibid.*, p. 366.
[15] *Ibid.*, II, 292.

to produce the greatest quantity of happiness, he furnishes a set of practical rules. These include obedience to the scriptures, to the civil magistrate, and so forth, but among them is the typical utilitarian principle: ' It is very proper in all deliberate actions to weigh, as well as we can, the probable consequences on each side, and to suffer the balance to have some influence in all cases, and the chief where the other rules do not interfere much, or explicitly.' [16]

Thus Hartley has taken a decisive step in formulating for English thinkers a doctrine of progress and has determined its development along rationalistic, deterministic, and utilitarian lines.[17] Almost every important feature that that doctrine later assumed is present at least in embryo in the *Observations on Man*. It is interesting to note, however, that Hartley himself, in spite of the optimistic prophecies of man's future already quoted, is much more conservative in his predictions when he comes to the discussion of the future of political states. Hartley, still in the grip of orthodox Christianity, would not admit the possibility of a state of felicity on earth that might rival the felicity of heaven. He predicts the overthrow of ' all the present civil Governments ' [18] for the reason so often advanced in primitivistic and anti-luxury discussions, that all the known governments of the world have the evident principles of corruption in themselves.[19] ' Thus all bodies politic seem, like the body natural, to tend to destruction and dissolution, as is here affirmed, through

[16] *Ibid.*, p. 294.

[17] For a descussion of the earlier eighteenth-century attempts to apply the conception of evolution to human history by John Edwards, William Worthington, and Edmund Law, see R. S. Crane, ' Anglican Apologetics and the Idea of Progress,' *loc. cit.*

[18] *Ibid.*, p. 366.

[19] *Ibid.*

vices public and private, and to be respited for certain intervals, by partial, imperfect reformations. There is no complete or continued series of public happiness on one hand, no utter misery on the other; for the dissolution of the body politic is to be considered as its death.   It seems as romantic therefore for any one to project the scheme of a perfect government in this imperfect state, as to be in pursuit of an universal remedy, a remedy which should cure all distempers, and prolong human life beyond limit.' [20]   He predicts the future Christianization of the world,[21] but concludes that ' It is not probable, that there will be any pure or complete Happiness, before the Destruction of this World by Fire.' [22]

III

In the direct line of influence of Hartley, and representative of the professed progressivists, is Joseph Priestley.   A statement of his position in regard to progress may well be used as a kind of touchstone for other versions of the theory of perfectibility.   I choose Priestley as representative of the progressivists rather than Godwin because, although his name is not so familiarly associated with the idea of progress as that of Godwin, I consider that he has the more logically consistent theory.

Priestley was the interpreter of Hartley to his generation by presenting to it the principle of association without the incubus of the doctrinal discussion and of the somewhat difficult and cumbersome theory of vibrations; not that Priestley could be said, however, to be ' abandoning' the doctrine of vibrations, as Halévy has said,[28] by

[20] *Ibid.,* p. 369.
[21] *Ibid.,* Prop. LXXXIV.
[22] *Ibid.,* Prop. LXXXV.
[28] *The Growth of Philosophical Radicalism,* London, 1928, p. 193.

thus summarizing it in a prefatory essay, for he expressly states in his Preface, ' I am far from being willing to suppress the doctrine of vibrations; thinking that Dr. Hartley has produced sufficient evidence for it, or as much as the nature of the thing will admit of at present.' [24] Priestley is, indeed, a faithful disciple of Hartley, and freely acknowledges his indebtedness to *Observations on Man,* a book, as he says, ' to which I owe much more than than I can express.' [25]

Like Hartley he adopts the principle of necessity, being first impelled thereto by reading Collins's *Philosophical Inquiry concerning Human Liberty,* published in 1717, but ' much more confirmed in the principle ' by Hartley.[26] More closely than does Hartley, however, Priestley links the operation of the mechanism of the mind with the inevitable chain of cause and effect ' from the beginning of the world to the consummation of all things '; ' . . . there will,' he writes, ' be a necessary connection between all things past, present, and to come, in the way of proper *cause and effect,* as much in the intellectual, as in the natural world; so that, how little soever the bulk of mankind may be apprehensive of it, or staggered by it, according to the established laws of nature, no event could have been otherwise than it *has been, is,* or *is to be,* and therefore all things past, present, and to come, are precisely what the Author of nature really intended them to be, and has made provision for.' [27] Priestley even goes a step beyond Hartley in abolishing the distinction between matter and

---

[24] *Hartley's Theory of the Human Mind, on the Principle of Association of Ideas. With Essays Relating to the Subject of it,* London, 1775, p. iv.

[25] *The Doctrine of Philosophical Necessity,* London, 1777, p. xxx; see also *Miscellaneous Observations Relating to Education,* Bath, 1778, pp. xii-xiii.

[26] *Doctrine of Philosophical Necessity,* p. xxx.

[27] *Ibid.,* p. 8.

spirit, thus following the lead of the Encyclopaedists, but not going the whole way with them, for he, like Hartley, keeps God, as the above quotations show, as the creator of the system. ' In fact,' he writes in *Disquisitions Relating to Matter and Spirit,* ' the system now held forth to the public, taken in its full extent, makes the Divine Being to be of as much importance in the *system,* as the apostle makes him when he says, *In him we live, and move, and have our being.'* [28] ' The principal object is, to prove the uniform composition of man, or that what we call *mind,* or the principle of perception and thought, is not a substance distinct from the body, but the result of corporeal organization.' [29] Thus Priestley by virtue of his more extreme determinism is in an even better position than Hartley for developing a program of progress on the basis of the external influences that can be brought to bear on man. It is just at this point that one sees, in the age-old duel between art and nature, art winning an ascendancy over nature. The position of the primitivists is now reversed and ' natural man ' has nothing to recommend him to one of Priestley's views: ' Idleness, treachery and cruelty are predominant in all uncivilized countries; notwithstanding the boasts which the poets make of the *golden age* of mankind, before the creation of empires.' [30] Nature is to him at best a bungling teacher compared with art that is based on the true mechanism of mind. With nature as tutor man could not expect to rise above mediocrity; with art there seems no limit to the progress he may make: ' Moreover, by *art* we not only anticipate the course of *nature,* but may communicate knowledge in an easier, because a more *regular* method than nature

---

[28] *Op. cit.,* London, 1777, p. 354.
[29] *Ibid.,* p. 355.
[30] *Lectures on History,* London, 1788, p. 323.

employs. . . . Indeed, without these advantages, no man, in this advanced age of the world, could possibly attain to what would be called even a mediocrity in improvements, and must fall prodigiously short of the eminence to which great numbers now attain. But by means of art we are not only enabled to go far beyond that low mediocrity in every thing, to which nature alone would train mankind, but the whole human species is put in a progressive state, one generation advancing upon another, in a manner that no bounds can be set to the progress. And this progress is not *equable,* but *accelerated,* every new improvement opening the way to many others; so that as men a few centuries ago could have no idea of what their posterity are at this day, we are probably much less able to form an idea of what our posterity will attain to as many centuries hence.' [31] Not only is this progress brought about by formal education, but by the influence also of society and government, two factors which are as inoperative as education in a state of nature, but which in the civil state insure the progress of the species as well as that of the individual: 'The next advantage . . . is, that the human species itself is capable of a similar and unbounded improvement; whereby mankind in a later age are greatly superior to mankind in a former age, the individuals being taken at the same time of life. . . . The great instrument in the hand of divine providence, of this progress of the species towards perfection, is *society,* and consequently *government.* In a state of nature the powers of a single man are dissipated by an attention to a multiplicity of objects. The employments of all are similar. From generation to generation every man does the same that every other does, or has done; and no person begins where another ends; at least, general improvements are exceeding

[31] *Miscellaneous Observations Relating to Education,* pp. 2-4.

slow, and uncertain. This we see exemplified in all barbarous nations, and especially in countries thinly inhabited,
where the connections of the people are slight, and consequently society and government very imperfect; and it
may be seen more particularly in North America, and
Greenland. Whereas a state of more perfect society admits
of a proper distribution and division of the objects of
human attention. In such a state men are connected and
subservient to one another; so that, while one man con-
fines himself to one single object, another may give the
same undivided attention to another object. Thus the
powers of all have their full effect: and hence arise improvements in all the conveniences of life, and in every
branch of knowledge.' [32]

There is another point in the doctrine of associationism
where Priestley has gone further and been more consistent
than Hartley. A fundamental principle of associationism
is that the intellectual development of the individual is
necessarily a process of increasing complexity: simple
ideas are compounded to form complex ones, and complex ideas to form decomplex ones; and the process of
increasing complexity in the individual intellect would just
as necessarily mean increasing diversity in mankind as a
whole. Now this fact Priestley sees even more clearly
than Hartley. Hartley had somewhat chimerically thought
that by complete control of external influences all ' particular Differences will, at last, be over-ruled ' and men
will become ' perfectly similar.' [33] Priestley, relinquishing
the impossible, sees not only that the logic of progress
demands increasing complexity and diversification, but
that diversification is one of the principal benefits of
progress: '. . . the great excellence of human nature

[32] *An Essay on the First Principles of Government*, London, 1768, pp. 4-7.
[33] *Observations on Man*, I, 83.

consists in the variety of which it is capable. Instead then of endeavouring by uniform and fixed systems of education, to keep mankind always the same, let us give free scope to every thing which may bid fair for introducing more variety among us. . . . Uniformity is the characteristic of the brute creation. Among them every species of birds build their nests with the same materials, and in the same form; the genius and disposition of one individual is that of all; and it is only the education which men give them that raises any of them above the others. But it is the glory of human nature, that the operations of reason, though variable, and by no means infallible, are capable of infinite improvement. . . . Have we, then, so little sense of the proper excellence of our natures, and of the views of divine providence in our formation, as to catch at a poor advantage adapted to the lower nature of brutes. Rather, let us hold on in the course in which the divine being himself has put us, by giving reason its full play, and throwing off the fetters which short-sighted and ill-judging men have hung upon it. Though, in this course, we be liable to more extravagancies than brutes, governed by blind but unerring instinct, or than men whom mistaken systems of policy have made as uniform in their sentiments and conduct as the brutes, we shall be in the way to attain a degree of perfection and happiness of which they can have no idea.' [34] I make especial note of Priestley's reasoning on this point because it is one of the most vulnerable points in the whole theory of progress. Many a progressivist, as we shall see, who is otherwise logically consistent in his system of ideas, is too much intrigued with the idea of simplicity to see that not a uniform simplicity but diversification is the logical outcome of the premises with which he has started.

[34] *First Principles of Government*, pp. 78-80.

Priestley, again, not only builds on the foundation of Hartley's psychology but carries on to further development his utilitarian principles. Indeed, Bentham says that it was from Priestley's *Essay on the First Principles of Government* that his ' principles on the subject of morality, public and private together were determined. It was from that pamphlet and that page of it [that contained the phrase " the greatest happiness of the greatest number "] that I drew the phrase, the words and import of which have been so widely diffused over the civilized world.' [35] Priestley's motive for giving the preference to the utilitarian criterion of right and wrong is exactly what Hartley's had been before him and Bentham's was to be after him: its greater exactness and ease of application: ' To make the *public good* the standard of right or wrong,' he writes in his *Letters to the Right Honourable Edmund Burke,* ' in whatever relates to society and government, besides being the most natural and rational of all rules, has the farther recommendation of being the easiest of application. Either what *God has ordained,* or what *antiquity* authorises, may be difficult to ascertain; but what regulation is more conducive to the *public good,* though not always without its difficulties, yet in general it is much more easy to determine.' [36] One of the reasons for Priestley's tremendous enthusiasm for the new government of France is that here, as in America, he sees a government established on the principle of the general good. ' How glorious, then, is the prospect, the reverse of all the past, which is now opening upon us, and upon the world.' [37] Thus is utilitarianism almost necessarily linked with the idea of progress.

[35] *Deontology, or the Science of Morality,* London, 1834, I, 300.
[36] *Op. cit.,* 2nd ed., Birmingham, 1791, p. 23.
[37] *Ibid.,* p. 145.

As to the extent of the perfectibility of man Priestley is somewhat vague. In the passages already quoted he seems to suggest an unlimited progress toward perfection. In another passage he goes back to the older terminology of the infancy, youth, and manhood of humanity and calculates the probable longevity of the world on the basis of the length of time it will take humanity to reach manhood: '. . . allowing a period of *manhood*, in proportion to this long *infancy* of the human species, three hundred and sixty thousand years will not be deemed a disproportioned age of the world.' [38]

IV

A discussion of the backgrounds of radical thought on the subject of society and government in the late eighteenth and early nineteenth century would not be complete without a view of the contribution of Burke, but I shall postpone a discussion of him until we have traced the development of utilitarianism in the work of Bentham and his school, so far as it is of importance for the present problem.

A study of the differences between the utilitarianism of Hume and Adam Smith on the one hand, and that of Bentham on the other, yields an interesting index of the change in the temper of the century. While the primitivists might still force a drop of comfort out of the theories of the former, however repugnant primitivism might be to Hume himself, the utilitarianism of Bentham was bone-dry to any but the progressivists. In the first place, although Hume finds himself forced out of rationalism by his scepticism of the powers of the intellect, he attempts to

[38] *Institutes of Natural and Revealed Religion*, Birmingham, 1782, II, 418-19.

formulate a pleasure-pain criterion of right and wrong without at the same time admitting egoism as the sole principle of human action. If even animals, he argues, show a disinterested benevolence where one could not by the slightest possibility derive their sentiments from the ' refined deductions of self-interest,' are we to deny the presence of benevolence in human beings where it shows itself so much more indubitably? The reduction of the principle of human action to the single basis of self-interest is merely a product, Hume feels, of that ' love of *simplicity,* which has been the source of much false reasoning in philosophy.' [39] If one wants merely simplicity, a hypothesis based on disinterested benevolence ' has really more *simplicity* in it, and is more conformable to the analogy of nature, than that which pretends to resolve all friendship and humanity into this latter principle.' [40] Thus one has in Hume a perfect basis for an anti-rationalistic type of primitivism: an ethics based on feeling that admits benevolence as one of the ruling motives of human actions.

In Bentham, on the other hand, the long fight against the egoistic hedonism championed by Hobbes ended in complete surrender. The opening sentences of his *Introduction to the Principles of Morals and Legislation* read: ' Nature has placed mankind under the governance of two

---

[39] Appendix, Sect. II, ' Of Self Love,' *Enquiry concerning the Principles of Morals,* in, *Essays Moral, Political, and Literary,* London, 1882, II, 269. Cf. Hutcheson, ' Some strange Love of *Simplicity* in the Structure of human Nature, or Attachment to some favourite *Hypothesis,* has engaged many *Writers* to pass over a great many *simple Perceptions,* which we may find in ourselves. . . . Had they in like manner considered our *Affections* without a previous Notion, that they were all from *Self-Love,* they might have felt an *ultimate Desire* of the Happiness of others as easily conceivable, and as certainly implanted in the human Breast, though perhaps not so strong as *Self-Love.' Essay on the Passions,* pp. x-xi.

[40] *Ibid.,* p. 271. See also Sect. V, ' Why Utility Pleases,' Pt. II. Cf. Halévy, *op cit.,* p. 14.

sovereign masters, *pain* and *pleasure*. It is for them alone
to point out what we ought to do, as well as to determine
what we shall do. On the one hand the standard of right
and wrong, on the other the chain of causes and effects,
are fastened to their throne. They govern us in all we do,
in all we say, in all we think: every effort we can make to
throw off our subjection, will serve but to demonstrate and
confirm it. In words a man may pretend to abjure their
empire: but in reality he will remain subject to it all the
while. The *principle of utility* recognizes this subjection,
and assumes it for the foundation of that system, the object
of which is to rear the fabric of felicity by the hands of
reason and law. Systems which attempt to question it,
deal in sounds instead of sense, in caprice instead of
reason, in darkness instead of light.' [41] On no other basis
did Bentham feel that he could find a principle both
universal and definite enough on which to found a scien-
tifically objective system of morality.

Further, the thing that Hume was particularly trying to
avoid—the swinging of his anti-rationalistic ethics based
on feeling back into a rationalistic ethics by the necessity
of arriving at some sort of a method of evaluation of
pleasures—Bentham not only did not have the same reason
for avoiding but on the contrary actually sought. To Hume
the evaluation of pleasures by the calculation of consequences would defeat the very purpose with which he
started, the demonstration of the possibility of a system
of morality not based on our fallible intellect. Far, therefore, from allowing a pleasure-pain calculus such as Bentham evolved, he insisted that actions must be judged not
by their consequences but by their motives: ' 'Tis evident,

[41] *Op. cit.*, Oxford, 1829, pp. 1-2. The first edition was printed in
1780, and published in 1789. The first edition of the revision was
published in 1823.

that when we praise any actions, we regard only the
motives that produced them, and consider the actions as
signs or indications of certain principles in the mind and
temper. . . . We must look within to find the moral
quality . . . the virtuous motive must be different from
the regard to the virtue of the action. A virtuous motive
is requisite to render an action virtuous. An action must
be virtuous before we can have a regard to its virtue.
Some virtuous motive, therefore, must be antecedent to
that regard. . . . In short, it may be established as an
undoubted maxim, *that no action can be virtuous, or
morally good, unless there be in human nature some
motive to produce it, distinct from the sense of its
morality.'* [42] Obviously this principle admitted an element
of uncertainty distasteful to seekers after scientific objec-
tivity and was a far less infallible prescription than the
Benthamite one on which to guarantee social progress.
For Bentham lays down the purely objective rule that
' The general tendency of an act is more or less pernicious,
according to the sum total of its consequences: that is,
according to the difference between the sum of such as
are good, and the sum of such as are bad.' [43] He does
admit that in estimating the consequences one must take
the intention, among other things, into consideration, but
he works everything back to a calculable basis, first by
estimating the intention as good or bad partly on the
consequences and partly on the motives,[44] and second, by
reducing motives in turn to a pleasure-pain formula. ' A
motive is substantially nothing more than pleasure or
pain, operating in a certain manner . . . *there is no such
thing as any sort of motive that is in itself a bad one.*

[42] *A Treatise of Human Nature,* London, 1739, Bk. III, Pt. II, pp. 38-40.
[43] *Principles of Morals and Legislation,* p. 70.
[44] *Ibid.,* p. 88.

. . . With respect to goodness and badness, as it is with everything else that is not of itself either pain or pleasure, so is it with motives. If they are good or bad, it is only on account of their effects: good, on account of their tendency to produce pleasure or avert pain.' [45] Hume's cogent criticism—written almost forty years before Bentham's book was first published—of the very position which Bentham has here adopted is of interest. Hume sees clearly that reasoning such as Bentham's made the principle of human action in the last analysis rational, whereas the premise had been that it was non-rational. ' Nature has placed mankind under the goverance of two sovereign masters, *pain* and *pleasure*,' Bentham had said. Hume's criticism in his own words is as follows: ' One principal foundation of moral praise being supposed to lie in the usefulness of any quality or action, it is evident that *reason* must enter for a considerable share in all decisions of this kind; since nothing but that faculty can instruct us in the tendency of qualities and actions, and point out their beneficial consequences to society and to their possessor. In many cases this is an affair liable to great controversy: doubts may arise; opposite interests may occur; and a preference must be given to one side, from very nice views, and a small overbalance of utility. . . . But though reason, when fully assisted and improved, be sufficient to instruct us in the pernicious or useful tendency of qualities and actions; it is not alone sufficient to produce any moral blame or approbation. Utility is only a tendency to a certain end; and were the end totally indifferent to us, we should feel the same indifference toward the means. It is requisite a *sentiment* should here

[45] *Ibid.*, p. 102.

display itself, in order to give a preference to the useful above the pernicious tendencies.' [46]

Finally, in the problem raised by every hedonistic ethics of the harmonizing of private with public interests, Hume's solution was again of more use to the primitivists and Bentham's to the progressivists. Mandeville's solution to the problem in his ' private vices, public benefits ' formula that the pursuit of self-interest would automatically result in public good found some favor during the century but was not adopted to any great extent by either Hume or Bentham.[47] Hume, true to his principle that the main spring of action must be derived from feeling, infers, somewhat tentatively and not without contradictions in the *Treatise,* but with much more finality later, that it is through sympathy that we are brought to a desire for the public good even when it conflicts with private good. His most positive statement in the *Treatise* occurs in connection with the problem of justice and the other virtues named by him ' artificial.' Why is it, he there asks, that we should esteem such a moral virtue as justice? A quality or an act can only be agreeable when the end is agreeable, and in the case of an act of justice our own interests are often not concerned. The act is directed solely toward the good of mankind as a whole. The explanation is that through the power of sympathy we participate in the passions—the pleasure or pain—of other people, for the ' minds of all men are similar in their feelings and operations; nor can any one be actuated by any affection of which all others are not, in some degree susceptible. . . . Thus it appears, *that* sympathy is a very powerful principle in human nature, that it has a great

[46] Appendix I, ' Concerning Moral Sentiment,' *Enquiry concerning the Principles of Morals,* London, 1751, pp. 285-86.

[47] Cf. Halévy, *op. cit.,* p. 17.

influence on our taste of beauty, and *that* it produces our
sentiment of morals in all the artificial virtues. From
thence we may presume, that it also gives rise to many of
the other virtues; and that qualities acquire our approbation, because of their tendency to the good of mankind.' [48]
Hume is far, however, at the period of the *Treatise,* from
generalizing the feeling of sympathy into one of benevolence toward society in general. On the contrary he says
that ' experience sufficiently proves, that men, in the
ordinary conduct of life, look not so far as the public
interest, when they pay their creditors, perform their
promises, and abstain from theft, and robbery, and injustice of every kind. That is a motive too remote and too
sublime to affect the generality of mankind, and operate
with any force in actions so contrary to private interest as
are frequently those of justice and common honesty. In
general, it may be affirm'd that there is no such passion in
human minds, as the love of mankind, merely as such,
independent of personal qualities, of services, or of relation to ourself.' [49] By the time he wrote the *Enquiry concerning the Principles of Morals* he had somewhat shifted
his position. In the section on ' Benevolence,' in the section
called ' Why Utility Pleases,' the sections, ' Concerning
Moral Sentiment' and ' Of Self-Love,' and in the ' Conclusion,' he argues for the universal presence in human
nature of the sentiment of benevolence, of a disinterested
concern for the public good. In ' Why Utility Pleases ' he
speaks of it as the ' natural sentiment of benevolence.' [50]
His moderate statement in the ' Conclusion ' is as follows:
' It is sufficient for our purpose, if it be allowed, . . . that

[48] *Op. cit.,* London, 1739, pp. 204-7.
[49] *Ibid.,* p. 44.
[50] *Op. cit.,* p. 230.

there is some benevolence, however small, infused in our bosom; . . . Let these generous sentiments be supposed ever so weak; let them be insufficient to move even a hand or finger of our body, they must still direct the determinations of our mind, and where everything else is equal, produce a cool preference of what is useful and serviceable to mankind, above what is pernicious and dangerous. A *moral distinction*, therefore, immediately arises; a general sentiment of blame and approbation; a tendency, however faint, to the objects of the one, and a proportionable aversion to those of the other.' [51] It is this assumption that the sentiment of sympathy and benevolence will bring private interest into harmony with public that Adam Smith, following Hume, makes his starting point in the *Theory of Moral Sentiments* and works out into a somewhat more elaborate social ethics than Hume had evolved. How this emphasis on sympathy and benevolence might be drawn on by the primitivists, and especially by those who championed the rightness of the natural feelings, may clearly be seen in a passage by Hume himself: ' The social virtues must, therefore,' he writes, ' be allowed to have a natural beauty and amiableness, which, at first, antecedent to all precept or education, recommends them to the esteem of uninstructed mankind, and engages their affections. And as the public utility of these virtues is the chief circumstance, whence they derive their merit, it follows, that the end, which they have a tendency to promote, must be some way agreeable to us, and take hold of some natural affection.' [52]

Now Bentham, on the other hand, makes almost no use of the principle of sympathy and relies on the power of the educator and the legislator to bring about an identifica-

[51] *Ibid.*, p. 271.   [52] *Ibid.*, p. 214.

tion of private and public interests. [53] His discussion of benevolence is most full and definite in the *Deontology*.[54] He there defines the term benevolence as the ' disposition to do the acts of beneficence.' [55] A person may obviously have this disposition without actually performing the acts, but for the benevolence which issues in nothing Bentham has so little use that he relegates it to the sentimentalists. He uses the term ' effective benevolence ' for the only kind that he considers worth discussing. He is chiefly interested in effective benevolence for its net results to society rather than as a spring of action. As a motive force he regards it as weak and ineffective. When the interests of self are in hostility to the benevolent sympathies the ' benevolent sympathies must succumb. There is no help for it; they are the weaker.' [56] And rightly so according to Bentham, for ' The good produced by effective benevolence is small in proportion to that produced by the personal motives. The sympathetic affections are not, cannot be, as strong as the self-regarding affections.' [57] Even the quality of benevolence, weak as it is, Bentham struggles to get into a mathematical formula: ' Benevolence and beneficence are maximized when, at the least expence to himself, a man produces the greatest quantity of happiness to others.' [58] All this hard reasoning about benevolence could be of small comfort to the primitivists, but on the other hand the power which Bentham and his followers attributed to the educator and legislator in moulding

[53] Hume, it should be noted, does not ignore the possibility of the artificial identification of interests. See ' Of Political Society,' *Enquiry concerning the Principles of Morals*, and the essay, ' Of Parties in General.'

[54] London, Edinburgh, 1834. According to Halévy, *op. cit.*, p. 455, Bentham was working on the *Deontology* as early as 1814.

[55] *Ibid.*, I, 176.   [57] *Ibid.*, p. 176.

[56] *Ibid.*, p. 181.   [58] *Ibid.*, p. 190.

human nature and controling human action was exactly what the progressivists sought. Bentham was influenced in this principle by his early discipleship of Helvétius. In fact it is in his treatment of this point that Helvétius seems to have had his greatest influence on English thought. The educational experiments of the Benthamites, did they not carry us far beyond our period, would make an interesting companion-piece to those of the Rousseauists. It is a subject which cries out for investigation, for far too much of English educational theory of the period has been loosely attributed to Rousseau. I shall hope to untangle the strands in a future study, but here there is space for the details of neither the educational nor the legislative theory. It is the principle which is of most importance in this particular problem, and the principle that the Benthamites attempted to establish was that the welfare of the state, when it was not brought about by a natural identification of interests, could be assured by an artificial identification.

V

In returning to Burke one has to remind oneself that the ' return,' chronologically speaking, is scarcely a step, for although most of Bentham's work was published much later than that of either Priestley or Burke, the earliest period of his influence, the period of the first publication of the *Introduction to the Principles of Morals and Legislation,* was contemporaneous with both. But why return to Burke at all in a discussion of progressive thought of the late eighteenth century? The proposal to do so defies an age-long assumption of Burke's conservatism. Even the recent bi-centenary has called forth a new book on *Burke: the Founder of Conservatism.*[59] While it would of course

[59] A. A. Baumann, London, 1929.

be absurd to deny the fact that there are certain conservative aspects in Burke's thought throughout, and that he
adopts many a reactionary attitude in his agitated response
to the French Revolution, I hope to be able to show that in
some strains of thought he lines up with the best progressive thought on the subject of society and government,
and that in one aspect at least he is actually somewhat in
advance of the thinkers of his time. It is really surprising
that the tradition of conservatism should have got itself
attached to Burke's reputation to the exclusion of every
other quality of his thought, when even his own contemporary adversaries—such an adversary as Priestley for instance—recognised the generally progressive trend of his
thought, in spite of the stand that he took in the matter of
the French Revolution. ' It is with very sensible regret,'
writes Priestley, commenting on what he considers a
sudden change in Burke's point of view in his *Reflections
on the Revolution in France,* ' that I find Mr. Burke and
myself on the two opposite sides of any important question, and especially that I must now no longer class him
among the friends of what I deem to be *the cause of
liberty, civil* or *religious,* after having, in a pleasing
occasional intercourse of many years, considered him in
this respectable light.' The Dissenters, continues Priestley,
' many of whom were enthusiastically attached to him '
lament his ' fall,' as they consider it, as ' that of a friend
and brother.' [60] Now Burke himself argues in the *Appeal
from the New to the Old Whigs* that there is no essential
inconsistency between the point of view of the *Reflections*
and his earlier writings and speeches, and if his contemporaries had not been so blinded by certain of his aberra-
tions called out by panic over the Revolution—in his
unfairness to the General Assembly, his position in regard

---

[60] *Letters to Edmund Burke,* pp. iii-vi.

to monastic orders, to mention no others—they would have seen that he was at least partly right: in certain important strains of thought, certainly in those that are of most interest to us in connection with the history of the idea of progress, there is no real contradiction between his earlier and later writings: he merely goes on to develop his ideas more surely and fully in his later work.

There is, to begin with, considerable harmony between the thought of Burke and that of both Priestley and Bentham. All three, like Hume before them, repudiate purely speculative treatments of government, arguments from rights based on a presupposition of a social contract; [61] all of them are advocates of the historical method as opposed to that of *a priori* reasoning. From a study of history only, writes Priestley, ' can be derived all future improvements in the science of *government*. . . . Human nature, with the various interests and connexions of men in a state of society, is so complex a subject that nothing can be safely concluded *a priori* with respect to it. Every thing that we can depend upon must be derived from *facts*.' [62] Bentham makes *a priori* reasoning about the social contract one of the centers of his attack on Blackstone's *Commentaries*.[63] And with Burke the appeal to history

[61] Burke, it is true, in some of his later writings tacitly assumes a contractual basis of society. For the special interpretation which he gives to the idea of contract, see C. E. Vaughan, *Studies in the History of Political Philosophy before and after Rousseau*, Manchester, 1925, II, 52 ff.

[62] *Lectures on History*, pp. 12-13. Here one sees without question the direct influence of Bolingbroke whom Priestley quotes in this connection: ' " He who studies history as he would philosophy, will distinguish and collect certain general principles, and rules of life and conduct, which always must be true; because they are conformable to the invariable nature of things; and by doing so he will soon form to himself a general system of ethicks and politicks on the surest foundations, on the trial of these principles and rules in all ages, and on the confirmation of them by universal experience." ' *Ibid.*, p. 7.

[63] Halévy, *op. cit.*, pp. 133-34.

and repudiation of abstract reasoning is the consistent basis
of his doctrine of expediency. ' Nothing universal can
be rationally affirmed on any moral or any political subject.
Pure metaphysical abstraction does not belong to these
matters. The lines of morality are not like the ideal lines
of mathematics. They are broad and deep as well as long.
They admit of exceptions; they demand modifications.
These exceptions and modifications are not made by the
process of logic, but by the rules of prudence.' [64] He has
studied with attention and disinterest, he tells us in the
' Appeal,' the forms of government, ancient and modern,
and ' He is, indeed, convinced that the science of government would be poorly cultivated without that study.' [65]
' In history a great volume is unrolled for our instruction,
drawing the materials of future wisdom from the past
errors and infirmities of mankind.' [66] It will be seen that
all these men are in their method consciously in line with
the inductive methods of science as they had been developed. ' The science of constructing a commonwealth,'
writes Burke, ' or renovating it, or reforming it, is, like
every other experimental science, not to be taught *a
priori.*' [67] ' The legislators who framed the antient repub-
lics knew that their business was too arduous to be
accomplished with no better apparatus than the metaphysics of an undergraduate, and the mathematics and
arithmetic of an exciseman. They had to do with men,
and they were obliged to study human nature.' [68] Inferences are to be drawn from the long experience of the
ages and history is the political thinker's laboratory.

Again Priestley, Burke, and Bentham are in harmony in

[64] ' Appeal from the New to the Old Whigs,' *Works,* Boston, 1866, IV,
80-81; cf. *ibid.,* p. 134.
[65] *Ibid.,* p. 109.
[66] ' Reflections,' *Works,* III, 418.
[67] *Ibid.,* p. 311.
[68] *Ibid.,* p. 476.

their utilitarianism, Burke developing the doctrine in the form of a philosophy of expediency. The kinship of his thought to Bentham's may be seen in the following clear-cut statement: 'The practical consequences of any political tenet go a great way in deciding upon its value. Political problems do not primarily concern truth or falsehood. They relate to good or evil. What in the result is likely to produce evil is politically false; that which is productive of good, politically true.' [69] The course of Burke's thought on the subject of expediency has been so ably discussed by C. E. Vaughan in his very suggestive article on Burke in his *Studies in the History of Political Philosophy before and after Rousseau* that I shall not go further into the subject, except to note the point in Burke's utilitarianism at which he departs from Priestley and Bentham. We have seen how Priestley's discipleship of Hartley led him into an extreme rationalistic position; we have seen further that Bentham, who started with a hedonistic ethics, went over into a virtual rationalism by way of his pleasure-pain calculus. In this rationalism Priestley and Bentham are at one with the most radical progressivists—Godwin and his school. Now Burke, like Hume, never lets himself be betrayed into this extreme rationalistic point of view. He sees that one cannot leave out the province of the feelings, as did Godwin, and trust to reason alone. ' We are afraid,' he writes, ' to put men to live and trade, each on his own private stock of reason; because we suspect that the stock in each man is small.' [70] Wise moralists and statesmen have aimed, rather, at ' improving instincts into morals, and at grafting the virtues on the natural affections.' [71] Even in this age of

[69] ' Appeal,' *Works,* IV, 169.
[70] ' Reflections,' *Works,* III, 346.
[71] ' Letters on a Regicide Peace,' *Works,* V, 311.

enlightment, remarks Burke somewhat sarcastically, we are creatures of feeling and have to call in nature's ' unerring and powerful instincts, to fortify the fallible and feeble contrivances of our reason.' [72] This difference in their psychological interpretation of man is one reason why Burke's theory of progress is less spectacular than Godwin's or even Priestley's. Not having the mathematical certainty of a rationalism based on the mechanism of association as a guarantee, Burke saw no way to predict an infallible and accelerating progress.

That Burke was without a theory of progress could be maintained, however, only by those who mean by progress only the extreme of infinite perfectibility. In some ways Burke, like Priestley, has a more consistent conception of progress, one more nearly in line with later thought, than the radicals. Like Priestley he sees, what few of his generation saw, that progress must necessarily be in the direction of greater complexity and diversification. The very thing that recommended the new constitution in France to many of its advocates, its simplicity, was to Burke its greatest defect. ' The very idea of fabrication of a new government ' filled him with horror because he saw, from the point of view of his rich store of historical fact, what an increasingly intricate process must be the fitting of any government to the needs of an advancing civilization. A government ' is the result of the thoughts of many minds in many ages. It is no simple, no superficial thing, nor to be estimated by superficial understandings. An ignorant man, who is not fool enough to meddle with his clock, is, however, sufficiently confident to think he can safely take to pieces and put together, at his pleasure, a moral machine of another guise, importance,

[72] ' Reflections,' *Works,* III, 276; cf. pp. 345-46, 344-45.

and complexity, composed of far other wheels and springs and balances and counteracting and coöperating powers.' [73] Again he writes, ' Indeed, in the gross and complicated mass of human passions and concerns, the primitive rights of men undergo such a variety of refractions and reflections, that it becomes absurd to talk of them as if they continued in the simplicity of their original direction. The nature of man is intricate; the objects of society are of the greatest possible complexity; and therefore no simple disposition or direction of power can be suitable either to man's nature, or to the quality of his affairs. When I hear the simplicity of contrivance aimed at and boasted of in any new political constitutions, I am at no loss to decide that the artificers are grossly ignorant of their trade, or totally negligent of their duty. The simple governments are fundamentally defective, to say no worse of them.' [74] A new and simple scheme of government may correct one or two evils, it may provide for a single class, perhaps better than a government that has been evolved by a slow process of growth, but it will be a misfit in almost every other respect. ' The states of the Christian world,' on the other hand, ' have grown up to their present magnitude in a great length of time and by a great variety of accidents. They have been improved to what we know them with greater or less degrees of felicity and skill. Not one of them has been formed upon a regular plan or with any unity of design. As their constitutions are not systematical, they have not been directed to any *peculiar* end, eminently distinguished, and superseding every other. The objects which they embrace are of the greatest possible variety, and have become in a manner infinite. In all these old countries, the State has been made

[73] ' Appeal,' *Works*, IV, 209.   [74] ' Reflections,' *Works*, III, 312.

to the people, and not the people conformed to the State.' [75]

Burke was led to this view of the necessarily increasing complexity of a progressing state by his interpretation of the nature of the state—and in this he out-distances both Priestley and Bentham, not to speak of the Godwinians. While other writers were talking as if the state were a mechanism that could be adjusted or made over at will, Burke is one of the first, as Vaughan has already pointed out, to approach the theory of the state as organism;— or rather, I prefer to modify the view of Vaughan, and put it that Burke falls neither into the false analogy of the state with a living organism, nor the equally false analogy of mechanism, but that he develops the idea of corporateness.[76] Certainly Burke himself would be the last to agree with Vaughan's statement that ' in the spirit, if not in the letter, we have the whole theory of the State as an organism.' [77] In regard to the analogy of the state with organism he writes shrewdly enough, ' Parallels of this sort rather furnish similitudes to illustrate or to adorn

[75] ' Letters on a Regicide Peace,' *Works*, V, 373.

[76] Since writing this section I note that Mr. Cobban in his recent study of Burke also takes issue with the statement that Burke's theory is that of organism, but as nearly as I can tell—the passage is somewhat ambiguous—he seems to confuse the idea of corporateness with that of organism and denies the one with the other. In the sentence which he quotes from the speech on Representation of 1782, ' By *nature* there is no such thing as politic or corporate personality; all these ideas are mere fictions of law, they are creatures of voluntary institution; men as men are individuals, and nothing more,' Burke throws the emphasis on the phrase ' By *nature* ' by his own italics. In his later writing he would not have gone even this far in disparaging the idea of corporateness, as we shall see. As his thought develops, that idea, while kept always distinct from that of organism, comes to underly his whole conception of the state. Cf. Cobban, *Edmund Burke and the Revolt against the Eighteenth Century*, London, 1929, pp. 89-90.

[77] *Op. cit.*, II, 26.

than supply analogies from whence to reason. The objects which are attempted to be forced into an analogy are not found in the same classes of existence. Individuals are physical beings, subject to laws universal and invariable. The immediate cause acting in these laws may be obscure: the general results are subjects of certain calculation. But commonwealths are not physical, but moral essences. They are artificial combinations, and, in their proximate efficient cause, the arbitrary productions of the human mind. We are not yet acquainted with the laws which necessarily influence the stability of that kind of work made by that kind of agent. There is not in the physical order [note Burke's use of " physical " above] (with which they do not appear to hold any assignable connection) a distinct cause by which any of those fabrics must necessarily grow, flourish, or decay; nor, in my opinion, does the moral world produce anything more determinate on that subject than what may serve as an amusement . . . for speculative men.' [78] Burke, as I have suggested, avoids the false implication of the term ' organism ' by using the more accurate and even more modern term of corporateness to define the quality of the organized state. Without corporateness, according to Burke, there is no state. ' In a state of *rude* Nature there is no such thing as a people. A number of men in themselves have no collective capacity. The idea of a people is the idea of a corporation.' [79] Again, locality does not make a corporate state: ' Nation is a moral essence, not a geographical arrangement, or a denomination of a nomenclator.' [80] The fact that a number of people live together in a specified locality does not insure their cor-

[78] ' Letters on a Regicide Peace,' *Works,* V, 234-35.
[79] ' Appeal,' *Works,* IV, 169.
[80] ' Letters on a Regicide,' *Works,* V, 326.

porateness, for the body politic of any country is only
built up during a long course of time of innumerable
' *moleculae* ' that are ' so many deposits and receptacles
of justice.' [81] If the members of the state violate the corporateness thus gradually built up, the state falls apart
as truly as if the people were scattered in distant lands.
' If men dissolve their ancient incorporation in order to
regenerate their community, in that state of things each
man has a right, if he pleases, to remain an individual.' [82]
And if they do so dissolve their incorporation, let them
well consider what they are doing, for they little know
' how many a weary step is to be taken before they can
form themselves into a mass which has a true political
personality.' [83] For ' Men are not tied to one another by
papers and seals. They are led to associate by resemblances, by conformities, by sympathies.' [84] It is this ' mysterious incorporation ' of a people that brings the process
of growth of a state in line with the order of Nature:
' Our political system is placed in a just correspondence
and symmetry with the order of the world, and with the
mode of existence decreed to a permanent body composed
of transitory parts; wherein, by the disposition of a stupendous wisdom, moulding together the great mysterious
incorporation of the human race, the whole, at one time,
is never old, or middle-aged, or young, but in a condition
of unchangeable constancy, moves on through the varied
tenour of perpetual decay, fall, renovation, and progression. Thus, by preserving the method of nature in the
conduct of a state, in what we improve we are never

[81] *Ibid.*, p. 326.
[82] ' Appeal,' *Works*, IV, p. 172.
[83] *Ibid.*, p. 170.
[84] ' Letters on a Regicide Peace,' *Works*, V, 317.

wholly new; in what we retain we are never wholly obsolete.' [85]

Are we to conclude from all this that C. E. Vaughan is right when he says that ' Burke never reached the conception of progress,' [86] that ' he did not realize its importance either for purposes of speculation, or for purposes of practice; that he made no attempt to bring it into harmony with those secondary conceptions on which, as was not unnatural in a practical statesman, he laid exaggerated stress ' ? [87] That a process of melioration in a state such as Burke describes it would necessarily be a more gradual progress than certain enthusiasts of the period were willing to admit is self-evident. Any progress that is to be real and lasting, Burke thought, must be an evolution from existing materials, not a mechanical remaking of a people. This point we should all now readily grant. But to deny that Burke has reached the conception of progress is to follow him in his reasoning about the necessarily increasing complexity of a state without seeing that that very theory presupposes progress as its basis. The assumption of progress, in fact, underlies Burke's thinking on political matters. Far from holding change as an ' object of suspicion,' far from attempting to exclude the idea of growth and development, as Vaughan has said, [88] Burke expressly says that ' A state without the

[85] ' Reflections,' *Works*, III, 274.

[86] *Op. cit.*, II, 59.

[87] *Ibid.*, p. 62. Again I find that Mr. Cobban has also taken issue with Vaughan for denying Burke the principle of growth, but he himself writes, ' At the same time it must be noted that Burke's theory does not at all imply the doctrine of progress.' *Op. cit.*, p. 90. Just how he differentiates between growth and progress he does not make clear. If he means that growth is mere change and adaptation to circumstance without progress some of the following quotations will amply refute that view.

[88] *Op. cit.*, II, 30.

means of some change is without the means of its con-
servation.' [89] That he did not feel that that change should
extend to the actual ' decomposition of the whole civil
and political mass' does not alter the fact that Burke
cannot conceive of a state without a means of development. One of his criticisms of the new constitution of
France was that its framers looked on it as fixed and
final, that they were too unwilling to consider changes in
it, whereas the first essential of a government not miracu-
lously perfect to start with is ' that it is not only by possibility susceptible of improvement, but that it contains in
it a principle tending to its melioration.' [90] Further he
sharply satirizes the narrow view of English law which has
drawn the study of law into such ill repute in England,
namely, the view that attributed to the law a ' species of
eternity' and valued it for ' having remained without any
change in all the revolutions of government.' [91] ' Hardly
can we find in these old collections,' he writes, ' a single
title which is law today. . . . This is a truth which
requires less sagacity than candor to discover.' Thus in
Burke's view progress, however gradual, was necessary
to political health. He has described in the ' Reflections '
the slow but constant improvement of political society
as he sees it: ' Political arrangement, as it is a work for
social ends, is to be only wrought by social means. There
mind must conspire with mind. Time is required to produce that union of minds which alone can produce all the
good we aim at. . . . By a slow, but well-sustained progress, the effect of each step is watched; the good or ill
success of the first gives light to us in the second; and so,
from light to light, we are conducted with safety through

[89] ' Reflections,' *Works,* III, 59.
[90] ' Appeal,' *Works,* IV, 82.
[91] ' Abridgement of the English History," *Works,* VII, 478.

the whole series. We see that the parts of the system do not clash. The evils latent in the most promising contrivances are provided for as they arise. One advantage is as little as possible sacrificed to another. We compensate, we reconcile, we balance. We are enabled to unite into a consistent whole the various anomalies and contending principles that are found in the minds and affairs of men. From hence arises, not an excellence in simplicity, but one far superior, an excellence in composition.' [92] Finally, that Burke assumed a progress toward perfection not only for the state but for the individual through the agency of the state comes out clearly in his discussion of the relation of church and state. Society in its corporate capacity, he says, performs its homage to the ' Institutor and Author and Protector of civil society, without which civil society man could not by any possibility arrive at the perfection of which his nature is capable, nor even make a remote and faint approach to it. They conceive that He who gave our nature to be perfected by our virtue willed also the necessary means of its perfection: He willed, therefore, the state: He willed its connection with the source and original archetype of all perfection.' [93] Indubitably the idea of progress underlies Burke's political and moral philosophy, and if he did not preach the doctrine as noisily as some of his contemporaries it was only because he was too occupied with refuting *their* notion of progress and the methods which they were advocating for attaining it.

[92] *Works*, III, 456-57.
[93] ' Reflections,' *Works*, III, 361.

CHAPTER VII

Transitional Steps in the Popularization of the Idea of Progress

I

What's worse—this pestilent explosion
Of Controversy puts in motion
The spawn of Godwin and Tom Payne.[1]

We surveyed, in the last chapter, England's best contributions to the idea of progress in the eighteenth century. We now turn to the troop of popularizers who followed in the wake of Priestley and other leaders of revolutionary thought. The relation between Priestley and the more popular Paine was recognized even by their contemporaries. 'The doctrines so earnestly inculcated by Priestley and his class of enemies to our establishments,' wrote Robert Bisset, historian of the reign of George III, 'tended to promote the success of Paine's political lessons. Priestley was more fitted for forming visionary and sophistical speculatists among men of superficial literature, whereas Paine was well qualified for effecting a change on the vulgar and ignorant. Priestley dealt chiefly in prescription; his nostrum to be applied to every case was *alterative*: Paine was operatical and proposed *immediate incision.* From Priestley proceeded such philosophers as Godwin and Holcroft, from Paine such practical reformers as Watt and Thelwall. Priestley, to use his own words, had laid the train, Paine's desire was to light the match.' [2]

---

[1] [George Huddesford], *Bubble and Squeak, a Gallimaufry of British Beef with the Chopp's Cabbage of Gallic Philosophy and Radical Reform,* [London], 1799, Pt. I, p. 33.

[2] *The History of the Reign of George III to the Termination of the Late War* . . . , London, 1802, V, 227-28.

It was seen to be no protection to the public that the original statement of a dangerous doctrine was both voluminous and difficult, for a man like Thomas Paine ' with a vulgar but impressive language, may blend the substance of the opinions with his own, and in a short popular tract make them familiar and intelligible to every apprehension.' [3]

In the dissemination of the idea of progress, the writers whose work we shall review in this chapter, Godwin, Price, Mackintosh, Paine, and Mary Wollstonecraft, stand midway between the thinkers considered in the last chapter and the writers who sought to popularize the conception of perfectibility through the more widely read genre of the novel. The latter we shall consider in the chapter following this. In the work of the semi-popularizers before us we shall see the intermediary steps in the breaking up of more logical systems of thought and the mixture of primitivistic presuppositions with ideas of perfectibility.

There may seem to be more incongruity than there really is in including *An Enquiry concerning Political Justice* in a consideration of even the semi-popular publications on the theory of progress—and this in spite of the prohibitive price of the first edition. There would have been no incongruity in the inclusion in Godwin's mind. In the preface to his *Thoughts on Man* he says not only that he has aimed at a popular and interesting style in this work, but that ' I have always regarded it as my office to address myself to plain men, and in clear and unambiguous terms. It has been my lot to have occasional intercourse with some of those who consider themselves as profound, who deliver their oracles in obscure

[3] Mathias, *Pursuits of Literature,* London, 1797, Advertisement to the Third Part, p. 2.

phraseology, and who make it their boast that few men can understand them, and those few only through a process of abstract reflection, and by means of unwearied application. To this class of the oracular I certainly did not belong. I felt that I had nothing to say, that it should be very difficult to understand. I resolved, if I could help it, not to " darken counsel by words without knowledge." This was my principle in the Enquiry concerning Political Justice. And I had my reward. I had a numerous audience of all classes, of every age, and of either sex. The young and fair did not feel deterred from consulting my pages.' [4]

Godwin lines himself up definitely in the *Enquiry concerning Political Justice* with the speculative writers rather than with those, like Priestley and Burke, who proceed by the historical method. He recognizes both modes of studying society and government, the historical and the philosophical, but gives his preference to the latter: ' The first of these subjects is not without its use; but the second is of a higher order and more essential importance.' [5] But if he does not adopt Priestley's method, he does adopt the same basis for his theories in the principles of Locke and Hartley. With Locke he agrees that ' We bring into the world with us no innate principles: consequently we are neither virtuous nor vicious as we first come into existence.' [6] The moral qualities of men, therefore, are the product of the impressions made on them. ' Our virtues and vices may be traced to the incidents which make the history of our lives, and if these incidents could be divested of every improper tendency, vice would be extirpated from the world.' [7] ' From these simple prin-

[4] London, 1831, p. iv.   [6] *Ibid.*, I, 12.
[5] *Op. cit.*, London, 1793, I, 78.   [7] *Ibid.*, p. 18.

ciples we may deduce the moral equality of mankind. We are partakers of a common nature, and the same causes that contribute to the benefit of one contribute to the benefit of another. Our senses and faculties are of the same denomination. Our pleasures and pains will therefore be the same. We are all of us endowed with reason, able to compare, to judge, and to confer. The improvement therefore which is to be desired for the one is to be desired for the other.' [8] One notes in the above quotations that this Lockean premise that is here used as the starting point of equalitarianism and progress is the same that had been used by some writers as a basis of primitivism. In fact, Godwin himself goes even further in his later writing than the negative statement that men are neither good nor evil at birth, and adopts the point of view of natural goodness: ' " God made man upright." Every child that is born, has within him a concealed magazine of excellence. His heart beats for every thing that is lovely and good; and whatever is set before him of that sort in honest colours, rouses his emulation.' [9] But his inference from this natural goodness is a theory of progress, not primitivism. ' Let then no man, in the supercilious spirit of a fancied disdain, allow himself to detract from our common nature. We are ourselves the models of all the excellence that the human mind can conceive. . . . And it is but just, that those by whom these things are fairly considered, should anticipate the progress of our nature, and believe that human understanding and human virtue will hereafter accomplish such things as the heart of man has never yet been daring enough to conceive.' [10]

[8] *Ibid.*, p. 106. Cf. *The Enquirer: Reflections on Education, Manners, and Literature*, London, 1797, p. 15.
[9] *Thoughts on Man*, p. 457.　　　　　[10] *Ibid.*, p. 470.

To the Lockean premise, Godwin, like Priestley, adds the Hartleian doctrine of associationism and adopts without hesitation the view that the mind is a mechanism.[11] He rejects, it is true, the theory of vibrations, but his conception of the building up of the complex fabric of the mind and of the importance of the control of impressions is essentially that of Hartley and Priestley. Finally, like Hartley and Priestley, he adopts the corollary of the doctrine of moral necessity which he reached by way of Socinianism, being influenced thereto by Priestley himself.[12]

So far Godwin is essentially in agreement with Hartley and Priestley. From this point on, however, he proceeds through a tangle of paradoxes. To begin with, he puts moral truth on an empirical basis by adopting without reservation the doctrine of utility. Utility, he writes, ' as it regards percipient beings, is the only basis of moral and political truth.'[13] Conduct to be virtuous must be determined by a calculation of consequences: ' Virtue cannot exist in an eminent degree, unaccompanied by an extensive survey of causes and their consequences, so that, having struck an accurate balance between the mixed benefits and injuries that for the present adhere to all human affairs, we may adopt that conduct which leads to the greatest possible advantage.'[14] Having established

[11] Political Justice, I, 318 ff.

[12] ' Till 1782,' he writes, ' I believed in the doctrine of Calvin, that is, that the majority of mankind were objects of divine condemnation, and that their punishment would be everlasting. The " Système de la Nature," read about the beginning of that year, changed my opinion and made me a Diest. I afterwards veered to Socinianism, in which I was confirmed by " Priestley's Institutes," in the beginning of 1783. I remember the having entertained doubts in 1785, when I corresponded with Dr. Priestley. But I was not a complete unbeliever till 1787.' C. Kegan Paul, William Godwin; his Friends and Contemporaries, London, 1876, I, 26.

[13] Political Justice, I, 201.   [14] Ibid., p. 232.

utility and expediency, however, as the sole principle of approbation, Godwin, falling apparently into a species of hypnosis induced by the contemplation of abstract truth, which with both Godwin and Holcroft almost reaches to apotheosis of it, arrives at something that looks very much like the ' eternal and immutable ' truth of the late seventeenth-century rationalists. ' Truth is in reality,' Godwin writes, ' single and uniform. There must in the nature of things be one best form of government, which all intellects, sufficiently roused from the slumber of savage ignorance, will be irresistibly incited to approve. . . . Truth cannot be so variable, as to change its nature by crossing an arm of the sea, a petty brook or an ideal line, and become falsehood. On the contrary it is at all times and in all places the same.' [15] These sentences might have been written by any one of a half-dozen writers a century earlier and express a doctrine incompatible with the utilitarian test of right which Godwin has adopted.

In the second place, Godwin drops into another paradox, again in relation to his utilitarianism, when he treats of the rôle played by government in the forming of society. It will be remembered that Bentham, following Helvétius, adopts the principle of the artificial identification of private and public interests through the agency of education and government; and while he is not so extravagant in his claims for the power of government as Helvétius he attributes to it enormous influence. Now Godwin goes even further than Bentham in the influence which he attributes to political institutions.[16] He considers government of far more importance than education in this harmonizing of interests, because it is more universal in its

[15] *Ibid.*, pp. 181-82.
[16] Cf. *Political Justice*, I, Bk. I, Ch. V, ' The Influence of Political Institutions Exemplified.'

influence.[17] The influence of political institutions forms indeed one of the two premises of his whole argument as he gives them at the beginning of his *Enquiry*: ' FIRST, that the moral characters of men are the result of their perceptions: and, SECONDLY, that of all the modes of operating upon mind government is the most considerable.' [18] But having built up a conception of the power of government, Godwin finds that after all he does not need it. It becomes, indeed, an increasing embarrassment to him as he proceeds in *Political Justice*. He does not need government for the artificial identification of interests for which Bentham had used it, because he has in the meantime adopted Hume's principle that an act must be judged by its motives, rather than Bentham's that it is to be judged by its consequences. In his definition of virtue as the ' desire to promote the benefit of intelligent beings in general ' he measures the quantity of virtue not by the quantity of resulting good but by the 'quantity of desire.' [19] Obviously a system like Bentham's which insures the greatest good of the greatest number by governmental rewards and punishments, does something too unpleasant to the motives of actions for even Godwin to ignore the difficulty.[20] Imperceptibly Godwin drops into the language of reprobation when he speaks of government. Starting with the postulate that government is the most powerful influence both for good and evil, he finds in the end very little use for it even for good. ' By its very

[17] *Ibid.*, pp. 26 ff.
[18] *Ibid.*, p. 11.
[19] *Ibid.*, p. 254.
[20] *Ibid.*, pp. 122-23. Godwin repudiates both natural and artificial identification of interests in his essay ' Of Self-Love and Benevolence,' *Thoughts on Man*, pp. 205 ff., but he tacitly adopts the theory of the natural identification in the essay ' Of Human Innocence,' *ibid.*, pp. 112 ff.

nature political institution has a tendency to suspend the elasticity, and put an end to the advancement of mind.' [21] We should actually be better off without it: 'All vice is nothing more than error and mistake reduced into practice, and adopted as the principle of our conduct. But error is perpetually hastening to its own detection. Vicious conduct is soon discovered to involve injurious consequences. Injustice therefore by its own nature is little fitted for a durable existence. But government " lays its hand upon the spring there is in society, and puts a stop to its motion." It gives substance and permanence to our errors.' [22] The ' grand instrument for forwarding the improvement of mind' is now not government but the propagation of truth by discussion.[23]

Now the explanation of this second paradox in *Political Justice* is to be found in Godwin's third paradox. The power of government to secure the identification of interests, indeed any external influence for that purpose, becomes unnecessary in a system of extreme rationalism such as Godwin works out. Unlike Hume, he has no scruples against making the principle of action entirely rational. As I have said above, he followed Hartley and Priestley in rejecting the doctrine of free will. He echoes the very phrases of Hartley in the following passage: ' A mysterious philosophy taught men to suppose, that, when the understanding had perceived any object to be desirable, there was need of some distinct power to put the body in motion. But reason finds no ground for this supposition. . . . We need only attend to the obvious meaning of the terms in order to perceive that the will is merely, as it has been happily termed, the last act of the understanding, one of the different cases of the association of ideas. . . .' [24]

[21] *Political Justice*, I, 185.   [23] *Ibid.*, p. 186.
[22] *Ibid.*, p. 31.   [24] *Ibid.*, pp. 302-3.

And he finds the same advantages in moral determinism that Hartley and Priestley had found; namely, that human material is much more manipulable when conceived to be subject to the laws of necessity rather than under the dominance of a capricious power of will. ' Man being, as we have now found him to be, a simple substance, governed by the apprehensions of his understanding, nothing farther is requisite but the improvement of his reasoning faculty, to make him virtuous and happy. But, did he possess a faculty independent of the understanding, and capable of resisting from mere caprice the most powerful arguments, the best education and the most sedulous instruction might be of no use to him.' [25]   He proves from the mechanism of the mind that thought is the ' real and efficient source of animal motion ' without any further spring of action: ' If the perception of some-thing as true, joined with the consciousness of my capa-city to act upon its truth, be of itself sufficient to produce motion in the animal system, then every perception so accompanied has a tendency to motion.' [26] This holds true whether the act is to benefit oneself or someone else. But not only does Godwin make thought a sufficient spring of action without any call on the feelings; in *Political Justice,* at least, he actually denies the name of virtue to any act which is not rational. He distinguishes for instance between innocence and virtue: ' Innocence is not virtue. Virtue demands the active employment of an ardent mind in the promotion of the general good.' [27] He even goes so far in his rationalism as to say that a disinterested act that is instigated by sympathy is not virtuous.[28]   And what an elaborate calculation he does

[25] *Ibid.*, pp. 303-4.
[26] *Ibid.*, p. 342.
[27] *Ibid.*, p. 71.
[28] *Ibid.*, p. 254.

impose upon the reason in the genesis of any virtuous action! 'But how extensive must be the capacity that comprehends the full value of that benefit which is the object of virtue! It must begin with a collective idea of the human species. It must discriminate, among all the different causes that produce a pleasurable state of mind, that which produces the most exquisite and durable pleasure. Eminent virtue requires that I should have a grand view of the tendency of knowledge to produce happiness, and of just political institution to favour the progress of knowledge.' [29] Now here is the paradox. It will be remembered that Hume, believing that reason is always an inert principle and can never be the spring of action felt it necessary to evolve an ethics based on feeling and called in the principle of sympathy and benevolence to explain disinterested actions. Now this principle of sympathy and benevolence Godwin has made unnecessary by making reason the spring of all action both interested and disinterested; but having made it unnecessary, in fact incompatible with his rationalism, having said moreover that an act instigated by sympathy is not virtuous, he proceeds to adopt it! What is more, he adopts the principle of sympathy in the later more extreme form which Hume had given it in the *Enquiry concerning the Principles of Morals* rather than the earlier moderate form of the *Treatise*. He opposes the theory of self-love with many of the arguments that Hume had used, repeating Hume's explanation that the theory of self-love had probably won favor from a love of simplification, forgetting that he himself, unlike Hume, is simplifying by denying self-love altogether and adopting benevolence as the sole principle. [30] Again he ridicules

[29] *Ibid.*, p. 255.
[30] *Ibid.*, p. 355. Godwin in *Pol. Just.* makes no acknowledgment of

the supposition that one stops to calculate the consequences to oneself before he performs a disinterested act, say an act of pity, forgetting the elaborate calculation of consequences to society that he himself had insisted on. The very form in which he couches this criticism shows the extent to which he now admits feeling as a spring of action: ' Surely nothing can be more contrary to any thing we are able to observe of ourselves, than to imagine, that in every act, of pity suppose, we estimate the quantity of benefit to arise to ourselves, before we yield to the emotion.' [31] While this contradiction between rationalism and the principle of benevolence seems to have been unnoticed by Godwin when he was writing *Political Justice,* it was not many years after its publication that he radically modified his doctrine and admitted feeling by the front door instead of the back. His note for a projected revision of *Political Justice* is as follows: ' The voluntary actions of men are under the direction of their feelings. . . . Reason, accurately speaking, has not the smallest degree of power to put any one limb or articulation of our bodies into action. Its province, in a practical view, is wholly confined to adjusting the comparison between different objects of desire, and investigating the most successful mode of attaining those objects.' [32] The revision of *Political Justice* was never completed but Godwin published a similar repudiation of his extreme rationalism in the preface to *St. Leon.*

The explanation of this third paradox is simple enough. A theory of universal benevolence may have been super-

his indebtedness to Hune, but he does so quite fully in his later essay, Of Self-Love and Benevolence,' *Thoughts on Man,* p. 225.

[31] *Ibid.,* p. 348.

[32] Quoted by Ford K. Brown, *Life of William Godwin,* London, 1926, p. 135.

fluous for Godwin's utilitarianism which was apparently self-starting and self-operating, and it may have been incompatible with his rationalism, but it was necessary for his theory of progress towards the simplified community which he conceived as the goal of political development; for that community, difficult enough to conceive under any circumstances, would be quite impossible unless one assumed an extreme form of altruism as a universal ingredient of human nature in general, as in the following: ' The system of disinterested benevolence proves to us . . . that, all which has been said by philosophers and moralists respecting impartial justice is not an unmeaning rant; and that, when we call upon mankind to divest themselves of selfish and personal considerations, we call upon them for something which they are able to practice.' [33]

But this leads us to the fourth and final paradox. Godwin having started with the principle of associationism, which, as we have seen, is a system of progress by increasing complexity, having illustrated that increasing complexity himself by the evolution of language,[34] outlines a theory of social progress in the direction of increasing simplicity. Not having the wide factual background in the history of society that Burke had, he sees the intricate problem of social organization in over simplified terms. Society to him is ' nothing more than an aggregation of individuals. Its claims and its duties must be the aggregate of their claims and duties.' [35] Instead of seeing that diversification in society increases the necessity for greater complexity in the government, he sees government as progressing in the opposite direction. He was betrayed into this inconsistency partly no doubt by his hatred of political ob-

[33] *Political Justice,* I, 359.   [34] *Ibid.,* p. 47..   [35] *Ibid.,* p. 90.

scurantism,[36] but partly also by the worship of abstract truth which we noted before. 'The road to the improvement of mankind,' he writes, ' is in the utmost degree simple, to speak and act the truth.' [37] He had over and over, it is true, made deductions such as the following against eternal and immutable principles, ' It is the characteristic of mind to be capable of improvement. An individual surrenders the best attribute of man, the moment he resolves to adhere to certain fixed principles, for reasons not now present to his mind, but which formerely were. . . .' [38] But now, forgetting such statements, he lets himself be led by his glorification of truth to the conception that ' there must be one best method of advancing these common purposes, one best mode of social existence deducible from the principles of their nature. If truth be one, there must be one code of truths on the subject of our reciprocal duties.' [39] And so he sees society progressing toward greater and greater simplicity. Although he had started with the conception that a ' sound political institution was of all others the most powerful engine for promoting individual good,' [40] he now simplifies government to the point of elimination. ' Did we leave individuals,' he writes, ' to the progress of their own minds, without endeavouring to regulate them by any species of public foundation, mankind would in no very long period convert to the obedience of truth. The contest between truth and falsehood is of it self too unequal, for the former to stand in need of support from any political ally. The more it be discovered, especially that part of it which relates to man in society, the more simple and self evident will it appear; and it will be found impossible

[36] *Ibid.*, II, 561.
[37] *Ibid.*, pp. 494-95.
[38] *Ibid.*, p. 668.

[39] *Ibid.*, I, 237.
[40] *Ibid.*, p. 2.

any otherwise to account for its having been so long concealed, than from the pernicious influence of positive institution.' [41]

In the end Godwin almost works round to a species of primitivism. It would in some ways have been better, he remarks somewhat wistfully, if men had never gone beyond their simple communal organization to form themselves into nations. But then, he adds, they would never have progressed to the present degree of civilization. The truth is that Godwin, like many of his contemporaries, would have liked to have things both ways. He would have liked to preserve or return to the simplicity of semi-primitive social organization, yet he could not bring himself to relinquish the intellectual fruits of civilization. He got an aesthetic satisfaction from the contemplation of eternal, immutable and *a priori* moral truths which he was loath to give up, yet he was equally devoted to the principle of utility. He was committed to a system of rationalism as the very foundation of his theory of progress, yet he was equally charmed with the idea that human behavior is controlled by an emotion of universal benevolence. It was the attempt to have things both ways that spoiled the logic of his social theories.

II

I have chosen to discuss Godwin's *Political Justice* first, in spite of the fact that many of the other titles on our list come considerably earlier, because Godwin's very eclecticism made of the book a repository for most of the leading conceptions which had been connected with the theory of progress. There are few other writers who offer such a rich assortment of ideas. Of the others, each is

[41] *Ibid.*, II, 495-96. Cf. II, 600 ff.

likely to develop a single favorite prescription. The current attack on institutions—government, marriage, the Church—drew out from some a scheme of progress through legal reform. The deification of the reason called forth on the one hand a profound belief in the efficacy of education and accumulated learning, and on the other hand an almost superstitious reverence for the abstract idea of truth.

In dealing with the revolutionary group of writers who were contemporary with Godwin, it will obviously be impossible to discuss all of them, or indeed any of them, in full. I shall merely select a few representatives already mentioned, for their theories are of the most interest in connection with the idea of progress.

Richard Price is usually credited with initiating English revolutionary propaganda with his *Discourse on the Love of Our Country* delivered at the Old Jewry soon after the fall of the Bastille. It is to some of his works written before this, however, that we must look for the most interesting illustrations of his ideas about progress. One of the two most important, in this connection, is the book written shortly after the American revolution at the request of the Americans who sought his advice as to how to effect a corresponding revolution in their principles and manners. It is called, *Obserbations on the Importance of the American Revolution, and the Means of Making it a Benefit to the World.*[42] The other is an Old Jewry discourse, preached in 1787 before the Society for Commemorating the Revolution in Great Britain, *The Evidence for a Future Period of Improvement in the State of Mankind.* With Price we shall find no such building up of mechanistic social and psychological theories as in

[42] London, 1784.   Cf. a bibliographical note in Roland Thomas, *Richard Price, Philosopher and Apostle of Liberty*, Oxford, 1924, pp. 96-97.

Priestley. He had a much more simple faith in human nature than the other members of the revolutionary groups, and a serene optimism that did not bother much with how and why. One is not to gather however that he was not a well-informed man of many interests, scientific and otherwise. In fact his book on the principles of actuarial mathematics, *Observations on Reversionary Payments,* was a distinguished and important pioneer work in its field.[43] He was, moreover, a great friend and admirer of Priestley, and carried on with him a friendly debate in print in *A Free Discussion of the Doctrines of Materialism and Philosophical Necessity* (1778). For all this, Price's approach to the idea of progress is a very simple and unphilosophical one. It seems indeed to be largely a product of wishful thinking bred of his interest in political and religious tolerance and education.

Not an associationist like Priestley and Godwin, Price was a rationalist of the Cudworth and Clarke school of eternal and immutable morality—certainly not a very promising foundation for a philosophy of change.[44] Again, he is an opponent of Priestley's theory of natural and moral necessity,[45] yet, without any philosophical basis in associationism and mechanism for a theory of progress, he nevertheless has caught enough of the language of the times to tell us that his belief in human progress is based partly on tradition and scripture, and partly on ' reason and the necessary tendencies of things.' [46] ' Such are the natures of things,' he writes in another place, ' that this progress must continue. During particular intervals it

[43] Thomas, *op. cit.,* pp. 54-55.
[44] *Observations on the American Revolution,* pp. 61-62, and *A Review of the Principal Questions and Difficulties in Morals,* London, 1769 (first ed. 1758), especially pp. 21, 39, 57-68, 73, 195.
[45] *Observations,* pp. 31-32.
[46] *Evidence for a Future Period of Improvement,* p. 6.

may be interrupted, but it cannot be destroy'd. Every present advance prepares the way for farther advances; . . . For this reason, mankind may at last arrive at degrees of improvement which we cannot now even suspect to be possible. A dark age may follow an enlightened age; but, in this case, the light, after being smothered for a time, will break out again with a brighter lustre.' [47] Every object in nature, he reasons, grows gradually to an improved state of being; so likewise is the individual man and the species brought gradually through states of preparation to states of greater dignity and happiness. His theory of progress is thus a vague evolutionism.[48] Progress, he reasons, becomes automatically more rapid as it proceeds: ' It deserves particular consideration here, that it is the nature of improvement to increase it self. Every advance in it lifts mankind higher, and makes them more capable of farther advances; nor are there, in this case, any limits beyond which knowledge and improvement cannot be carried.' [49] He sums up the progress of past ages and concludes: ' The observations now made may be of use in assisting you to form just ideas of the progressive course of human improvement. Such has it hitherto been; and such the natures of things assure us it must continue to be. Like a river into which, as it flows, new currents are continually discharging themselves, it must increase till it becomes a wide-spreading stream, fertilizing and enriching all countries, and *covering the earth as the waters cover the sea.*' [50]

But belief in progress is combined oddly with a primitivism of the anti-luxury variety already noted in Chapter II. Price, having said that unlimited progress toward

---

[47] *Observations*, p. 4.
[48] *Evidence for a Future Period of Improvement*, pp. 11, 18.
[49] *Ibid.*, p. 12.   [50] *Ibid.*, p. 20.

perfection is inevitable, having hailed the scientific discoveries and the steps toward political and religious
liberty that were helping to accelerate it, fears in the next
breath that the Americans *will* progress; that they will
lose with the development of their country ' that simplicity of character, that manliness of spirit, that disdain
of tinsel in which true dignity consists.' [51]   The progress
which he has predicted with so much enthusiasm ought
really to have been the subject of lament to Price in view
of his belief that ' The happiest state of man is the middle
state between the *savage* and the *refined,* or between the
wild and the luxurious state.   Such is the state of society
in Connecticut, and some others of the *American* provinces; where the inhabitants consist, if I am rightly informed, of an independent and hardy *Yeomanry,* all nearly
on a level—trained to arms,—instructed in their rights—
cloathed in home-spun—of simple manners—strangers to
luxury—drawing plenty from the ground. . . .' [52]   The
evidence of past progress is now changed for the evidence
of degeneration: ' There is danger that a state of society
so happy will not be of long duration; that simplicity and
virtue will give way to depravity; that equality will in
time be lost, the cursed lust of domineering shew itself,
liberty languish, and civil government gradually degenerate into an instrument in the hands of a *few* to oppress
and plunder the *many.*—Such has hitherto been the progress of evil in human affairs.' [53]

As usual, there is no attempt to reconcile these conflict-
ing points of view. They were both current in Price's day;
they both found their way into his books and sermons.
Richard Price is then a typical agent for the confusion
of the two systems of thought as those systems made their
way to the people.

[51] *Observations,* p. 77.   [52] *Ibid.,* p. 70.   [53] *Ibid.*

III

I have said that most of the other writers besides Godwin tended to reflect one or two facets only of revolutionary thought. Of the writers who concentrated on government in its relation to perfectibility I have chosen James Mackintosh and Thomas Paine. Of the two, Mackintosh, in spite of the great promptness of his reply to Burke, is the more substantial and judicious thinker. It is interesting to note that in the eight years that intervened between the publication of the *Vindiciae Gallicae* in 1791 and the publication of *A Discourse on the Study of the Law of Nature and Nations* in 1799 he came round almost entirely to the side of Burke.

His point of view in the *Vindiciae Gallicae* was that one could expect a very marked progress toward perfection through the reform of government. ' Who will be hardy enough to assert, that a better Constitution is not attainable than any which has hitherto appeared? Is the limit of human wisdom to be estimated in the science of politics alone, by the extent of its present attainments? Is the most sublime and difficult of all arts, the improvement of the social order, the alleviation of the miseries of the civil condition of man, to be alone stationary, amid the rapid progress of every other art, liberal and vulgar, to perfection?' [54] And again, ' It is absurd to *expect,* but it is not absurd to *pursue* perfection. It is absurd to acquiesce in evils, of which the remedy is obvious. . . . If indeed the sum of evil produced by political institutions, even in the least imperfect Governments, were small, there might be some pretence for this dread of innovation, this horror at remedy, which has raised such a clamor over Europe: But, on the contrary, in an estimate of the

[54] Dublin, 1791, pp. 48-49.

sources of human misery, after granting that one portion
is to be attributed to disease, and another to private vices,
it might perhaps be found that a *third equal* part arose
from the oppressions and corruptions of Government,
disguised under various forms.' [55] But this progress in
political organization could not safely be left to the gradual process of peaceful reform. 'No hope of great
political improvement' is to be entertained from tranquillity.[56] All the interests of the state tend to hold
political organization static in times of peace; progress can
only be achieved 'by the shock of revolution.' [57] At such
a time only can the liberal and enlightened experience
'which hears the testimony of the nations, and collects
from it the general principles which regulate the mechanism of society' [58] substitute an enlightened government
for the one which had come into being from the blunders
and accidents of the past. The new government will have
the virtue of simplicity, for 'Primary political truths are
few and simple. It is easy to make them understood, and
to transfer to government the same enlightened self-
interest that presides in the other concerns of life.' [59]

Thus wrote the youthful Mackintosh, allowing himself
to be mesmerized like so many of his contemporaries by
the attractions of simplicity. By the time he wrote his
prospectus for a series of lectures on the *Law of Nature
and Nations,* however, the idea of simplicity had revealed
itself to him as a snare and a delusion. He is ready now
to admit that progress, if it is to come at all, must be
accomplished by a gradual change and that that change is
necessarily in the direction of increasing complexity.
Going completely over to the side of Burke, ' a writer who

[55] *Ibid.,* pp. 50-51.
[56] *Ibid.,* p. 48.
[57] *Ibid.,* p. 47.

[58] *Ibid.,* p. 50.
[59] *Ibid.,* p. 145.

is admired by all mankind for his eloquence, but who is, if possible, still more admired by all competent judges for his philosophy,' [60] he now agrees that of the two evils, over-complexity and over-simplicity, the latter is more to be feared than the former,[61] for a body of political laws ' must in all countries arise out of the character and situation of a people; they must grow with its progress, be adapted to its peculiarities, change with its changes, and be incorporated in its habits. Human wisdom cannot create the materials of which it is composed. The attemp , always ineffectual, to change by violence the ancient habits of man, and the established order of society, so as to fit them for an absolutely new scheme of government, flows from the most presumptuous ignorance, requires the support of the most ferocious tyranny, and leads to consequences which its authors can never foresee; generally, indeed, to institutions the most opposite to those of which they profess to seek the establishment.' [62] Thus did Burke win a silent victory over one of his most virulent opponents.

IV

' Society in every state is a blessing, but government, even in its best state, is but a necessary evil; in its worst state an intolerable one. . . . Government, like dress, is the badge of lost innocence; the palaces of kings are built upon the ruins of the bowers of paradise.' [63] These are the words of Thomas Paine at the beginning of his career, and the statement shows the strain of primitivism that his

[60] London, 1799, p. 59.
[61] Ibid., p. 58.
[62] Ibid., pp. 50-51.
[63] Thomas Paine, ' Common Sense,' in *Writings of Thomas Paine*, ed. M. D. Conway, New York and London, 1894, I, 69. (Originally published in 1776.)

writings never lost, in spite of the fact that he is classed as one of the most radical of the progressivists. One searches for the wider philosophical basis of Paine's political thought through a mass of discussions of particular problems, but what one finds reveals the astonishing fact that Paine uses nearly every one of the primitivistic presuppositions as the basis of a prophecy of unlimited progress. His panacea is the characteristic primitivistic one: go back to nature; study man in the earliest stages of his existence; find out the laws of nature; simplify! His chief links with Godwin are his utilitarianism and his belief in the power of reason.

'The error,' writes Paine, 'of those who reason by precedents drawn from antiquity, respecting the rights of man, is that they do not go far enough into antiquity. They do not go the whole way. They stop in some of the intermediate stages, of a hundred, or a thousand years, and produce what was then done, as a rule for the present day. This is no authority at all . . . but if we proceed on we shall at last come out right; we shall come to the time when man came from the hand of his Maker. What was he then?—MAN. . . . We are now got at the origin of Man, and at the origin of his Rights.' [64] If we go back to primitive society we learn, first, that men were created equal without distinction of rank—' The artificial NOBLE [of an hereditary aristocracy] shrinks into a dwarf before the NOBLE of Nature'; [65] and second, that he was created both with wants that drove him into society and with social affections that made society his greatest source of happiness. ' There is no period in life when this love for society ceases to act. It begins and ends with our being.' [66]

[64] ' Rights of Man,' *Writings*, II, 303.
[65] *Ibid.*, p. 323.
[66] *Ibid.*, p. 407.

If governments had not started as a usurpation of power
instead of a delegation of power all would have been
well.[67] It is only false systems of government that have
made man the enemy of man. ' The more perfect civilization is, the less occasion has it for government, because
the more does it regulate its own affairs and government
itself. . . . Man, with respect to all those matters, is
more a creature of consistency than he is aware, or than
governments would wish him to believe. All the great
laws of society are laws of nature.' [68] The example of the
settling and organizing of the government in America has
shown the enlargement of mind that comes from contact
with nature and points the way to regeneration: ' In such
a situation man becomes what he ought. He sees his
species, not with the inhuman idea of a natural enemy,
but as kindred; and the example shews to the artificial
world, that man must go back to Nature for information.' [69] The central principle that nature has to teach is
simplicity. ' I draw my idea of the form of government
from a principle in nature which no art can overturn,
viz. that the more simple a thing is, the less liable it is to
be disordered, and the easier repaired when disordered.' [70]

All this is about as pure primitivism as one could
wish for. And yet like a gloss over this primitivism are
spread cant phrases about progress: ' Reason, like time,
will make its own way, and prejudice will fall in a combat
with interest.' [71] ' I am well aware that the moment of
any great change, such as that accomplished on the 10th
of August, is unavoidably the moment of terror and con-

[67] *Ibid.,* p. 413.
[68] *Ibid.,* p. 408.
[69] *Ibid.,* p. 402.
[70] ' Common Sense,' *Writings,* I, 71-72; cf. p. 116.
[71] ' Rights of Man,' *Writings,* II, 403.

fusion. The mind, highly agitated by hope, suspicion and apprehension, continues without rest till the change be accomplished. But let us now look calmly and confidently forward, and success is certain. It is no longer the paltry cause of kings, or of this, or of that individual, that calls France and her armies into action. It is the great cause of ALL. It is the establishment of a new aera, that shall blot despotism from the earth, and fix, on the lasting principles of peace and citizenship, the great Republic of Man.' [72]

One of Paine's followers, Elihu Palmer, wrote much more truly of him than he was aware when he said, ' he reasons without logic, and convinces without argumentation—he strangles error by his first grasp, and developes truth with much simplicity.' [73]

It would be of interest to analyze the intellectual vagaries of Paine's host of followers were sufficient space allowed. The inquiry would keep us too long from the main line of our investigation; but I cannot resist pausing for Elihu Palmer's *Principles of Nature*. Elihu Palmer was an American, a ' violent political agitator and head of the society of Columbian illuminati.' [74] He is said to have been a favorite with the Painites.[75] He was educated for the ministry but soon turned deist, of the late eighteenth-century variety, and wrote his book, *Principles of Nature*, 1801, largely in the interests of deism. But what an odd defence of deism his book is! Falling into the current of mechanistic doctrine developed by the

[72] ' Address to the People of France,' *Writings*, III, 97-98.
[73] *Principles of Nature; or, a Development of the Moral Causes of Happiness and Misery among the Human Species*, New York, 1801, p. 158.
[74] Appleton's *Cyclopaedia of American Biography*.
[75] J. M. Robertson, *A History of Freethought in the Nineteenth Century*, London, 1919, p. 60.

French, he evolves a complete theory of materialistic monism. All life in his system is reduced to matter and motion, motion being inherent in matter from the beginning, ' co-essential and co-eternal with it.' [76] ' There must be in the essence of matter, a capacity when combined in certain forms, to produce specific results. The principle of life must be essentially inherent in the whole system and every particle thereof.' [77] Man and the larger animals must have been created, he thinks, at a time when the earth was nearer to the sun than it is now, a position which gave nature power of ' " inconceivable exertion " such as she has not since been able to exert.' [78] Mind has an equally mechanistic origin: ' A certain portion of matter organized upon a certain specific plan, produces in the animal we denominate man, all the energetic and astonishing effects of mind.' [79] Further, ' The human mind is incapable of forming any conception of that which is not material; man is a being whose composition is purely physical, and moral properties or intellect, are the necessary results of organic construction.' [80] The chief characteristic of creation is constant change.

So far Palmer has been a consistent materialist, but quite unexpectedly, in spite of the complete mechanism of his system of nature, he refuses to accept the doctrine of necessity because ' It is essential to the dignity of man, that he be free and independent both morally and politically.' [81] Not only does he thus force free will into his materialistic monism, but he even superimposes a deity on his self-sufficient universe—and that in spite of the statement quoted above that mind can form no con-

[76] *Principles of Nature*, p. 25.
[77] *Ibid.*, p. 250.
[78] *Ibid.*, pp. 79-80.
[79] *Ibid.*, p. 252.
[80] *Ibid.*, p. 232.
[81] *Ibid.*, p. 256.

ception of anything but matter![82] He echoes the earlier deists when he writes of deism that it is a religion ' not confined to any age or country, it is established over the face of the whole earth, it is complete and universal, it is comprehensible by every mind.' [83] And he echoes the primitivists when he says that man must get back to the simple laws of nature ' from which, in all his enquiries, he has so long deviated.' [84] With this primitivism are combined the revolutionary glorification of reason and prophecy of progress.[85] Thus Elihu Palmer includes within the cover of one book materialistic monism, free will, deism, primitivism and progressivism.

V

Mary Wollstonecraft's nervous and energetic mind played over the current ideas of her time at will, choosing now this popular conception, now that, for her vigorous and eruptive prose, but shaping her thought always to the pattern of progressivism.[86] Like the younger Mackintosh she has much to say about the corruptions of modern governments and the necessity of simplification. Burke's reverence for tradition is incomprehensible to her: ' Are we to seek for the rights of men in the ages when a few marks were the only penalty imposed for the life of a man, and death for death when the property of the rich was touched? when—I blush to discover the depravity of our nature—when a deer was killed! Are these the laws that it is natural to love, and sacrilegious to invade?

[82] *Ibid.*, p. 204.
[83] *Ibid.*, p. 218.
[84] *Ibid.*, p. 191.
[85] *Ibid.*, pp. 221, 270.
[86] For the latest biographical study, see H. R. James, *Mary Wollstonecraft*, Oxford, 1932.

—Were the rights of men understood when the law authorized or tolerated murder?—or is power and right the same?'[87] This repudiation of the sacredness of tradition was the more possible for her because, among the primitivistic conceptions at her command, there were only a few that were attractive to her. She lapses into a praise of primitive man in her attack on the corruptions which follow refinement of manners: ' Let us examine the catalogue of the vices of men in a savage state, and contrast them with those of men civilized; we shall find that a barbarian, considered as a moral being, is an angel, compared with the refined villain of artificial life. Let us investigate the causes which have produced this degeneracy, and we shall discover, that they are those unjust plans of government, which have been formed by peculiar circumstances in every part of the globe.'[88] In general, however, she saw the primitive social state as a state of war,[89] with a government that developed crudely and imperfectly, so crudely and imperfectly as to carry no implication of finality with it. ' When society was first regulated, the laws could not be adjusted so as to take in the future conduct of its members, because the faculties of man are unfolded and perfected by the improvements made by society: consequently the regulations established as circumstances required were very imperfect. What then is to hinder man, at each epoch of civilization, from making a stand, and new modelling the materials, that have been hastily thrown into a rude mass, which time

[87] A Vindication of the Rights of Men, in a Letter to Edmund Burke, London, 1790, pp. 18-19.

[88] An Historical and Moral View of the Origin and Progress of the French Revolution; and the Effect It Has Produced in Europe, London, 1794, p. 521. See also A Vindication of the Rights of Woman: with Strictures on Political and Moral Subjects, London, 1792, pp. 397-98.

[89] French Revolution, pp. 3-8.

alone has consolidated and rendered venerable?'[90] At the same time, however, that Mary Wollstonecraft was thus fearlessly proclaiming the wholesomeness of change and welcoming the new, she was also quite capable of arguing back to 'immutable truth'[91] and considering the time it will take to bring men's minds, 'warped by custom,' back to nature.[92] Especially was she intrigued, like the younger Mackintosh and like Godwin, by the idea of simplicity. Simplification was to be the great panacea for political ills. 'But when courts and primogeniture are done away, and simple equal laws are established, what is to prevent each generation from retaining the vigour of youth? . . . The french revolution is a strong proof how far things will govern men, when simple principles begin to act with one powerful spring against the complicated wheels of ignorance.'[93] Complexity of laws has merely bewildered the judgment of men and has furnished a shield for the unscrupulous politician.[94] As governments progress simplification becomes more and more possible. 'And we ought not to be discouraged from attempting this simplification, because no country has yet been able to do it; since it seems clear, that manners and government have been in a continual progressive state of improvement, and that the extension of knowledge, a truth capable of demonstration, was never at any period so general as at present.'[95] 'If philosophy at length have simplified the principles of social union, so as to render them easy to be comprehended by every sane and thinking being; it appears to me, that man may contemplate with benevolent complacency and becoming pride, the approaching reign of reason and peace.'[96] In fact Mary

[90] *French Revolution*, pp. 14-15.
[91] *Rights of Men*, pp. 8, 36.
[92] *Ibid.*, pp. 11, 41.
[93] *French Revolution*, pp. 19-20.
[94] *Ibid.*, p. 218.
[95] *Ibid.*, p. 219.
[96] *Ibid.*, pp. 6-7.

Wollstonecraft's position in regard to simple and immutable truth, like that of Godwin, was almost identical with that of the philosophy of the Enlightenment: ' A few fundamental truths meet the first enquiry of reason, and appear as clear to the unwarped mind, as that air and bread are necessary to enable the body to fulfil its vital functions; but the opinions which men discuss with so much heat must be simplified and brought back to first principles; or who can discriminate the vagaries of the imagination, or scrupulosity of weakness, from the verdict of reason? ' [97]

But along with this echo of a belief in eternal and immutable truths is an acceptance of the principle of associationism,[98] and a profound belief in the progress attainable by the cultivation of the understanding.   Thoroughly rationalistic in her ethics, she asks of Burke: ' What do you mean by inbred sentiments? From whence do they come? How were they bred? . . . If these sentiments are not acquired, if our passive dispositions do not expand into virtuous affections and passions, why are not the Tartars in the first rude horde endued with sentiments white and *elegant* as the driven snow? ' [99] It is only in the sovereignty of the reason over the passions that man rises above the ' brutes ' and attains to any thing that can be called virtue.[100] The cultivation of the understanding has been the only means of civilizing primitive man,[101] but so far civilization has been superficial because it has cultivated the manners more than the reason [102]—' yet, I feel confident of being able to prove, that the people are essentially good, and that knowledge is rapidly advancing to that degree of perfectibility, when the proud distinctions of sophisticating fools will be eclipsed by the mild

[97] *Rights of Men*, p. 36.
[98] *Rights of Women*, pp. 259 ff.
[99] *Rights of Men*, p. 70.
[100] *Ibid.*, pp. 67-68.
[101] *French Revolution*, pp. 20-21.
[102] *Ibid.*, pp. 223, 225-26.

rays of philosophy, and man be considered as man—acting with the dignity of an intelligent being.' [103]

This belief expressed by Mary Wollstonecraft and Godwin in the power of the mind to control the other faculties and to assure an unlimited progress in wisdom became a very popular one. In its crudest forms it led to a naïve identification of learning with goodness and a calculation of the rapidity of progress on the basis of the accumulation of fact and of inductions therefrom. When one believed, as did John Aiken, for instance, in agreement with the Jacobean rationalists, that the mind had only to distinguish a desirable end to feel completely assured of gaining that end and attaining a future perfection in human relationships, then one could neglect the problem of selfishness and disrupting passions: ' if the *end* be first precisely laid down, and if experience be faithfully consulted as to the success of different *means,* it is scarcely possible that continual progress should not be made, as the world advances in reason and knowledge, towards a perfect coincidence of means and end.' [104] ' That the world may grow better as it grows wiser,' writes William Jackson of Exeter in *The Four Ages,* wherein he puts the Golden Age in the future, ' may be inferred from the property of knowledge to purify the heart while it enriches the mind.' [105] There were those who questioned with William Johnson Temple ' Whether the Multiplication of Books and Increase of Knowledge be favourable to Piety and Love of Public Good,' [106] but there were more

---

[103] *Ibid.,* p. 72.

[104] *Letters from a Father to His Son, on Various Topics, Relative to Literature and the Conduct of Life,* London, 1793, pp. 41-42.

[105] *The Four Ages; together with Essays on Various Subjects,* London, 1798, p. 83. See also ' Enquirer, No. 1. Question I. *Ought the Freedom of Enquiry to be restricted?'* *Monthly Magazine,* I (1796), 2-5.

[106] *Moral and Historical Memoirs,* London, 1779, pp. 175 ff.   This

people in the nineties who were occupied with calculating the results of mere increase in knowledge. The Enquirer in the *Monthly Magazine* discussing the advance in knowledge, especially scientific and political, writes, ' The experience of different men not only carries each individual, more or less towards perfection, during the course of his life, but may be conceived to serve as a common stock of improvement, which it is the interest of all to preserve and increase; which, therefore, may be reasonably expected to be transmitted from age to age, not only without loss, but with perpetual accumulation.' [107] And later on he, or someone else writing under his name, wonders if wisdom may not actually be hereditary: ' My idea is this: That by a proper manner of unfolding and perfecting the faculties and dispositions of the individual, the early custom (and education is nothing more) will, in time, become the moral habit, and the moral habit will at length grow into the physical constitution, which, after a few generations, will devolve in succession, with at least as great certainty as hereditary maladies.' [108]

A lively debate went in the *Edinburgh Magazine* in 1801 and 1802 on the subject of perfectibility. A. M. starts it by a prediction of unlimited progress in philosophy on a gradually accelerating scale.[109] Scoto-Britannus

book is attributed to Temple without any question by the DNB. The British Museum Catalogue attributes it to H. C. Jennings, but the style is quite different from that of other works by Jennings.

[107] ' The Enquirer, No. X,' *Monthly Magazine*, II (1796), 871. Cf. Sir William Drummond, *Philosophical Sketches of the Principles of Society and Government*, London, 1795, p. 31.

[108] ' Enquirer, No. XXV,' *Monthly Magazine*, XII (1801), 14. Unfortunately the writer uses as proof the apparent inheritance among the Quakers of ' innate innocence ' and instinctive aptitude for the truth. Cf. ' Thoughts on Hereditary Virtue,' *Monthly Magazine*, XIII (1802), 22-24.

[109] *Ed. Mag.* n. s., XVII (1801), 301-2.

replies that perfectibility in this life is inconsistent with a future state; we must only expect periods of advance and retrogression.[110] Urbanus, in two articles, comes to the defence of perfectibility on the ground that belief in it greatly strengthens our faith in a beneficent deity and impels us to acts of heroic virtue ' by the certainty of their successive issue.' [111] He deduces the progress of mind from the fact that it is active. Each individual is constantly acquiring knowledge and passing it on to the next generation.   Scoto-Britannus, somewhat chagrined by the eloquence of Urbanus, replies that he never said that he did not believe in perfectibility; he merely questioned the theory of infinite perfectibility, ' that is whether the human mind will arrive in this life at the highest perfection of which its nature is capable.' [112] A new writer signed R. now comes into the controversy to further refine on the definition of perfectibility and make a distinction without a difference.[113] Scoto-Britannus then comes back strongly with an attack on R.'s identification of philosophy and virtue, and prophesies the undermining of religion and morality by philosophy and the degeneration of civilization by luxury. ' It is the luxury and immorality of the inhabitants,' he writes, ' which are the chief causes of the decline of empires, and which operate with equal energy in the most enlightened and scientific nations; and when the seeds of decay are once sown, science, philosophy, and reason, will totter with the fabric that supported them. . . .' [114] Thus the good old stage property of anti-luxury propaganda is once more brought into play to oppose a new theory.[115]

[110] Ibid., pp. 374-76.
[111] Ibid., pp. 439-44, and XVIII (1801), 35-42.
[112] Ibid., p. 93.   [114] Ibid., XIX (1802), 200.
[113] Ibid., XIX (1802), 89-90.   [115] Cf. ibid., pp. 171-77.

CHAPTER VIII

FICTIONAL PROPAGANDISTS

I

It is sometimes difficult to distinguish the dividing line between polemic and fiction at the end of the eighteenth century. The ' new philosophy,' as it was called, with its happy, fairy tale ending for its hero, mankind, reads like romance in many of its versions, while the romances based on it or satirizing it march with the ponderous tread of the philosophical treatise. The novelist afforded the political speculator a prompt and multiple extension of his influence such as he has seldom had.

> Godwin's dry page no statesman e'er believ'd,
> Though fiction aids what sophistry conceiv'd.[1]

Thus deplores Mathias in *Pursuits of Literature.*

There must have been a great deal of ephemeral literature of propaganda that is now impossible to trace. Playfair, in his *History of Jacobinism,* gives some idea—perhaps exaggerated by fear—of the quantity of this radical literature when he says, ' He who pleaded the cause of murder and plunder saw his work distributed by thousands and hundreds of thousands, and himself enriched.' [2] At a time when the newspaper was a much less powerful agent for the dissemination of new ideas than it is today, the pamphlet was of course a much used means of public discussion, but the novel was also of singular importance. ' Novels, which chiefly used to be dangerous in one re-

---

[1] T. J. Mathias, *Pursuits of Literature,* London, 1797, Pt. III, pp. 32-33.

[2] William Playfair, *History of Jacobinism, Its Crimes, Cruelties and Perfidies* . . . , Philadelphia, 1796, I, 98.

spect, are now become mischievous in a thousand,' laments Hannah More. 'They are continually shifting their ground, and enlarging their sphere, and are daily becoming vehicles of wider mischief. Sometimes they concentrate their forces, and are at once employed to diffuse destructive politics, deplorable profligacy, and impudent infidelity.' [3] There may have been few people who, like the heroine of one of these novels, lived on an exclusive diet of 'novels and metaphysicks,' but one comes across too frequent remarks on the pernicious effect of 'philosophical novels' to doubt of their influence whether for good or ill.[4] 'Wherever the freedom of the press exists . . . I must assert *that*, LITERATURE, *well or ill conducted*, IS THE GREAT ENGINE *by which, I am fully persuaded, all* civilized *states must ultimately be supported or overthrown!*' This is the reflection of Mathias as he contemplates the literature of his day, especially the novels of the 'unsex'd female writers.' [5]

What is the fate of the family of ideas that we have been following when they fall into the hands of the popular novelists? In answering this question it is not my purpose to give a comprehensive review of all of the novels either of radical reform and perfectibility or of satire and criticism. I am more interested in following more minutely than would be possible in such a survey the com-

---

[3] *Strictures on the Modern System of Female Education, Works,* London, 1830, V, 22. First published in 1799 but said by her to have been written early in the French Revolution. See *ibid.,* p. 3.

[4] See besides the remarks already quoted in the preface and elsewhere, Elizabeth Hamilton, *Memoirs of Modern Philosophers,* second edition, Bath, 1800, I, xv.

[5] Mathias, *op. cit.,* Advertisement to the Third Part, p. 1; and *ibid.,* Pt. IV, p. ii. See also Richard Polwhele, *The Unsex'd Females: a Poem,* London, 1798. This poem, inspired by *Pursuits of Literature,* is directed chiefly against Mary Wollstonecraft, but the writer runs over the list of most of the women writers of the time.

plex of ideas characteristic of a few of the most popular novels. In general we find in these novels what we have come to expect in popular literature—that the popular writer hates to relinquish any idea that is in vogue, however much it clashes with his main thesis. He catches at the cant phrases of rationalism and utilitarianism, but can hardly be prevailed on to give up sensibility. Helen Maria Williams, one of the early writers on the Revolution, for instance, gives us the astonishing information that 'however dull the faculties of my head, I can assure you, that when a proposition is addressed to my heart, I have some quickness of perception. I can then decide, in one moment, points upon which philosophers and legislators have differed in all ages.' [6] In fact there seems to have been a group of writers to whom the liberty promised by the French Revolution seemed to mean liberty for more indulgence in feeling rather than for the development of reason. For this we have the contemporary corroboration of the historian, Bisset. 'There were in the literary class, as in other bodies,' writes Bisset, 'persons who, from a benevolent enthusiasm, hoped that the French constitution would extirpate vice and misery, and diffuse over the world philanthropy and happiness. Among the literary producers, there was one set who thought the highest perfection of the human character was sensibility; and that the restraints of religion and moral precepts, as well as of political establishments, were harsh and tyrannical, because they so often contradicted the impulse of sentimental feeling; these praised the French revolution in the belief that it was inimical to austere restrictions. Under this class were to be ranked various female votaries of literature, and at their head Mary Ann Wollstonecraft,

Letters on the French Revolution, Boston, 1791, p. 121.

who produced, as a counterpart to the Rights of Man, a performance entitled the Rights of Woman. . . .' [7]

Not only does sensibility hold its own with rationalism, but pro-luxury and anti-luxury ideas jostle each other on the page, and simplicity remains a favorite. One of the most curious phenomena of these novels is that ' beautiful souls ' are of even more frequent appearance than in the more sentimental literature of primitivism—or perhaps they only stand out more clearly in their sinister surroundings. That they should appear in the satires on the progressivists like *The Infernal Quixote* of Charles Lucas or Sophia King's *Waldorf, or the Dangers of Philosophy* is not surprising, but they also appear in the more radical novels. Robert Bage, for instance, like Lucas, chooses the Welsh variety of beautiful soul in Miss Fluellen, ' the child of pure nature. All red and white, and kind and coming.' [8] Likewise, Edmund Oliver's sister in Charles Lloyd's novel of that name was ' the child of nature; the virtues which she possessed seemed to have sprung spontaneously in her bosom.' [9] But beautiful souls most flourish in the rich soil of Charlotte Smith's novels. The mind of Monimia of *The Old Manor House* was like that of Miranda on her desert island; the world past and present was unknown to her. ' Enchanted with her native rectitude of heart and generosity of spirit, Orlando rapturously exclaimed, " Charming girl! how every sentence you utter, every sentiment of your pure and innocent mind delight me!" ' [10] Even Orlando himself comes near to being one of the few masculine beautiful souls: ' But

---

[7] Robert Bisset, *The History of the Reign of George III to the Termination of the Late War . . .* , London, 1802, V, 229.

[8] *Man as He Is,* London, 1792, III, 28.

[9] London, 1798, I, 16.

[10] London, 1820, I, 54-55.

when he saw, and only for a moment conversed with Orlando, he perceived that he was one of those beings for whom education can do little, and whom nature has so highly favoured that nothing can be added by art.' [11] But of Charlotte Smith's novels, more later.

II

Of all the followers of Godwin, Mary Hays is perhaps the most faithful and the least discriminating, although even she takes issue with *Political Justice* at one vital point. Biographical information about Mary Hays is not readily accessible, but we learn from her *Love Letters* and their preface [12] that she was closely associated with the group that we are interested in—Godwin, Mary Wollstonecraft, whose death-bed she attended,[13] Priestley, Coleridge, the Lambs, and Charles Lloyd. *The Memoirs of Emma Courtney,* that lurid tale of infatuation based on Mary Hays's own unrequited passion, actually contains some of her own letters to Godwin who appears in the book in the character of Mr. Francis, the elderly philosophical adviser of Emma Courtney.[14]. Thus the novel comes out of the very heart of radicalism.

The theme of progress forms rather the underlying assumption of *Emma Courtney* than the main issue. It is almost as though Mary Hays had absorbed the supposition of perfectibility so thoroughly from her social environment that support of the idea seems superfluous. To her, progress is inherent in the very nature of man,[15] and her heroine, Emma Courtney, quite as a matter of course,

[11] *Ibid.,* II, 37.
[12] Ed. A. F. Wedd, London, 1925.
[13] C. Kegan Paul, *William Godwin* . . . , London, 1876, I, 282.
[14] *Love Letters,* p. 7.
[15] *Letters and Essays, Moral and Miscellaneous,* London, 1793, p. 13.

makes it her objective in life to increase the happiness and contribute to the improvement of individuals, and thus widen the circle that will ' operate towards the grand end of life—*general utility.*' [16] That she chose to accomplish her share in the amelioration of society by courting a man unresponsive to her tireless efforts to win his affections was her misfortune. ' A solitary enthusiast,' sighs Emma after almost the last repulse, ' a child in the drama of the world, I had yet to learn, that those who have courage to act upon advanced principles, must be content to suffer moral martyrdom.' [17] Mr. Francis holds forth at length on the progress that may be expected from the overthrow of old institutions and the gradual enlightenment of reason.[18] It is interesting that, though Mary Hays makes Mr. Francis more emphatic on the subject of mutability than Godwin ordinarily was,[19] she herself falls elsewhere into the fallacy of which he had been guilty in praising the uniformity, simplicity, and immutability of truth. ' When,' she exclaims, ' will mankind be aware of the uniformity, of the importance, of truth? When will they cease to confound, by sexual, by political, by theological, distinctions, those immutable principles, which form the true basis of virtue and happiness? ' [20]

More interesting than any direct discussion of the idea of progress in *Emma Courtney* is the shaping influence of the philosophical premises on the form of the fiction itself. However crude stylistically *Emma Courtney* may be, however unhealthy in tone, the fact remains that, with the possible exception of *Caleb Williams,* it comes nearer to achieving pure naturalism in fiction than any novel before the end of the nineteenth century. Adopting the idea,

---

[16] N. Y., 1802, I, 36. First published, London, 1796.
[17] *Ibid.,* II, 61.   [19] *Ibid.,* p. 64.
[18] *Ibid.,* I, 63-67.   [20] *Ibid.,* II, 106.

apparently from Helvétius whom she quotes in this connection,[21] that there can be a science of mind as exact as the physics of Newton, adopting the principle of associationism and of necessity, she takes as much care to relate the minutest formative influences on the mind of Emma as any French naturalist of the late nineteenth century. ' The events of my life have been few, and have in them nothing very uncommon, but the effects which they have produced on my mind; ' writes Emma to her adopted son, ' yet, that mind they have helped to form, and this in the eye of philosophy, or affection, may render them not wholly uninteresting. While I trace them, they convince me of the irresistible power of circumstances, modifying and controuling our characters, and introducing, mechanically, those associations and habits which make us what we are; for without outward impressions we should be nothing.' [22]

The amoral tendency of the doctrine of moral determinism observable in nineteenth-century naturalistic fiction is to be seen in *Emma Courtney* also. The whole implication of the book is that every man is what he is by a train of circumstances largely out of his control, and moral blame for what he does amiss is therefore ruled out of court.[23] Emma replies to the criticisms of Mr. Francis, ' To what purpose did you read my confessions, but to trace in them a character formed, like every other human character, by the result of unavoidable impressions, and the chain of necessary events.' [24] With admirable consistency she proceeds, ' You will tell me, It remains with myself whether I will predetermine to resist such impressions. Is this true? Is it philosophical? Ask yourself. What!—can *even you* shrink from the consequences of

---

[21] *Ibid.*, I, 4.
[22] *Ibid.*, p. 5.   Cf. II, 10.
[23] *Ibid.*, p. 3.
[24] *Ibid.*, II, 82-83.

your own principles?' [25] 'The capacity of perception, or
of receiving sensation, is (or generates) the power; into
what channel that power shall be directed, depends not
on ourselves. Are we not the creatures of outward impressions?' [26]

But besides this tendency of the principles of associationism and necessity to relieve the individual of moral
responsibility, a tendency so shocking to the conservative
eighteenth-century mind, Mary Hays has another strain
equally interesting in the light of later nineteenth-century
fiction. When she looked not backward to the origin of
our actions but forward to their consequences, she developed very much the same stern moral law, analogous to
the natural law of the physical world, that became such
an important factor in the sombre ethics of George Eliot.
' I cannot exactly tell the extent of the injury I may have
done him,' writes Emma of the man she had pursued for
three years, not knowing that he was already married. ' A
long train of consequences succeeds, even, our most indifferent actions.—Strong energies, though they answer not
the end proposed, must yet produce correspondent effects.
Morals and mechanics are here analogous.' [27] This
acknowledgment of the inevitable train of consequences
both to ourselves and others of all our deeds reads almost
like a passage from *Romola* or *Middlemarch*. Thus Mary
Hays anticipates both the weakest and the strongest points
in the ethics of naturalistic fiction.

There is another ethical problem in *Emma Courtney*
that is of interest. It has to do with that moot problem of
utilitarians, the motivating force of actions. As has been
sufficiently indicated without giving the details of the plot,
the whole novel turns on the pursuit of a man by a

[25] *Ibid.*, p. 83.   [26] *Ibid.*, p. 82.   [27] *Ibid.*, p. 79.

woman, the reversal of courtship being apparently one of the author's ' advanced principles ' that will have to make its warlike way against the prejudices of the world. Now the woman, Emma Courtney, is only a thin disguise for the author, and the novel is a novel of self-justification. How was Mary Hays to justify letting passion rule so much of her life in the face of a rationalism as extreme as Godwin's? She took the simplest way—she both accepted and rejected Godwin's rationalism without heeding the contradictions. As we have seen, she is rationalistic in her determinism. She is even, when it suits her, as rationalistic as Godwin at his most rationalistic in her utilitarianism. The following definition of virtue is almost copied from *Political Justice*: ' What is virtue, but a calculation of the *consequences of our actions?* Did we allow ourselves to reason on this principle, to reflect on its truth and importance, we should be compelled to shudder at many parts of our conduct, which, *taken unconnectedly,* we have habituated ourselves to consider as almost indifferent. Virtue can exist only in a mind capable of taking comprehensive views. How criminal, then, is ignorance!' [28] ' Let us remember,' she lets Mr. Francis write to Emma, ' that vice originates in the mistakes of the understanding. . . . Our duties, then are obvious— If selfish and violent passions have been generated by the inequalities of society, we must labour to counteract them, by endeavouring to combat prejudice, to expand the mind, to give comprehensive views, to teach mankind their truest interest, and to lead them to habits of goodness and greatness.' [29] But when the story turns, as it inevitably does in the end, to a discussion of passion, there is too much desire for self-justification for Mary Hays to accept God-

[28] *Ibid.*, p. 65; cf. p. 69.   [29] *Ibid.*, I, 66-67.

win's doctrine of the supremacy of the reason. She criticizes, it is true, in the person of Emma, her own passion, and many of her actions motivated by it,[30] but in her correspondence with Mr. Francis on the subject she gives herself and not Mr. Francis the last word, and the conclusion seems to be one of justification for following the ' voice of her heart ' and regret that the world was not yet ready for ingenuousness and honesty in passion such as hers.[31] ' From the miserable consequences of wretched moral distinctions, from chastity having been considered as a sexual virtue, all these calamities have flowed. Men are thus rendered sordid and dissolute in their pleasures; their affections vitiated, and their feelings petrified; the simplicity of modest tenderness loses its charm; they become incapable of satisfying the heart of a woman of sensibility and virtue.' [32] Thus Mary Hays preserves in the midst of rationalism the language of sensibility and the doctrine of the importance of the passions. The following quotation that she makes from Rousseau might have been more at home in one of our primitivistic novels: ' To those who are strangers to these delicate, yet powerful sympathies, this may appear ridiculous—but the sensations are not the less genuine, nor the less in nature. I will not attempt to analyse them. . . . Yet, affections like those are not so much weakness, as strength perhaps badly exerted. Rousseau was, right, when he asserted, that, " Common men know nothing of violent sorrows, nor do great passions ever break out in weak minds. Energy of sentiment is the characteristic of a noble soul." ' [33] Yet however inconsistent Mary Hays is, her criticism of Godwin's extreme rationalism is well-taken. Emma labors to show Mr. Francis that passion had been the stimulating principle of her

---

[30] *Ibid.*, especially II, 116. [32] *Ibid.*, p. 77.
[31] *Ibid.*, II, 158. [33] *Ibid.*, p. 95.

reason. Had she not been aroused by passion she might have ' domesticated, tamely, in the lap of indolence and apathy.' [34] ' Are not passions and powers synonymous— or can the latter be produced without the lively interest that constitutes the former? Do you dream of annihilating the one—and will not the other be extinguished?' [35] She even works up a case of Godwin vs. Godwin by quoting *Caleb Williams* in support of her side.[36]

III

Of an altogether different stamp from Mary Hays is the fellow-thinker with Godwin, Thomas Holcroft. With less mind and more vehemence than Godwin, Holcroft caught the revolutionary enthusiasm from Godwin and had in turn no small share in the genesis of *Political Justice*. ' My mind,' writes Godwin, ' became more and more impregnated with the principles afterwards developed in my Political Justice; they were the almost constant topic of conversation between Holcroft and myself: and he, who in his *Skeptic* and other writings had displayed the sentiments of courtier, speedily became no less a republican and a reformer than myself.' [37] And again, ' My mind, though fraught with sensibility and occasionally ardent and enthusiastic, is perhaps in its genuine habits too tranquil and unimpassioned for successful composition, and stands greatly in need of stimulus and excitement. I am deeply indebted on this point to Holcroft.' [38] It is pleasant to think of the excitable, benevolent but irritable and quick-tempered Holcroft cutting capers about the ponderous

[34] *Ibid.*, p. 75.
[35] *Ibid.*, p. 82.
[36] *Ibid.*, pp. 73, 77.
[37] *Life of Thomas Holcroft Written by Himself Continued to the Time of his Death . . . by William Hazlitt*, ed. Elbridge Colby, London, 1925, II, 32.   [38] *Ibid.*, II, 33.

and egocentric author of *Political Justice*. Mary Shelley's picture of Holcroft is after all the best:

The name of Holcroft at once gives rise to a crowd of recollections to those who are conversant with the history of the times, and that particular circle of literary men of which my father was one. The son of a shoemaker, he rose to eminence through the energy of his character, and the genius with which nature had endowed him. To think of Holcroft as his friends remember him, and to call to mind whence at this day he principally derives his fame as an author, present a singular contrast. He was a man of stern and irascible character, and from the moment that he espoused liberal principles, he carried them to excess. He was tried for life as a traitor on account of his enthusiasm for the objects of the French Revolution. He believed that truth must prevail by the force of its own powers, but he advocated what he deemed truth with vehemence. He warmly asserted that death and disease existed only through the feebleness of man's mind, that pain also had no reality. Rectitude and Courage were the gods of his idolatry, but the defect of his temper rendered him a susceptible friend. His Comedy, "The Road to Ruin," will always maintain its position on the English stage, so long as there are actors who can fitly represent its leading characters. He was a man of great industry, unwearied in his efforts to support his family. When they first became acquainted neither he nor Mr. Godwin had yet imbibed those strong political feelings which afterward distinguished them. It required the French Revolution to kindle that ardent love of Political Justice with which both were afterwards, according to their diverse dispositions, warmed.[39]

When one analyzes Holcroft's writing, one finds it an emotional and imaginative version of Political Justice with the highlights drawn in somewhat differently and with some modifications of outline. Perhaps the most welcome difference between his writing and Godwin's is the addition of a touch of humor and caricature here and there—

[39] C. Kegan Paul, *op. cit.*, I, 25-26.

or what seems to us humor and caricature. It is sometimes a delicate matter to distinguish between intentional humor on the author's part in these eighteenth-century novels and the contribution from one's own sense of the ridiculous.

Perhaps it will be best to start with Holcroft's finest contribution to the fiction of revolutionary propaganda, *Anna St. Ives.* As Mary Wollstonecraft somewhat humorously remarks in her review of the book, ' The story is not intangled with episodes, yet, simple as it is, it carries the reader along, and makes him patiently swallow not a few improbabilities.' [40] The situation is a favorite one in revolutionary novels—the bright young son of a member of the lower classes cultivates his mind, becomes an advocate of equal rights and the perfectibility of man, and converts and marries the rich and beautiful heiress of his father's employer. In this case the young man is Frank Henley, whose father is Abimelech Henley, gardener to Sir Arthur St. Ives. A variant on the usual pattern is provided by the fact that by the time Anna is ready to marry Frank the unscrupulous Abimelech, one of the best characters in the book, has got the whole of Sir Arthur's fortune into his own hands, so that the marriage becomes a marriage of convenience after all. The complication in the story is provided by the young profligate, Coke Clifton, the favored suitor. Like so many eighteenth-century heroines, Anna, though really in love with Frank, quite easily persuades herself that duty to the ' author of her being ' dictates her marriage to the rich suitor. She not only persuades Frank that she and he can keep their love on a plane of pure intellectuality, but that their noblest line of behavior is to unite in educating Coke Clifton up to their principles. When she had wrung an unwilling consent

[40] *Analytical Review,* XIII (1792), 72.

from Frank, ' I wished to confirm the noble emulation, to
convince him how different the pure love of mind might
be from the meaner love of passion, and I kissed him! I
find my affections, my sensibilities, peculiarly liable to
these strong sallies.' [41] And the two of them set to work
upon Coke. Naturally the high-spirited young gallant was
somewhat irritated to be told even by the beautiful Anna
that ' In the progress toward truth, I have presumed to
think you several steps behind me. . . .' [42] But being an
intriguer like his predecessor, Lovelace, he smothered his
outraged pride and pretended a gratifying conversion to
the principles of truth and justice. And many were the eloquent flights he had to listen to. Here is a sample:

Dare you receive a blow, or suffer yourself falsely to be called
liar, or coward, without seeking revenge, or what honour calls
satisfaction? Dare you think the servant that cleans your shoes
is your equal, unless not so wise or good a man; and your
superior, if wiser and better? Dare you suppose mind has no
sex, and that woman is not by nature the inferior of man? . . .
Dare you think that riches, rank, and power, are usurpations; and
that wisdom and virtue only can claim distinction? Dare you
make it the business of your whole life to overturn these prejudices, and to promote among mankind that spirit of universal
benevolence which shall render them all equals, all brothers, all
stripped of their artificial and false wants, all participating the
labour requisite to produce the necessaries of life, and all com-
bining in one universal effort of mind, for the progress of knowledge, the destruction of error, and the spreading of eternal
truth? [43]

Patiently he lets his two reformers work on him until he
gets them to the point where he wants them, and then he
has them separately abducted. But things go wrong with

[41] *Anna St. Ives, A Novel,* London, 1792, III, 30.
[42] *Ibid.,* IV, 228.
[43] *Ibid.,* III, 156-57.

his plan. Frank is nearly murdered by his hired abductors and Clifton, in trying to rescue him, is seriously injured. And then what a glorious time his victims have forgiving Clifton and saving him from despair! There is much the same glorification of the passions in this section as we saw in the samples of sentimental primitivism. The argument seems to be that the tremendous wickedness and perversity of Clifton's past life only tended to prove how tremendously good he could be if he wanted to. Yet his errors, in the Godwinian language, had been errors of the understanding. He was convicted of ' ignorance, mistakes of the understanding, false views, which you wanted knowledge enough, truth enough, to correct.' [44] The old Clifton, taken at such a disadvantage by the enthusiasts, disappears ' and in his stead an angel of light is come! ' [45] But nevertheless Anna marries Frank and not Clifton. ' Let us,' writes the now wiser Anna, ' never cease our endeavours to reform the licentious and the depraved, but let us not marry them.' [46] One cannot help feeling that the author secretly sympathizes with Coke Clifton during much of his ordeal, but his sense of humor completely deserts him at the end, and the book closes with the victory of Truth and the tearful conversion of the sinner.

It will be seen from the above that Holcroft's psychology is less theoretical and even less consistent with itself than Godwin's. He subscribes tacitly to Godwin's rationalism and professes to believe that our errors come from ignorance and mistakes in judgment. This rationalism makes its appearance again and again. He tells us in *A Narrative of Facts Relating to a Prosecution for High Treason* that ' man is happy in proportion as he is truly informed; that his ignorance is not a fault but a misfor-

---

[44] *Ibid.,* VII, 250-51.   [45] *Ibid.,* p. 256.   [46] *Ibid.,* V, 217.

tune, because his quantity of knowledge is inevitably the
result of the circumstances under which he exists; that to
be angry with him therefore, to treat him unkindly, and
to punish him, is criminal, in other words, is erroneous;
that to instruct him, and while instructing to convince him
of the benevolence of the teacher's intentions, is the only
way to cure him of his mistakes and diminish the commis-
sion of crimes.' [47] In *Hugh Trevor* again, a later and
wiser novel than *Anna St. Ives,* Holcroft repeats the reasoning that lay behind the conversion of Coke Clifton:
'Man becomes what the mistaken institutions of society
inevitably make him: his tendency is to promote his own
well being, and the well being of the creatures around
him; these can only be promoted by virtue; consequently,
when he is vicious it is from mistake, and his original sin
is ignorance.' [48] With an occasional glimmer of the difficulty of changing, by the mere force of reason, opinions
that have been dictated by prejudice and self-interest,[49]
Holcroft is nevertheless as hypnotized as Godwin with the
idea of truth and its power. 'Is this the age of Reason?'
he writes in his *Letter to the Right Honourable William
Windham.* 'Exert yourselves, summon your fortitude, ye
lovers of truth, proclaim her benevolent tenets, promul-
gate her peaceful precepts, or the age of Reason will never
be here. Seek no personal vengeance, be guilty of no intentional insult, but declare your thoughts; and if perse-
cution come, because you have openly and honestly warned
men against their errors, give it welcome.' [50] Holcroft
believed, Hazlitt tells us, that 'truth had a natural superiority over error, if it could only be heard; that if once

[47] London, 1795, pp. 3-4.
[48] *The Adventures of Hugh Trevor,* London, 1794-97, I, 169-70.
[49] *Anna St. Ives,* III, 110-11.
[50] London, 1799, p. 34.

discovered, it must, being left to itself, soon spread and triumph.' [51]

Yet with all of this professed belief in the power of reason, Holcroft avoids, as we have seen in *Anna St. Ives,* the extreme rationalism of Godwin. Without taking pains to reconcile one point of view with another, he gives full recognition to the power of passion there, and later in *Hugh Trevor* he goes so far as to name friendship and love, rather than reason, as the great agencies that are to civilize the world: 'Of all the pleasures of which the soul is capable, those of friendship for man and love for woman are the most exquisite. They may be described as—" the comprehensive principle of benevolence, which binds the whole human race to aid and love each other, individualized; and put into its utmost state of activity." . . . This is the spirit that is to harmonize the world; and give reality to those ideal gardens of paradise, and ages of gold, the possibility of which, as the records of fable shew, could scarcely escape even savage ignorance.' [52]

More surprisingly, he relinquishes the Godwinian premise that man is neither good nor bad at birth and actually goes back to the orthodox eighteenth-century premise of the goodness of the human heart: '. . . I am firmly persuaded that goodness can never be wholly driven from the human heart. It is the necessity of man's nature to be good: he feels it so thoroughly that he delights in being good.' [53] There is even to be found an idealization of the North American Indian in his writings. Frank Henley, despairing of winning Anna, looks around for a field in which the 'energies of mind might be most productive of good' and decides that the savages of America

---

[51] *Life of Thomas Holcroft,* II, 12-13.
[52] V, 37-38. Cf. *Anna St. Ives,* III, 23-24.
[53] *Memoirs of Bryan Perdue: a Novel,* London, 1805, III, 85.

will offer him the best material for the founding of an ideal society.[54] Anna moreover talks of 'her beloved golden age, her times of primitive simplicity.' [55] Twelve years later, however, Holcroft pulls himself out of this sentimentality and repudiates both the fable of the golden age and the current idealization of the Hottentots and Esquimaux.[56]

Holcroft is indeed a curious example of the follower who catches up the key words of the echo but loses the connecting links. He does not go into the logic of associationism or the metaphysics of mechanism. He is a child on the subject of necessity. Nevertheless he picks up the idea of eternal and infinite change and a consequent natural and inevitable progress. 'By the laws of necessity,' he writes, 'mind, unless counteracted by accidents beyond its control, is continually progressive in improvements.' [57] To this view, in spite of inconsistencies in logic, he remained loyal. 'Saw Dr. Towers at Debrett's . . . ,' he wrote in his diary, November 14, 1798. 'He asked me if the universal defection had not made me turn aristocrat. I answered, that I supposed my principles to be founded on truth, that is in experience and fact: that I continued to believe in the perfectibility of man, which the blunders and passions of ignorance might apparently delay, but could not prevent; and that the only change of opinion I had undergone was, that political revolutions are not so well calculated to better man's condition, as during a cer-

[54] *Anna St. Ives,* V, 78-79. Cf. 'Parental Feelings: or the Benakee Indian,' *The Family Picture,* London, 1783, I, 227 ff.

[55] *Ibid.,* V, 91.

[56] *Travels from Hamburg, through Westphalia, Holland, and the Netherlands, to Paris,* London, 1804, I, 137.

[57] *Anna St. Ives,* V, 87. Cf. *Hugh Trevor,* I, iii, and 'Review of Dugald Stewart, Elements of the Philosophy of the Human Mind,' *Monthly Review,* X (1793), 59.

tain period I, with almost all the thinking men in Europe, had been led to suppose.' [58]

IV

Other novelists of a more temperate disposition than Mary Hays and Holcroft were inclined to adopt a more moderate view of the future felicity of man and a more practical view of present distress. They relinquished less of the old for the speculative new. Representative of such writers are Charles Lloyd, Charlotte Smith, Robert Bage, and the anonymous author of *Berkeley Hall, or the Pupil of Experience.*

Charles Lloyd, as a matter of fact, goes so far, in his novel *Edmund Oliver,* in his criticism of the extreme radical position as set forth by Mary Hays and Godwin that it is a question whether he does not rather belong with the satirists than the advocates of progress. The scales are tipped in favor of putting him in this rather than the later chapter by the fact that most of his satire is directed only toward the radical views on the relation of the sexes in and out of marriage. Certainly his mind was early prepared for the reception of original ideas by a bad case of Rousseauism in his early youth,[59] an influence which bore fruit much later in his morbid novel of passion, *Isabel.* A letter to his brother, written when he was twenty, testifies to his early absorption of radical ideas. ' The pure ardour of universal benevolence,' writes the young enthusiast, ' does not abate at the sight of a Lutheran or a Quaker, a Catholic or an Unbeliever. No! it considers all the petty, paltry distinctions of parties and sects, which would separate man from man and brother from brother, as originating in the weaknesses and prejudices of mankind; it de-

[58] *Life of Thomas Holcroft,* II, 195.
[59] E. V. Lucas, *Charles Lamb and the Lloyds,* London, 1898, p. 16.

spises them all, and simply seeks by active usefulness, not by unintelligible dogmas, to diffuse good and enlarge the confin'd limit of human felicity.' [60] He then recommends to his brother's earnest attention such books as Holcroft's *Anna St. Ives,* Godwin's *Political Justice,* and Priestley's *Letters to a Philosophical Unbeliever.* He wrote *Edmund Oliver* three years later, after he had come under the influence of Coleridge. Perhaps the best known fact about the book is that the too evident reminiscences of some of Coleridge's early experiences and the implied criticism of his emotional and impulsive nature in the character of Edmund Oliver was one factor in the triangular quarrel between Coleridge, Lloyd, and Lamb. However that may be, the association with Coleridge lent new impetus to the traditional theme of the simplicity of country life which, with an adherence to the 'inflexible rules of right and wrong,' [61] forms the strongest strain in the book and gives it its conservative color. There is even a Shaftesburian note in his praise of the simple life: 'Oh man, how mistaken art thou with regard to thy true interest, when thou forsakest the simplicity of a country life! . . . How can a being who has nothing but distortion around him, acquire a fondness for moral beauty?' [62] But with this faith in the simple life is combined a belief in gradual but persistent progress in mankind. He differed from most of the radicals in believing that amelioration could never be reached by political reform superimposed on the masses from above,[63] but must be a matter of gradual permeation from individual to individual. 'It must go through the patient discipline of domestic duty, and the unapplauded toils of retired life, ere it make a sure advancement.' [64] There is

[60] *Ibid.,* p. 14.
[61] London, 1798, II, 148 ff.
[62] *Ibid.,* I, 50-51. Cf. p. 102.
[63] *Ibid.,* p. 185.
[64] *Ibid.,* p. 131.

danger, he feels, in the generalizing spirit of contemporary philosophers. ' I think I can perceive,' he writes, ' in the introduction of concubinage, in the rejection of cohabitation, and in the character of that indefinite benevolence, which would respect the mass of existence without addressing its operations patiently to parts of that mass, principles, that would destroy the tranquillity of society, that, by means of annihilation all the dear " charities of father, son, and brother," would at last lead to a callousness that spurns at all affections, to a mad spirit of experiment, that would eradicate all the valuable feelings of man's nature. . . . ' [65]

The extremists are characterized in Lloyd's novel in the persons of Mr. Edward D'Oyley and Lady Gertrude Sinclair. So broad is the caricature that one sample is sufficient: ' "Are you to forget the indefinite and incalculable benefit that you will be of to society by trampling on the rubbish which fills the onward path of man, directing your eye singly to the distant horizon of human perfection? And even, Edward, should we conjecture falsely, (for finite existences are ever liable to mistake) we ought to bear in mind that the sacred spark of truth is frequently elicited in the collision of heterogeneous and opposing principles." ' [66]

V

Charlotte Smith's novels cover the period of the French Revolution and after, and deal more directly with reforms in France and their consequences than the other novels of this group. *Desmond* especially was considered so radically republican in tone that the respectable *Gentleman's Magazine* and the *Critical Review* passed it by in silent contempt, but the more liberal *Monthly Review*

[65] *Ibid.*, pp. vii-viii.   [66] *Ibid.*, pp. 35-36.

had the courage to champion Mrs. Smith's political discussion. ' Novels, which were formerly little more than simple tales of love,' writes the reviewer, 'are gradually taking a higher and more masculine tone, and are becoming the vehicles of useful instruction. Mrs. Smith, who has already favoured the public with several instructive as well as entertaining works of this kind, has in the present publication, ventured beyond the beaten track, so far as to interweave with her narrative many political discussions.' [67] Mrs. Smith, herself, while she defends her sex for their interest in politics, makes it quite clear in her prefaces that she wishes to be considered as remaining well within the pale of traditional respectability for a wife, it being more in the observance than in the breach of her domestic duties that she has sought novel-writing as a means of support for her family.[68] And indeed the flavor of her early ' republicanism ' is so very mild and her tone so moral that it is hard for us now to see why any of her novels should have cost her the good opinion of her friends, or have been regarded, to use the delightful eighteenth-century phrase, as ' not unexceptionable.'

As I have said, Charlotte Smith's novels cover the period of the French Revolution. *Desmond,* the first to show any marked political tendency, was published in 1792. *The Old Manor House* followed in 1793, *The Banished Man* in 1794, *Marchmont* in 1796, and *The Young Philosopher* in 1798. These novels show the characteristic fluctuation of opinion of the time. Already in *The Banished Man,* Mrs. Smith is writing from the point of view of the French aristocratic *émigré,* and in *Marchmont* she bitterly repudiates the republic that she had let Desmond so enthusiastically support in the earlier

---

[67] *Monthly Review or Literary Journal,* IX (1792), 406.

[68] See especially the prefaces to *Desmond* and *Marchmont.*

novel. There Desmond denies the false reports of anarchy
in France that had been spread in England by men whom
the English government was glad to make use of to
' impede a little the progress of that light which they see
rising in the world.' [69] He assures his correspondent,
Bethel, of the probable permanence of the new system
and of its importance to the happiness not only of France
but of the universe. He praises Paine's *Rights of Man*
for the truths in it which either had not been seen before
or had been carefully repressed; '. . . they are bluntly,
sometimes coarsely delivered, but it is often impossible
to refuse immediate assent to those which appear the bold-
est.' [70] He attacks Burke, deplores his shift from an earlier
more liberal position in his present support of ' principles
absolutely opposite to all the professions of his political
life,' [71] and cites in opposition to his picture of the French
mob the magnanimity shown by the French people to
their king on his re-entrance into Paris—' This will
surely convince the world, that the *bloody democracy* of
Mr. Burke, is not a combination of the swinish multitude,
for the purpose of anarchy, but the association of reasonable beings, who determine to be, and deserve to be,
free.' [72]

Mrs. Smith was of course only changing with the times
when she wrote four years later in *Marchmont*, ' Do not
imagine, however, my dear friend, that I have any intention to plead in favour of that universal license, that wild
and impracticable scheme of general equality, which has,
within a few years, gained ground from the writings of
visionary speculatists, and from the propensity of mankind to run into extremes, and to pervert the best general

[69] *Desmond*, London, 1796, I, 106. [71] *Ibid.*, III, 209.
[70] *Ibid.*, II, 116. [72] *Ibid.*, p. 89.

rules to the most unworthy private purposes.' [73]   And
'I had determined to leave Paris . . . because my very
soul was sick of the wild assemblage of ideotism and
phrensy which I every day saw; and was eager, at all
events, to quit people whose folly called for my contempt, while their ferocity excited my abhorrence.' [74]

Inasmuch as most of Charlotte Smith's political views
have to do with the problems of democracy, the unequal
division of property, the injustices of English law and
law courts, rather than with the theory of progress itself,
it is unnecessary to go into greater detail in regard to
them.   More important for us is the fact that along with
her early French enthusiasm, and becoming more and
more prominent, is a strong strain of praise of the simple
life according to nature.   I have already remarked on the
'beautiful souls' of *The Old Manor House*.   Perhaps
even more striking in that novel is the portrait of the
noble Indian, Wolf-hunter.   Mrs. Smith is not sentimental in her general picture of the Indians, but in Wolf-
hunter she creates such a noble and generous friend to
the hero that when Orlando returned to England, an
unwelcome wayfarer, he found himself 'mortified that
such brutish inhospitality as what he had just experienced
could exist in British bosoms, and lamenting that there
were Englishmen less humane than the rude savages of
the wilds of America.' [75]   Celestina, the heroine of another novel, reflects in the Hebrides, 'Alas! . . . if they
have not our enjoyments, they suffer not from those
sensibilities which embitter our days.   Their short summer
passes in laying up necessaries for their long winter; and
with what their desolate region affords them they are
content, because they know not that there are comforts

[73] London, 1796, IV, 37.   [75] London, 1820, II, 161, 120.
[74] *Ibid.*, III, 185.

and conveniences beyond what it affords them. Void of
the wish and the power to observe other modes of life,
they are content with their own, and though little superior
in point of intellect to the animal from which they derive
their support, yet they are happy, if not from the possession of good, at least from the absence of evil; and that
sickness of the soul which we taste from deprivation and
disappointment.' [76]   Such reflections occur frequently in
Marchmont. The hero contemplates, for instance, a peas-
ant of southern France. ' He, said I, meditates nothing
about Revolutions—he hardly understands the term.
Under the old government he worked hard;—the new
one has made to him (fortunate man!) no sensible
change: he still works hard for the daily bread he eats.
He has heard that mass is abolished—that the religion
of his country is annihilated; but *his* religion consisted
merely in one simple and uniform routine of the duties
necessary to enable his family to exist from one week to
another. . . . *Is* it good then to be such a being? When
I reflect on the vice, the folly of cultivated, of polished
life, I am ready to answer that it *is.* . . .' [77]   But he had
just enough feeling for progress and respect for the
human reason left to decide that ' I would *not* exchange
my sense of existence for his; ' but he adds reflectively,
' yet I think there can be no doubt but that his is the
happier.' [78]

The Young Philosopher, written to the tune of the
following motto,

> Of Man, when warm'd by Reason's purest ray,
> No slave of Avarice, no tool of Pride;
> When no vain Science led his mind astray,
> But NATURE was his law, and GOD his guide,

---

[76] *Celestina,* London, 1791, III, 71.   [78] *Ibid.,* pp. 52-53.
[77] *Ibid.,* IV, 51-52.

contains perhaps the most striking of the portraits of natural goodness in Medora, the 'little wild Caledonian American.' [79] Delmont, the young philosopher, falls in love with her precisely, as he says, because 'she is so entirely the child of nature.' [80] 'Delmont, as he looked at her, or listened to the artless yet just sentiments she uttered, when she was induced to talk to him, doubted whether more knowledge of the world, and more of that information which books are supposed to give, would not rather tarnish than heighten the beauty of a mind, that now seemed to resemble one of those lovely spots, where every object that enchants the sight, or delights the imagination, is assembled; but which, if once the hand of art is introduced, loses that *Arcadian* bloom for which no improvement in clearing its wild rocks, or calling in more extensive prospects, can compensate.' [81] But it is Medora's father who uses the most interesting reasoning. He is disgusted anew with the state of civilized Europe on his return from America; 'he envied indeed no one, but rather beheld with wonder the toil and fatigue which were incurred to make a splendid appearance at such an immense expence as would have supported in America fifty families in more real comfort and plenty. He saw men labouring in places like dungeons the greater and better part of their days in the hope of some future satisfaction which great riches were to bestow; but the means were seldom acquired till the end was lost, and till the powers of enjoyment existed no longer. He saw the continual and often successful effort of knaves to take advantage of fools, and beheld a spirit of quackery prevail from the state charlatan, exhausting and enfeebling the public constitution, to the advertising puffer of some poisonous

---

[79] London, 1798, I, 245.   [80] *Ibid.*, p. 244.   [81] *Ibid.*, III, 39.

nostrum; and hardly as he contemplated the humiliating scene of almost universal imposition and deception, knew whether most to despise or to pity those who acted and those who suffered.' [82] He proposes to return to America where he can live without being subjected to the degradations of civilized life. But curiously enough he also plans to take back the *arts of civilization* to the ' wild regions of the earth ' and rejoices in the state of ' progressive improvement' of the country of his adoption! [83] With this complicated solution to the problem of civilization we will leave Mrs. Smith for Robert Bage.

VI

Like Charlotte Smith, Bage tends to choose a middle course between radical and conservative positions. Like her he criticizes European civilization from the point of view of the ' natural man.' Like her he uses the Indians and the life of nature to evaluate the idea of progress, and like her he criticizes the extremes of sensibility but rather prefers an ethics of feeling to the calculations of the utilitarians. In connection with sensibility, at the moment just waning in its popularity, it is amusing to find Mrs. Smith and Robert Bage using exactly the same device. The former in *Desmond* and *Marchmont* and the latter in *Barham Downs* (1784) and *James Wallace* (1788) give themselves the luxury of heroes of extreme

---

[82] IV, 199-200.

[83] *Ibid.*, pp. 201-2. Mrs. Smith, in her preface (I, vi) explains that her opinions are not necessarily those of her characters; but her general preference for the simple life of nature is clear enough. She seems to indicate by the example of Glenmorris, Medora's father, that however preferable a man may find a life of freedom and simplicity, he will not be able, in the present state of society ' so entirely to emancipate himself, as not to be dragged back in some instance to the forms of society.' (I, 232)

sensibility, but they employ in each case another character to scold them throughout the novel for their over-sensitiveness. Thus Mr. Wyman writes to the distressful hero of *Barham Downs,* ' Were it not for those *sinkings of the mind,* so unworthy of a man that a woman might be ashamed of them, which appear in thy last letters, I could take an interest in them. But that confounded habit, acquired at the expense of common sense; that artificial mode of thinking, or feeling, I know not which, which those who have it, and those who would be thought to have it, agree to call by the flowing name of sensibility, spoils you for a Man, whether you act or write.' [84] Yet Bage is equally sarcastic on the subject of the regulation of the conduct by the calculation of the consequences: ' The conduct of an angel, who can see into futurity, may be directed with certainty to the greatest good. Men can only be guided by what they know. I am sure, Sir, it is no maxim of yours, that no one ought to attempt a probable and proximate good, for fear of producing a remote and improbable evil.' [85] He recommends instead a generally benevolent attitude toward society and a modified sensibility.[86] His villains are frequently converted to the theory of benevolence by the happiness of the more sociably minded characters.[87]

All of this seems far enough from Jacobinism, and yet even Godwin payed homage to him, along with Erasmus Darwin, as one of the leaders of progressive thought of the time. On a trip to the north Godwin writes to Mary Wollstonecraft in June, 1797, ' We bent

[84] London, 1784, I, 165-66.
[85] *James Wallace,* London, 1788, II, 37.
[86] *Ibid.,* p. 38, and *Barham Downs,* I, 166.
[87] E. g., Samuel Sutton in *Mount Henneth,* Sir George Ormond in *Barham Downs,* and the hero of *Man as He Is.*

our course for Derby, being furnished with a letter of introduction to Dr. Darwin, and purposing to obtain from him a further letter of introduction to Mr. Bage, of Tamworth, author of " Man as He Is," and " Hermsprong." Did we not well? Are not such men as much worth visiting as palaces, towns, and cathedrals?' He describes how he was determined not to be discouraged from his project of meeting Bage by finding Dr. Darwin out of town and his wife unwilling to give him a letter of introduction; how he drove to Elford where some of Bage's paper mills were located and was directed to meet Bage on the road thither; how he met him, a man of sixty-seven, short, ' with white hair, snuff-coloured clothes, and a walking stick,' [88] and walked and talked with him, so fascinated that, although he had started his journey that morning at six o'clock without breakfast, he ' felt no inconvenience in waiting for food till our dinner-time at two.'

In *Hermsprong, or Man as He Is Not* (1796), Bage's last novel, one finds the most radical ideas, this novel being, as the title suggests an attempt to picture an ideal man. The ideal man, Hermsprong, we ought not at this time to be surprised to hear, comes from America where he has been brought up among the Indians, though by his own father and mother. His mode of education has rendered him wholly without prejudice on all social questions, and it must be confessed that it is rather refreshing to see him play havoc with some of the principles of eighteenth-century ethics so long held sacred in novel tradition, especially that principle of unswerving filial obedience even though the parent in question is a brute and a rascal.

Hermsprong has been in France during the Revolution,

[88] C. Kegan Paul, *op. cit.*, I, 261-62.

and even at this date, 1796, retains his belief in the main purposes of the French.

Mr. Sumelin. " Have you left America long?

Mr. Hermsprong. " About five years.

S. " Since then you have resided in France?

H. " Properly speaking, I have not resided anywhere. Smitten with the love of being seen, I have shown myself to half Europe; returning occasionally to France as I was wanted.

S. " They are going on there in a strange way.

H. " Yes, strange and new. I speak of the causes which animate the French; for as to the means—the destruction of the human species—it has been a favourite mode with power of every denomination, ever since power was.

S. " What are these causes you speak of?

H. " To make mankind wiser and better.

S. " And do you approve the means?

H. " What all? Oh no! It is left to the loyal Englishman, and is, I am told, a new prerogative,—to approve by the lump.[89]

Hermsprong, moreover, has read the *Rights of Man,* apparently with approval, for he lent it to a friend; and he has radical ideas on rank, having been ' taught only to distinguish men by virtue.' [90]

There really was no fundamental inconsistency on Bage's part in this use of a man brought up among the Indians as an exponent of revolutionary principles. There is not even any inconsistency in such idealization of the Indians as one finds in the remark, for instance, of Hermsprong's father: ' I despised them myself, till I found them my equals in knowledge of many things of which I believed them ignorant; and my superiors in the virtues of friendship, hospitality, and integrity.' [91] For though the perfectionists, with their premises drawn from Locke and Hartley, did not have any logical right (although

[89] London, 1820, p. 40.   [90] *Ibid.,* p. 30.   [91] *Ibid.,* p. 238.

some of them helped themselves to it) to the primitivistic premise that man is innately good, at least they started with the principle that man was neither good nor bad at birth but had been corrupted by the institutions of civilization. The inconsistency comes when, forgetting their Hartleian principle of associationism and increasing complexity,[92] they propose to reform and perfect civilized man by turning him in the direction of primitive simplicity. And this is exactly what Bage did. Hermsprong, speaking apparently for Bage, distinguishes always between progress in material prosperity and progress in happiness. He will not allow that the former contributes to the latter.

> Grant, said Glen, that we have been in a progressive state of improvement for some centuries, and that the aborigines of America have not.
>
> I allow your progressive state, Mr. Hermsprong answered; and if you will have it, that all is improvement, be it so. You have built cities, no doubt, and filled them full of improvement, if magnificence be improvement; and of poverty also, if poverty be improvement. But our question, my friend, is happiness, comparative happiness, and until you can trace its dependence upon wealth, it will be in vain for you to boast your riches.
>
> It appears to me, said the reverend Mr. Woodcock, that we have all the requisites for happiness which the untaught races of mankind have, with the addition of all that can be extracted from art and science.
>
> This, said Glen, appears to me an uncontrovertible argument.
>
> And perhaps is so, Mr. Hermsprong replied; but of this addition your common people cannot avail themselves. . . . It should seem . . . that nature in her more simple modes, is unable to furnish a rich European with a due portion of pleasurable sensations. . . .

[92] See *Barham Downs*, I, 21.

In this comparison, Sir, said Mr. Woodcock, you seem to have forgot our greatest pleasures, those drawn from intellect.

They also have exertion of intellect, Mr. Hermsprong replied. Their two grand occupations require much of it, in their way; and who, think you, make their songs? They have indeed a different mode of using their understandings, and a less variety of subjects; but our point is happiness. I know not that they derive less from intellect than you.[93]

For anything that Hermsprong will agree to call real progress, simplicity in government and simplicity in social relationships is requisite. He seems to feel that the state of society and government in America come the nearest to affording each citizen a most perfect adjustment of his life. But England, he thinks, is too far gone in the corruptions of luxury to be satisfied with such simplicity.[94] Hermsprong, on the other hand, feels that he could never reconcile himself to life in England. 'I cannot eat for hours, nor love candles as well as the sun. I cannot, I fear, submit to be fettered and cramped throughout the whole circle of thought and action. You submit to authority with regard to the first, and to fashion with regard to the last. I cannot get rid of the stubborn notion, that to do what we think is right to do, is the only good principle of action. You seem to think the only good principle of action is to do as others do. . . . Servile compliance is crime, when it violates rectitude; and imbecility, at least, when it is prostituted to folly. When it has become habitual, what a thing it has made of man!'[95]

It is impossible not to see, Bage tells us elsewhere, that most of our calamities and distresses are due to human

---

[93] *Hermsprong*, pp. 123-24.
[94] *Ibid.*, pp. 188-90.
[95] *Ibid.*, p. 336.

conventions and arrangements. Nature every where combines her elements to the advantage of man. 'Kings, lords and lawyers, are made by man.' [96] At another point he remarks even more bitterly, '. . . . nature created no other evil for man but pain; all things else, which we call evil, spring from *improvement*.' [97]

Possibly Bage's own rustic isolation had forced on his mind the values of the simple life of nature and an undue apprehension of the complexities of civilization. ' I should have added to the account of Mr. Bage,' wrote Godwin in the letter cited above, ' that he never was in London for more than a week at a time, and very seldom more than 50 miles from his home. A very memorable instance, in my opinion, of great intellectual refinement, attained in the bosom of rusticity.' [98] From whatever source, there is certainly an unusually strong leaning toward primitivism in the works of Bage, but one turns the page from passages such as those I have just cited and comes upon the following parody on anti-luxury propaganda which convinces one anew of the futility of even looking for a consistent system of thought in the pages of a popular novel. The words of sarcasm are those of Mr. Wyman in *Barham Downs* who seems to be the mouthpiece for Bage throughout the novel: ' They [our statesmen] have opened the historic page, and find in every leaf, that Wealth is the father of Luxury; Luxury the mother of corruption, and corruption of political death. Wealth therefore is the grand object of their attack. If they can get rid of this, real and nominal, they lay their axe to the root. Men will return to their primitive virtues, by the kindly aid of poverty; and what is of still more consequence at court, poverty is the natural parent of humility,

[96] *James Wallace*, I, 164.   [97] *Ibid.*, p. 6.   [98] Paul, *op. cit.*, I, 264.

and unmurmuring obedience. This being the case, can men go more directly to the point? When the Barons build again their castles, and restore mankind once more to the happy state of villenage, then will the learned monk tread the licentious page of freedom in the dirt, and give to truth and day, the deep-penetrating politics of these times.' [99]

VII

The case of *Berkeley Hall, or the Pupil of Experience* is somewhat different. Containing as extravagant pictures of noble savages as the most primitivistic novel, it nevertheless rejects the theory of primitivism for that of progress. As the book is not very accessible I will review its contents. In manner and episodic material it is strongly reminiscent of *Tom Jones*—with a slight Shandean flavor. Tim is an even braver Tom, Letitia a fairer but less trusting Sophia, the villain, Squire Aaron, brother of Letitia, a more sadistic Blifil, Dr. Sourby, a Thwackum and Square in one, and the hero's grandfather, Dr. Homily, a more ecclesiastical version of Squire Allworthy and Uncle Toby. This imitativeness sounds inauspicious, but the book is not without a certain vigor. Written in 1796, it professes to deal with the restoration period, but beyond some ardent support of the church of England against the attacks of the dissenters it has little reference to that period. It opens with an argument over perfectibility, and it runs the gamut of the issues of the 1790's. The scene is laid entirely in America, Berkeley Hall, the residence of Dr. Homily, being located in New Jersey. In consequence of the intrigues of Aaron and the heroine's friend, Miss Moody, who is in love with Tim, Letitia is made to doubt the fidelity of Tim, and the hero in

[99] II, 33-34.

desperation undertakes a tour of North America with Dr. Sourby, his erstwhile tutor.   Dr. Sourby, whose disposition is sufficiently indicated by his name, thinks that he will find the antidote for all of the ills of an unappreciative civil society in the life of nature, and Tim, in the bitterness of his spirit, is not loath to make the experiment with him.

'"Here," cried Dr. Sourby, "nature reigns in true sublimity and lovely simplicity.   Here we shall meet men in their original innocence and independence, untrammelled by forms, or the yokes of ancient institutions. Here the heads of men will not be deluded by prejudices and falsehoods, nor their hearts corrupted by flattery, envy, pride, and ambition.   Here we shall find the true nature and life of man."   So saying, he dismounted his steed, and led him stalking triumphantly down the hill.' [100]

At one point in their adventures they were surrounded by a party of Indians and were about to be scalped when Tonondoric, an old chief, sprang forward and, embracing Tim, cried out, '"I had a son once: but he is no more. You shall succeed him.   From this moment consider me as your father."' [101]   Tim, thus providentially saved, sprang between a lifted tomahawk and Sancho, his negro servant. The Indians so much appreciated the magnanimity of his conduct that they granted an amnesty to Sancho also, whom they called the Raven Chief.   But the cowardly and useless Dr. Sourby, it was decreed, must satisfy their desire for revenge.   '"Let us sacrifice the pampered glutton, who burdens and impoverishes the earth—he who has no wind for the chase, no legs to pursue an enemy, and no heart or arms to subdue him—the stranger I mean, that resembles, with heavy paunch, the unwieldy

[100] London, 1796, II, 341.
[101] Ibid., III, 36.

moose labouring through the snow, or the greasy bear
clambering up a smooth tree; he uses neither the hatchet,
spade, nor musquet; and is not man, but a *squaw mon-
ster,* that lives by the hands and heads of other men." ' [102]

It is at this point that the great nobility of the slave,
Sancho, is featured. Of all of the fictional negroes that
I have run across, he is the most ingenious in thinking
up ways to sacrifice himself for the good of his master
and his friends. When Tim declared his intention of
staking his own life on the rescue of his friend, and
proposed that if the worst came to the worst they should
have Sancho kill them painlessly before the Indians had
a chance to torture them to death, Sancho, almost driven
crazy by the proposal, rushed to the council of Indians
and offered himself as the victim in place of Dr. Sourby.
' " I am young and brave: I will meet death like you;
but the poor *old white friend* of ours *has lived softly,*
always like a *woman;* he is good for *head-work,* but
cannot be an acceptable offering to heroes. They triumph
not in the slaughter of a lamb or a goat, but in the death
of the tiger, the bear, or the lion. Look at these scars
(shewing his face and breast), and let *me* be the victim
to your departed warriors. I killed them; *he* kills nothing
but *musquitoes or butterflies.*"

' This harangue, and the noble proposal, so pleased the
chiefs, that they embraced Sancho, exclaiming, " Young
Tonondoric [Tim] himself is not more a hero than his
brother the raven! No, we will not shed such gallant
blood; and, what is more, we will spare for your sake
and *Tonondoric's* the *black blood* of your ignoble friend;
you shall not exceed us in magnanimity." ' [103]

The friends were thus freed of anxiety for the moment,

---

[102] *Ibid.,* p. 51.   [103] *Ibid.,* pp. 60-61.

but as soon as the rum began to circulate they were all forced to flee. They were guided by Tonondoric and his beautiful daughter, Ancuna, who were disaffected with their tribe for deserting the English and going over to the side of the French. After many adventures in which Sancho and Tonondoric vied with each other in magnanimity they all finally reached Berkeley Hall, Ancuna having picked up her Mohawk lover, Hendrick, on the way. It was here that primitivistic talk ran most high. Dr. Sourby, now cured of *his* primitivism, asked Tonondoric patronizingly what he thought of the buildings, churches, furniture of civilization, the splendor of the dresses, tables, and carriages, and Tonondoric gave perhaps as unanswerable a reply as he could have found: ' "You have shewn me many *great houses, musquash!* but few such great men as *Hendrick, my son,* or the *raven chief.*" ' [104]

Dr. Homily attempted to explain to him some of the arts of civilization and accounted for the helplessness of Dr. Sourby in the wilderness by saying that he was out of his element there.

' "You would not laugh at a *whale-fish,* brother, because he could not fly; nor the eagle-bird for not swimming like a Dolphin."

' "Very true, brother," said *Tonondoric*; your knowledge and way are good for you; and ours for us. I see the *musquash chief* is at home now, in his own element. He has plenty of *tongue* and *tooth-work* and little for the *hands* and *feet.*—He has all *head and belly-work*— he is right, brother.—Say I right, *musquash?*" ' [105]

Sancho undertook to show them over the grounds and explain the advantages of the gardens and hot-houses.

<hr/>

[104] *Ibid.,* p. 171.   [105] *Ibid.,* p. 172.

Tonondoric shook his head and observed, ' " *Brother raven,* you and I have little, and we sit loose on the earth. These fine things are like the roots of the great tree; they fasten the man to the earth, and make it hard for him to quit it. He that has so much to love, and so much to lose, must have much to fear. You and I have *nothing to fear, but guilt and dishonour.*" ' And Hendrick added, ' " You may depend so much on horses to carry you, muskets to kill for you, glasses to see for you, and your gold to fight for you, that you may lose the use of your own legs, not be able to defend yourselves with your own arms, to see with your own eyes, or have hearts to fight for yourselves; like the *musquash chief,* who earns not his own meat, raises no corn, kills no game, fights no enemies, and gets no children. We wonder he hires nobody to eat and drink for him; but that he can do very well for himself." ' [106]

But in spite of all this orthodox primitivistic talk and the sympathetic picture of noble savages, the idea of progress carries off the honors. The victorious theory is, to be sure, a rather conservative theory of perfectibility. The unfortunate Dr. Sourby is made not only the scape-goat for the primitivistic ideas that do not meet with the approval of Dr. Homily and his cronies, but he is also loaded with the more radical and subversive of the revolutionary principles of the day. They meet with the same fate as his primitivistic principles. Progress through the increase of knowledge and the spread of commerce, both fostered by a liberal government, seems to be the creed of the author. To Dr. Sourby's ideal natural state, Dr. Bellamy replies: ' " I cannot believe . . . that men would be more happy in such a state of *ease and repose,* than in

[106] *Ibid.,* pp. 189-91.

the *active scenes* of commercial and civilized nations. It seems to be the universal law of nature, that nothing shall be *idle or useless*; and in particular with respect to man, that his duty and happiness shall consist in *a progressive course of improvement*; in the acquisition of knowledge; in ameliorating the fertility and beauty of the earth; in habits of industry, patience, and self-denial; and the exercise of the great virtues of fortitude, charity, magnanimity, forgiveness of injuries, honest industry, and public spirit." ' [107]

The book is very strongly pro-British. It was apparently written to counteract current criticisms of the English government and church. The final word seems to be that if Great Britain and America will only coöperate in the extension of ' civilization, commerce, religion, law, and freedom ' to the rest of the world, a ' greater progress will be made in *meliorating the condition* of mankind, than, perhaps, we have now an idea of. For every advance in this business, makes the next stage of progress easier, almost *ad infinitum*.' [108]

[107] *Ibid.*, I, 294-95.
. [108] *Ibid.*, III, 404.

CHAPTER IX

Attempts at Compromise

I

Before we turn to the companion picture to the last chapter—the novels and tales that satirize the idea of progress—let us look at another group of writers who have more claim to being professional thinkers than the last. They are a shade more scrupulous than the novelists, have some sense of the incongruity of adopting two antagonistic ways of thinking at one time, but see too many beauties in each point of view wholly to relinquish either. They work out, therefore, various stratagems of logic whereby they are enabled to keep both primitivism and the theory of progress. In some cases religious scruples, in other cases, a kind of religious mysticism, enter into consideration to force a compromise in logic. Representative of the former case is the reasoning of Lord Kames and of the latter, that of Lord Monboddo.

We have already seen how Kames's development of the idea that the moral sense is innate, universal, and invariable, ' the same hereafter as it is at present and as it was in the past, the same among all nations, and in all corners of the earth,' [1] gave him the foundation for primitivism, and that in the *Sketches* he does actually write primitivistic passages. He is further impelled toward primitivism by way of the doctrine of degeneration, for Kames accepts the current anti-luxury point of view. ' In all times,' he writes, ' luxury has been the ruin of every state where it prevailed. Nations originally are poor and virtuous. They advance to industry, commerce, and

[1] *Sketches of the History of Man,* Edinburgh, 1788, IV, 22.

perhaps to conquest and empire. But this state is never
permanent: great opulence opens a wide door to indolence, sensuality, corruption, prostitution, perdition.' [2]
He is, however, too faithful an adherent of the historical
method—the method of Montesquieu, whom he calls
the greatest genius of the present age [3]—to ignore as
easily as some of his contemporaries the actual historical
and travel records of the wide variation in primitive
tribes both in physique and disposition, a variation that
makes extremely difficult any general primitivistic interpretation. Viewing this variation, Kames is disturbed by
two things. He cannot conceive that God ever created
tribes as savage as some are known to be, and he cannot
see how so many distinct nationalities could have sprung
from the one original pair that his Bible told him God
had created; for he accepts only with large reservations
Montesquieu's theory of the influence of climate.[4] He
devotes a long section to the analysis of the differences
between races, and tribes within races. Again and again
he is brought up short by the observation ' That were all
men of one species, there never could have existed, with
out a miracle, different kinds, such as exist at present.' [5]
He finally formulates a hypothesis that seems to him to
explain satisfactorily the varying human types, namely,
' That God created many pairs of the human race differing from each other both externally and internally; that he
fitted these pairs for different climates, and placed each
pair in its proper climate; that the peculiarities of the
original pairs were preserved entire in their descendants;
who, having no assistance but their natural talents, were
left to gather knowledge from experience, and in par·
ticular were left (each tribe) to form a language for

[2] *Ibid.*, II, 153-54.   [4] *Ibid.*, pp. 59 ff.
[3] *Ibid.*, I, 315.   [5] *Ibid.*, p. 74.

itself.' [6] But again he finds himself face to face with the first chapter of *Genesis* which tells him that God created only one human pair in the beginning. ' Though we cannot doubt of the authority of Moses, yet his account of the creation of man is not a little puzzling,' confesses Kames.[7] The Biblical and the historical accounts do not harmonize. Man was not created savage, but every where there are savage tribes; the progeny of Adam must have resembled their begetter, yet there seem to be different species of man. Kames's solution is ingenious. Mankind must have suffered some terrible convulsion to bring about the change in his state and nature. What convulsion could explain the transformation better than that at the Tower of Babel. ' Here light breaks forth in the midst of darkness. By confounding the language of men, and scattering them abroad upon the face of all the earth, they were rendered savages. And to harden them for their new habitations, it was necessary that they should be divided into different kinds, fitted for different climates.' [8] The beauty of this solution is that it enables Kames to hold to the theories of primitivism and progressivism at the same time. Some tribes in favorable localities illustrate all the primitive virtues that the most ardent advocate of the golden age could desire; others, savage to begin with, are in a position to illustrate the principle of progress. The moral sense, he has to admit, has not been equally perfect at all times, nor in all countries,[9] but he conceives that it has the best chance to generate

[6] *Ibid.*, p. 76.

[7] *Ibid.*

[8] *Ibid.*, p. 78. Kames could not have more than half believed in this solution, however, for when he comes to discuss the tribes of American Indians he forgets all about it and argues for separate creation. See III, 148.

[9] *Ibid.*, IV, 19.

primitive goodness in countries where there is plenty of food and space. 'In a nascent society, where men hunt and fish in common, where there is plenty of game, and where the sense of property is faint, mutual affection prevails, because there is no cause of discord. . . .'[10]

Kames is on the whole, however, rather more interested in progress than in primitive man—a progress brought about by the gradual cultivation of the moral sense and of the benevolent affections.[11]   But even in the consideration of progress his religious convictions play their part in modifying his views. Will man ever reach a state of perfection in his social relationships, he asks with many of his contemporaries. 'How devoutly to be wished, (it will be said), that all men were upright and honest; and that all of the same nation were united like a single family in concord and mutual affection! Here indeed would be perpetual sunshine, a golden age, a state approaching to that of good men made perfect in heavenly mansions.'[12]   But his religious scruples immediately arise to defend the *status quo*. Providence has not endowed us with perfection; it is easy, therefore, for a man like Kames to convince himself that he does not want it. A state of perfection would be insipid and uninteresting. Not only that, but as natural evils would necessarily remain, 'the extreme delicacy, and softness of temper, produced by eternal peace and concord, would render such evils insupportable.'[13]   With no need for courage, moreover, man would come to 'rival a hare or a mouse for timidity.'[14] With no controversies and disagreements to sharpen men's reason, it would 'for ever lie dormant.'[15]   'How rashly do men judge of the conduct of Providence!' he

[10] *Ibid.*, II, 204.
[11] *Ibid.*, IV, 130 ff.
[12] *Ibid.*, II, 207.

[13] *Ibid.*, p. 208.
[14] *Ibid.*, p. 213.
[15] *Ibid.*, p. 214.

exclaims. '. . . A golden age would to man be more poisonous than Pandora's box; a gift, sweet in the mouth, but bitter, bitter in the stomach.' [16] It is much more salutary for man, concludes Kames, ' to rest on the faith, that whatever is, is the best!' [17]

II

Kames and Monboddo were both figures of considerable importance in their time. Of the two the former was perhaps more highly esteemed and the latter more widely known. Mathias, for example, writes of Monboddo, 'All the learned world knows *how* Lord Monboddo believed and still believes, that men had once *tails* depending from the *gable end* of their bodies, supposing them to go *upon all fours*.' [18] The fact, incidentally, that Monboddo did *not* believe this need not surprise us. As so often happens in the case of men who boldly broach new theories, Monboddo was better known by hearsay than by first-hand acquaintance with his works, and, like many another in his position, he was much more famous for what he did not say than for what he did. The two ideas that one finds most commonly attributed to Monboddo in the eighteenth century are, first, an evolutionary conception that man is descended from the monkeys, and second, an extravagant primitivism that was supposed to out-distance even that popularly attributed to Rousseau. As a matter of fact, Monboddo himself takes the utmost pains to point out the distinctions that separate animal and man, and his final word is not primitivism but progress.

First, as to the misconception about Monboddo's views on the descent of man. Monboddo of course gives plenty

[16] *Ibid.*, pp. 217-21.
[17] *Ibid.*, p. 222.
[18] *Pursuits of Literature*, London, 1797, Pt. IV, p. 36 note.

of occasion for this misconception by his enthusiasm for the orang-outang, the *Man of the Woods,* a creature whom he finds to be gentle and affectionate, social by disposition, endowed with a capacity for ' intellect and science'; and to have a sense of justice and honour, of the decent and becoming in behavior.[19] In fact in the orang-outang, Monboddo finds the last existing specimen of the true primitive man.[20] One can get some idea of the liveliness of the controversy over the question of the humanness of the orang-outang by glancing over the authorities whom Monboddo cites in his attempt to prove that the orang-outang is to be classified as a man—Buffon, Tyron, Gassendi, de la Brosse, and many others less well known.[21] One meets incidental references to the controversy again and again in popular literature. It is characteristic of Monboddo that he should have taken the more spectacular view.

I will only add further, upon the subject of the Oran Outan, that if an Animal, who walks upright,—is of the human form, both outside and inside,—uses a weapon for defence and attack,— associates with his kind,—makes huts to defend himself from the weather, better, I believe, than those of the New Hollanders,—is tame and gentle,—and, instead of killing men and women, as he could easily do, takes them prisoners, and makes servants of them;—who has what, I think, essential to the human kind, a sense of honour;—who, when he is brought into the company of civilized men, behaves with dignity and composure, altogether unlike a monkey . . . ;—who has so much of the docility of a man, that he learns, not only to do the common offices of a menial servant, . . . but also to play upon the flute . . . ;— and, lastly, if joined to all these qualities, he has the organs of

[19] *Antient Metaphysics,* Edinburgh, 1774-99, IV, 27, 55.
[20] *Of the Origin and Progress of Language,* Edinburgh, 1773-92, Pt. I, bk. ii, ch. 4, 5.
[21] *Origin and Progress of Language,* I, 270 ff.

pronunciation, and, consequently, the capacity of speech, though not the actual use of it;—If, I say, such an Animal is not a Man, I should desire to know in what the essence of a man consists, and what it is that distinguishes a Natural Man from the Man of Art? [22]

But to Monboddo classifying the orang-outang as a man does not presuppose evolution of man from the lower animals. In the first place, the orang-outang is the only one of the simian tribe that Monboddo admits into the *genus homo*. The monkey and ape, ' with or without a tail,' the baboon, however they may resemble the orang-outang in shape of body, do not measure up to Monboddo's high standard of benevolence and gentlemanliness, and so are excluded on the basis of that internal principle.[23] In the second place, Monboddo is too devoted to design and final causation, and to the doctrine of the chain of being, to drop into an evolutionary way of thinking. He deplores the fact that many people ' believe Man to be no more than a better sort of Brute, and that the difference is only in degree, not in kind.' [24] When he outlines the ' progress of *Being*' by which ' Nature ascends from unorganized Body, to Body best of all organized,' that is, from plant to animal and then to intellectual being,[25] he is not thinking of progression in a temporal sense but in the sense of formal gradation. One of the distinctions, he tells us, between man and the rest of nature is that man progresses but nature does not. For ' *nature* is permanent and unchangeable, like its *author*: And, accordingly, the wild animals, who are undoubtedly in a state of nature, still preserve the same oeconomy and manner of life with no

---

[22] *Antient Metaphysics,* III, 41-42.
[23] *Origin and Progress of Language,* I, 311.
[24] *Antient Metaphysics,* II, 64.
[25] *Ibid.,* p. 65. See also I, 100.

variation, except such as change of circumstances may make absolutely necessary for the preservation of the individual or the species; and the variation goes no farther than that necessity requires.' [26] Man alone progresses and that progress is of human institution, not nature. Monboddo is, on the whole, too good an Aristotelian to adopt an evolutionary point of view. As in Aristotle's mind, so in Monboddo's, the doctrine of design and that of immutable species are linked together. Everything on this earth, he observes, ' is perfectly well fitted to answer the purpose, for which by nature, it is intended.' [27] This fitness of the original creation is particularly evident in animals where everything is nicely adjusted not only for the preservation of the individual but of the species: ' Thus it appears, that in every species of animals there is a system, not only of the individual but of the kind, by which the animals of that species are more or less connected together; and the end proposed by that system is the preservation both of the individual and the kind.' [28] These specific Aristotelian premises of fixed species and design, which Monboddo shows no dispostion to relinquish even in his latest writing, make it difficult to assign to him any thing more than a theory of anthropological evolution. Biological evolutionism would of course involve mutation of species.[29]

Turning now to the other popular misconception, that of Monboddo's primitivism, we note that again Monboddo gives some foundation for that misconception. The very

[26] *Origin and Progress of Language,* I, 367, 1774 edition.

[27] *Antient Metaphysics,* VI, 112.

[28] *Ibid.,* p. 113.

[29] Professor A. O. Lovejoy has, however, recently pointed out several early passages which tend to show that Monboddo at least wavered on this issue, and at times implied an acceptance of biological evolutionism. (Monboddo and Rousseau,' *Mod. Phil.,* XXX (1933), 281 ff.)

terms of his description of the orang-outang would seem
to presuppose a primitivistic point of view. And indeed
the assumption that underlies the *Antient Metaphysics,*
that everything in nature is perfect as it issues from the
hands of the creator, is one that is familiarly associated
with primitivism. Monboddo does in fact draw the usual
inferences. His reasoning is as follows: ' Now, I lay it
down as a principle, that God is wise and good, and consequently that he has allotted to every animal an economy
and manner of life best suited to his nature, and which
will preserve him longer in health and strength than any
other manner of life. That this is the case of other animals has never, I believe, been disputed. Now, we cannot
suppose that man is an exception from this general law
of nature; And that he has invented another manner of
life for himself, better than that which God has allotted
him . . . is, I think, impious to maintain.' [30] The result
of living in the unnatural state of civil society with arts of
human contrivance is inevitable degeneration, he thinks,
leading in the end to actual extinction of the species. ' As
civil society . . . grows older, vices and diseases, the
natural consequence, as I have shown, of that society, increases; so that the progeny grows worse, and likewise is
not so abundant. . . . But I have said enough already
. . . upon the bad effects of civil society both upon the
health and morals of men, enough, I think, to prove it to
be impossible, by the nature of things, that man can sub-
sist long in that state: For vices and diseases, going on
from generation to generation, and always increasing,
must at last consume the species.' [31] Conversely man nearest the state of nature is the best fitted for healthful and
peaceful life on this earth. Primitive man ' has pleasures

---

[30] *Antient Metaphysics,* V, 235.   [31] *Ibid.,* pp. 248-49.

of the Mind, as I have elsewhere observed, as well as of the Body; nor is he afflicted with any pain of Mind worth mentioning. He, therefore, enjoys a tranquillity and composure of Mind, which is very rarely to be found in the civilized Man, whose Mind is disordered by various passions unknown to the mere animal, and who is often at variance with himself, being distracted and torn to pieces by different passions, each contending for mastery, which never happens to the animal in the natural state, who is perfectly one animal, without discord or division.' [32] Not only is primitive man attuned to a tranquil life; he has a strength of mind—for all his intellectual deficiencies— that enables him to act and suffer: ' Savages . . . are very much superior to us in natural strength and firmness of Mind. They are also superior to us in natural sagacity. . . . ' [33]

If Monboddo had written no more than this we should have classified him with the primitivists without scruple and used him as one of our prime examples. And he might have written no more than this if he had lived in the first half of the century; but we must remember that he was writing in the last quarter of the century when ideas of an opposite nature were current. The doctrine of biological evolution he resisted in spite of his affection for the orang-outang, but the idea of progress proved too alluring to be denied, and in truth it accorded too well with the facts he had collected to illustrate the history of man. [34] Indeed, if the orang-outang exemplifies the primitive state of man, a theory of progress was unavoidable, since Monboddo regards that as an ' abject and brutish condition.' A very large share of *Antient Metaphysics* is devoted to tracing the progress of the individual intellect

[32] *Ibid.*, III, 201-2.   [33] *Ibid.*, p. 218.   [34] *Ibid.*, p. 2.

from potentiality to actuality and the similar progress in the species.

But how reconcile the idea of progress with the theory of progressive degeneration? Monboddo's solution is even more ingenious than that of Kames. Man does indeed degenerate under the unnatural régime of civilization, Monboddo tells us, but that degeneration of the physical body and the animal mind is a sacrifice to the intellectual principle which can only progress as the body which impedes it dwindles and vanishes. In the end the body will disappear altogether and man will become pure mind. At the same time there will be a great convulsion of the earth, and a new heaven and a new earth will be created to house the new order of men who are 'more righteous and pious than the former, and who are therefore called Saints.'[35] This convulsion, which will happen in 'not many generations' will be an effect of the Divine Mercy because 'such a slow and lingering death, as that of a species dying out, must be accompanied with much pain and misery.'[36] By this simultaneous degeneration of the body and development to perfection of the mind are primitivism and the idea of progress made compatible.

Such is Monboddo's theory in its most logical form. Needless to say he involves himself in many contradictions in the development of it. In the first place he had said, it will be remembered, that man involved himself in misery in the civil state because he departed from the natural state which God had originally arranged for him. With his departure from that state, it would be impious to suppose, Monboddo had said, that man could be anything but miserable. Yet when he comes to speak of the progress of man, he says that that progress is an 'essential

[35] *Ibid.*, V, 238-39.   [36] *Ibid.*

part of his nature.' [37] In other words, God is put in the position of so fitting man for a natural state that inevitable retribution will come upon him if he departs from it and then making it *necessary to his nature* that he depart form it!

In the second place Monboddo's theory would logically demand that if the body is really at war with the mind and an impediment to its advance,[38] the dwindling of the body as it becomes subservient to the mind should be accompanied by a corresponding elevation and ennobling of the mind. That is indeed Monboddo's hypothesis, but alas, when he comes to expatiate on it, he lets eighteenth-century anti-luxury propaganda creep in almost unconsciously to denounce the ' vices ' as well as the ' diseases ' of civilization, and before he realizes it, he has involved the mind in as much degeneration as the body. In addition to what Monboddo has to say on this point in *Antient Metaphysics*, he left at his death an eighty page manuscript entitled *The Degeneracy of Men in a State of Society,* evidently a prospectus of a larger work on this subject.[39] Noting the phrase ' so disordered likewise in Mind,' which I have italicized in the following quotation, one sees a specimen of the contradiction: '. . . it is impious, in my opinion, to maintain, that a creature, so weak of body, so diseased, and so short lived, *so disordered likewise in Mind,* notwithstanding all our boasted improvements in Arts and Sciences, in short, an Animal so miserable as by far the greater part of Men in the civilized nations of Europe are, should have come, in that state, directly and immediately out of the hands of a Creator infinitely good as well as

[37] *Ibid.*, III, 269. Cf. IV, 32-33.
[38] *Ibid.*, III, 172-3.
[39] William Knight, *Lord Monboddo and Some of His Contemporaries,* London, 1900, pp. 276-77.

wise . . . ; whereas my philosophy is, that Man, as he came out of the hands of his Creator, was the most perfect of all the animals here on earth, and consequently the happiest, as happy as the mere Animal could be: But he was destined for a higher sphere and greater happiness. For this purpose, it was necessary that his nobler or intellectual part should be separated from his animal, with which, in this state of our nature, it is loaded and encumbered. . . . The Dissolution goes on quicker, or slower, from the moment the intellectual part begins to exert itself; for then it begins to prey upon the animal part in several ways, but chiefly by the invention of those arts which, I have shown, are so destructive to the Body.' [40]

Finally Monboddo is involved in a third contradiction when he is moved to defend the civil state. The civil state, he had told us, is contrary to what God had ordained and therefore necessarily evil in its effects. But in pursuance of his hypothesis he now says that ' if properly conducted ' it produces the greatest happiness that man enjoys in this life *and is to enjoy in the next*! Moreover it is only in that state that man is capable of religion and of forming any idea of God himself.[41] A strange God who so arranged things that man would necessarily be involved in vice and misery if he departed from his original state and yet made it impossible for him to know anything about his Creator unless he did! And all this intellectual manoeuvering to reconcile the two antagonistic ideas of primitivism and progress!

It is interesting to note that Monboddo's theory of simultaneous degeneration and progress was given much more plausible form by Hugh Murray, a prolific writer on geographical subjects and editor of travel material. His best

---

[40] *Antient Metaphysics*, III, 103.   [41] *Ibid.*, V, 88.

known achievement is his monumental *Encyclopaedia of Geography, a Description of the Earth, Physical, Statistical, Civil, and Political* (1834), which he wrote in conjunction with Sir W. Hooker, Professor W. Wallace, and W. W. Swainston. It is Murray's theory that the very tendencies that ultimately make for progress cause at first corruption and deterioration. We cannot overlook the fact, he says in his *Enquiries Historical and Moral Respecting the Character of Nations and the Progress of Society* (1808), that ' as nations advance in wealth and prosperity, their morals are corrupted instead of being improved.' [42] Nations far from the influences of civilization have ' a certain rude simplicity and native innocence, which, when contrasted with the numerous vices and disorders that spring up in a more advanced stage, merit a decided preference.' [43] These nations, on the other hand, as they advance in numbers and wealth are commonly found to become more dissolute and immoral. But in the course of time ' From amid this chaos, order begins to arise; a gradual refinement takes place; arts, sciences, and philosophy, rear their head; which, though in their imperfect and *crescent* state, they may tend rather to increase the disorder, yet, when improved and perfected, seem destined to raise the human race to a condition much superior to that crude simplicity from which they had emerged. This improvement springs up, as it were, in the bosom of the preceding corruption, and, for a long time, co-exists along with it. At first almost insensible, it prevails more and more, till there seems reason to hope, that it may at last attain a very considerable ascendancy.' [44] He formulates as the principles that first corrupt and then improve society, (1) numbers collected in one place; (2) ' free

[42] Edinburgh, 1808, p. 18.   [43] *Ibid.*   [44] *Ibid.*, pp. 19-20.

communication between different societies and different members of the same society'; (3) wealth; (4) great public events.[45] He finds that the principle of corruption proceeds much more rapidly than that of improvement and is only kept from choking 'the tender plants of improvement' by the necessity of labor and coercion.[46] Knowledge he finds to be the great instrument for the improvement of mankind.[47]

III

I shall close this discussion of the various kinds of compromises that were made in order to retain both primitivism and progress by an analysis of the work of a man who, in his own time, was almost as widely known, at least by reputation, as either Kames or Monboddo, but who now, as DeQuincey predicted when he wrote some memoirs of him, is almost forgotten. I refer to John Stewart, or 'Walking Stewart,' as he was universally called; and well did he deserve the title: across India and Persia, from Paris to Constantinople, from New York to Canada, he walked. Wishing on one occasion to consult Dugald Stewart about a philosophical question, he walked from London to Edinburgh as casually as any one else might have walked to the British Museum.[48] 'A terrestrial globe,' remarks DeQuincey, 'representing the infinite wanderings of Mr. Stewart, would have seemed belted and zoned in all latitudes, like a Ptolemaic globe of the heavens, with cycles and epicycles, approaching, crossing, traversing, coinciding, receding.'[49] In London his

---

[45] *Ibid.*, pp. 21-51.
[46] *Ibid.*, pp. 64 ff.
[47] *Ibid.*, pp. 108 ff.
[48] John Taylor, *Records of My Life*, London, 1832, p. 294.
[49] 'Walking Stewart,' *Collected Writings*, ed. David Masson, Edinburgh, 1890, III, 94.

ubiquity was no less famous than his habit of sitting con-templatively on Westminster Bridge or ' in trance-like meditation amongst the cows ' in St. James's Park.[50] The writer of his obituary notice in the *London Magazine* re-marks, ' Where really was he? You saw him on West-minster Bridge, acting his own monument; you went into the Park,—he was there, fixed as the gentleman at Charing Cross; you met him, however, at Charing Cross, creeping on like the hour-hand upon a dial, getting rid of his rounds and his time at once! Indeed, his ubiquity seemed enormous,—and yet not so enormous as his sitting habits. He was a profound sitter.' [51]

Friend of DeQuincey, John Taylor, Thomas Taylor the Platonist, Robert Owen, Thomas Rickman, admired by Wordsworth for his eloquence and many of his opinions,[52] he was regarded as a great, if eccentric and somewhat in-effectual genius, ' a sublime visionary,' as DeQuincey has called him. The public at large, judging him by his spec-tacular clothes, his eccentric behavior, his enormous self-esteem (he got his friends to promise to bury copies of his books in different parts of the earth so that when the world was spiritually ready for them they would still be in existence), his pompous and cloudy rhetoric, thought him half mad. ' But he was no madman,' declares De-Quincey, ' or, if he was, then I say that it is so far desir-able to be a madman.' [53] ' His mind was a mirror of the sentient universe—the whole mighty vision that had fleeted before his eyes in this world: the armies of Hyder Ali and his son Tippoo, with oriental and barbaric Pag-eantry; the civic grandeur of England; the great deserts

[50] DeQuincey, *op. cit.,* p. 108.
[51] Quoted by the editor, in DeQuincey, *op. cit.,* III, 119-20.
[52] *Ibid.,* pp. 96, 106, 107, 109.
[53] *Ibid.,* p. 103.

of Asia and America; the vast capitals of Europe; London, with its eternal agitations, the ceaseless ebb and flow of its "mighty heart"; Paris, shaken by the fierce torments of revolutionary convulsions; the silence of Lapland; and the solitary forests of Canada; with the swarming life of the torrid zone; together with innumerable recollections of individual joy and sorrow that he had participated by sympathy:—lay like a map beneath him, as if eternally co-present to his view.' [54] If anyone ever had a right to theorize about man, either primitive or civilized, Walking Stewart most certainly had.

Stewart was true to one tendency of his times in making materialistic mechanism the foundation of his system. He presupposes a duality of matter and power, modifying a famous line from Pope to read, 'a stupendous whole, whose body matter is, and power the soul.' [55] Man has no need to call on any being outside of himself, for the human mind, like every other phenomenon in nature, has power placed within:

> Rise then exalted man, thy station fill,
> Reason adore, and know thyself the God.

These lines are found in Stewart's *Revelation of Nature with the Prophecy of Reason* (1795), which is dated, like all of his books, from the year of publication of his first book, *The Apocalypse of Nature wherein the Source of Moral Motion Is Discovered* (1790), for he considered that the 'aera of intellectual existence' had started with that publication.[56] In *The Revelation of Nature* Stewart gives the first full exposition of the central idea which

[54] *Ibid.,* pp. 115-16.
[55] *Tocsin of Social Life,* London, 1803, p. 7.
[56] The British Museum misdates *The Revelation of Nature* 1813, mistaking *The Apocalypse of Perfectuability,* 1808, for *Apocalypse of Nature,* 1790.

runs through all his works, the essential homogeneity and unity of all nature. Characteristically he coins a new word to express his idea, ' homo-ousia,' which he takes to signify ' the conjunction or unity of all beings.' He proposes a homo-ousic society to which an individual may be admitted who has reached a comprehension that he is ' a constituent, co-equal, and co-eternal, part of the whole existence, or nature.' [57] By the time of the publication of *The Tocsin of Social Life, Addressed to All the Nations of the Civilized World; in a Discovery of the Laws of Nature Relative to Human Existence* (1803), he achieves a much clearer explanation of his theory: ' The important discovery which is to establish my high claim to universal attention, is simply this:—That all bodies are in a perpetual state of transmutation, in composition or decomposition, that is, life and death; that nothing can be created, and nothing annihilated; that what is called identity, or individuality of mode, is nothing but a succession of matter and its powers; and that when the clue of that succession breaks, identity ceases, while its substance, or essential matter that formed it, revolves in dispersed particles or atoms into states of new successions of matter and its powers, or identities, in an endless course of transmutations, or circulations throughout the universe.' [58]

What are the inferences which Stewart draws from this theory which, except for its materialism, is essentially that of Wordsworth? The inferences are very much the same as Wordsworth's. The reason for man's present misery is that he has lost the perception of the essential unity of all nature. If there are two things of which Walking Stewart is absolutely certain, they are, first, the fact that man has degenerated, and second, that he is inherently

---

[57] *Revelation of Nature,* p. 81.   [58] *Tocsin,* pp. 3-4.

perfectuable.' 'It is impossible to doubt a moment,' he writes in *The Scripture of Reason and Nature*, 'that human misery has increased in a parallel ratio with human refinement and civilization. I have travelled among the hordes of Turcomans, who are the modern Scythians, differing but little from their ancestors, and I have lived with savages, who differ but little from our native Britts and Picts; and I declare, in the sacred name of that nature I worship, . . . that these Scythians and savages apply the weak powers of their understanding better than civilized man to the purpose of human happiness.' [59] That man is capable of 'perfectuability' in spite of his degenerate condition, Stewart never doubts. But man has gone the wrong way about his improvements. It is at this point that Stewart's reasoning, for all the obscure phraseology in which it is couched, takes on a distinctly modern tone. His analysis of the reason why the enormous development of science has not induced more real human progress one meets often in social criticism at the present time: namely, that the advance of science, or to use Walking Stewart's more picturesque language, 'the morbid and rickety growth of science,' [60] has outstripped the growth of the wisdom of man. Man finds himself supplied with a stupendous new equipment of scientific facts and appliances with no correspondingly increased power of mind for the handling of it. 'In the civilized world,' he writes in *The Apocalypse of Human Perfectuability*, 'the progress of arts and sciences seems rather to have enveloped or contracted, than developed the capacities of human nature into their energies. The understanding has been cultivated into a sack of knowledge, not as an instrument of thought and sense, and has given to the will a restless fever of luxurious

[59] London, 1813, p. 184. [60] *Scripture of Reason*, p. xxvi.

wants, passions, and affections, that has generated a
selfishness far below that of savage life or even brute
instinct; for the savage loves his tribe, and the brute its
offspring; while the civilized man betrays his country for
sordid lucre, and tears his offspring from the mother's
breast, to be suckled for money by a sordid stranger.' [61]
Man has ' lost the rule of instinct ' and acquired in its
place only the ' technical power of the mind ' generated
by science instead of wisdom (Stewart's word for it is
' sense ') which can only be generated by ' the intense
exercise of the thoughts and faculties in reflection.' [62]

Parallel to the modern contraction of the intellectual
powers is the contraction of the moral nature of man—
and here again Stewart strikes a contemporary note—by
the transformation of morality into a system of puritani-
cal inhibitions. Instead of conceiving virtue as distinguished by thoughtfulness, sympathy, sincerity, fortitude,
and wisdom, the modern world has made morality a
' practical modification of truth ' by which it has enveloped
and contracted human nature.[63]

Stewart's solution is the development of wisdom or
sense through the education of the people in the doctrine
of the unity of self and nature. While we may not share
Stewart's enthusiastic conviction that ' This vast and important sentiment of the immortal connection of self and
Nature, regenerates the being in the instant of conception,
and effects what the ethics and example of ages could
never procure,' [64] yet one is forced to admit that Stewart
has shown considerable sagacity and has again antici-

[61] London, 1808, p. 14.
[62] *Scripture of Reason*, pp. 186, 147.
[63] *Apocalypse of Human Perfectuability*, pp. 5-6.
[64] *Travels over the Most Interesting Parts of the Globe to Discover the Source of Moral Motion*, 1790, II, 72-73.

pated a modern conception in the inferences which he draws from his doctrine. He feels that a sense of the unity of all life might have a greater humanizing effect than the system of negative morality in force. The result would be the building up of a social organization founded on the principle of ' co-operation in humanization ' rather than on the principle of ' competition ' based on the selfish interests of our present capitalistic civilization.[65] Not only might society thus acquire a corporate rather than a competitive character, but nations might be led to confederate.[66] All this has a familiar sound to our ears today, but in Stewart's time it was scarcely even understood. Perhaps it was in the bitterness of the conviction that he was not even taken seriously in his own time that he wrote these lines:

> Who dares to think, would rack the mind with pain,
> Who thinks aloud would torture all his kind.

---

[65] *Apocalypse of Human Perfectuability*, p. 11.
[66] *Ibid.*, p. 12.

CHAPTER X

FICTIONAL SATIRES ON THE IDEA OF PROGRESS

I

The Peers of Hell assembled;—by their Arch leader summoned.
Up Satan rose, Harrowed with doubt and soul-corroding
thought—the Pandaemonium attentive heard him speak.—
 ' My wiles and labours, restless subtilties, and never-ceasing
pains, in aid of our united cause 'gainst Heaven and Earth,
well do you know, ye Chiefs.
 ' Success—so long wavering—smiles on our efforts. The reign
of Antichrist is begun.—Thanks to the daring, restless sons of
France, inspired by me and mine!'¹

These are the words with which Charles Lucas introduces his Infernal Quixote, and the words are indicative
of the degree of concern that the ' New Philosophy' was
arousing among certain writers in England. The new doctrine received, of course, some opposition from the beginning, but the deposition of the French king and the
September massacres caused a vast multiplication of the
reactionary literature. In the words of Belsham, a contemporary historian, ' The nation was on a sudden struck
with terror at the idea of any political innovation of any
kind; and the very name of REFORM became the subject
of violent and indiscriminate reprobation. Under the impression of this prevailing prepossession, . . . an innumerable multitude of pamphlets, in the popular form of
letters, dialogues and narratives, were circulated by this
means throughout the kingdom, inculcating an unreserved
submission to Government, on the old exploded princi-

¹ Charles Lucas, *The Infernal Quixote: A Tale of the Day*, London,
1801, pp. iii-iv.

ples of Toryism and High Churchism.' [2] As Isaac D'Israeli
explains in the preface to his satirical novel, *Vaurien,* no
one could feel much concern as long as the metaphysi-
cians had confined themselves to the field ot nature, but
when they made man the object of their speculation, and
'in the temerity of their ignorance' pretended to have
found in him an infinite perfectibility; when they incorporated, moreover, the fruits of their labors into political
systems which they urged for immediate adoption, then it
was time for lovers of the commonwealth to bestir themselves.[3] 'This philosophy is imagined to have derived its
origin from the labours of Voltaire,' writes D'Israeli. 'It
is a calumny on that powerful genius. . . . Helvetius, Con-
dorcet, and Mirabeau are among those who have sought
celebrity by novel extravagancies. It is these men, who
have temerariously talked of *calculating events* which so
often depend on accident; have loudly triumphed in *first
principles,* ever concealed mysteriously from us; and of
the *infinite perfectibility* of our mind and organs, which,
scarcely arrived at their existence, perish before the eyes
of those who declaim on their eternity. . . . This doctrine
has been servilely followed by some living writers in this
country.' [4]

As the doctrines of the New Philosophy had been
spread through the medium of novels, they were also
opposed by the same means. As George Walker said of
his novel, *The Vagabond,* 'It is . . . an attempt to parry
the Enemy with their own weapons; for no channel is
deemed improper by them, which can introduce their

[2] W. Belsham, *Memoirs of the Reign of George III to the Session of
Parliament Ending A. D. 1793,* second ed., London, 1795, IV, 404.
    [3] *Vaurien: or, Sketches of the Times Exhibiting Views of the Phi-
losophies, Religions, Politics, Literature, and Manners of the Age,* London,
1797, I, vi-vii.   [4] *Ibid.,* pp. ix-xi.

sentiments.'[5] He feels that 'perhaps a *Novel* may gain attention, when arguments of the soundest sense and most perfect eloquence shall fail to arrest the feet of the *Trifler* from the specious paths of the new Philosophy.'[6] Mrs. Jane West, again, complains in the preface to *The Infidel Father* that 'The rage for novels does not decrease.' Though she does not feel that they are the best means for propagating the words of sound doctrine, yet 'while the enemies of our church and state continue to pour their poison into unwary ears through this channel, it behoves the friends of our establishments to convey an antidote by the same course; especially as those who are most likely to be infected by false principles, will not search for a refutation of them in profound and scientific compositions.'[7]

Few of the novels of attack on radicalism leave us in any doubt as to the authors they are satirizing, many of them being as liberally supplied with footnotes as this book. The writers most frequently named are Godwin, Helvétius, Rousseau, Hume, Paine, Holcroft, and Mary Hays, with Godwin well in the lead.

Many of these novels fall outside of this study because, while they dwell vaguely on political systems and progress, they are chiefly concerned with defending from the attacks of Godwin and his followers the principles of religious piety and domestic morality—the integrity of the family, the duty of submission of the daughter to her father and the wife to her husband, and the sacredness of the marriage vows. Such is the case, for instance, with Sophia King's *Waldorf, or the Dangers of Philosophy, A Philosophical Tale* (London, 1798) in which the hero is

[5] London, 1800, p. iii. First edition published in 1799.
[6] *Ibid.*
[7] London, 1802, I, ii.

so successfully converted to the new doctrines by the philosopher, Lok, that he seduces a succession of girls and is responsible for the death of two brothers who attempt to revenge their sister. Mrs. Jane West, again, in *A Tale of the Times,* tells the story of the undermining of the virtue of Lady Monteith and the ruining of her husband by Edward Fitzosborne, a brilliant young man who had picked up a set of wrong ideas of morality and politics in France during the revolution. The emphasis is on the domestic tragedy rather than on political theory, and the cause of the tragedy is traced to the materialistic utilitarianism of the ' enlightened,' a doctrine which deifies nature and its vicegerent, interest, and promulgates the ' monstrous doctrines, that " whatever is profitable is right," that " the end sanctifies the means," and that " human actions ought to be free." ' [8] ' Should it therefore be told to future ages, that the capricious dissolubility (if not the absolute nullity) of the nuptial tie and the annihilation of parental authority are among the blasphemies uttered by the *moral* instructors of these times: should they hear, that law was branded as a vain and even unjust attempt to bring individual actions under the restrictions of general rule; that chastity was defined to mean only individuality of affection; that religion was degraded into a sentimental effusion; and that these doctrines do not proceed from the pen of *avowed* profligates, but from persons *apparently* actuated by the desire of improving the happiness of the world: should, I say, generations yet unborn hear this, they will not ascribe the annihilation of thrones and altars to the successful arms of France, but to those principles which, by dissolving domestic confidence and undermining private worth, paved the way for universal confusion.' [9]

[8] London, 1799, II, 273.　　　　　[9] *Ibid.,* pp. 274-75.

The attack on Godwinian ideas in Amelia Opie's *Adeline Mowbray, or the Mother and Daughter* (1804), is a curious one; for Amelia Alderson, before her marriage to the painter, Opie, was brought up in all the enthusiasm of radical reform by her father, who retained his allegiance to French principles even during the dark days of the Reign of Terror. Amelia so far shared her father's enthusiasm for revolutionary political theory that she attended the trials of Hardy, Horne Tooke, and Holcroft in London, expressing her enthusiasm for the acquittal of Horne Tooke by walking across the table and kissing him![10] The following extract from one of her letters of this period testifies to the degree of her intimacy with the radical group in London. 'Godwin drank tea and supt here last night; a leave-taking visit, as he goes to-morrow to spend a fortnight at Dr. Parr's. It would have entertained you highly to have seen him bid me farewell. He wished to salute me, but his courage failed him. . . . You have no idea how gallant he is become; but indeed he is much more amiable than ever he was. Mrs. Inchbald says, the report of the world is, that Mr. Holcroft is in love with her, *she* with Mr. Godwin, Mr. Godwin with *me,* and I am in love with Mr. Holcroft! A pretty story indeed! This report Godwin brings to me, and he says Mrs. I. always tells him that when she praises *him,* I praise Holcroft. This is not fair in Mrs. I. She appears to me jealous of G.'s attention to me, so she makes him believe I prefer H. to him. She often says to me, " Now you are come, Mr. Godwin does not come near me." Is not this very womanish?'[11] It was very shortly after the writing of this letter that Godwin cleared up Mrs. I.'s doubts as to

[10] Cecilia Lucy Brightwell, *Memorials of the Life of Amelia Opie,* second ed., Norwich, 1854, pp. 40-41. and DNB.

[11] Brightwell, *op. cit.,* pp. 56-57.

the object of his affections by marrying Mary Wollstone-craft. With all this liberal political background, how-ever, *Adeline Mowbray* tells the tragic story of a girl who attempts to put into practice the Godwinian ideas about marriage. The story is suggested by the experiences of Mary Wollstonecraft, whom Amelia Opie very greatly admired,[12] and Godwin, as Glenmurray, figures as the philosophical villain of the piece. Now it is quite prob-able that if Amelia Alderson had become Mrs. Godwin or the second Mrs. Holcroft, instead of Mrs. Opie, *Adeline Mowbray* would not have been written; but I cannot think, from the tone of the letters of the period of her inti-macy with Godwin, that the novel, written ten years later after a happy marriage to a successful painter, was dictated by disappointed love. It seems on the other hand a testi-mony to the extent of concern even among the politically liberal over the moral implications of the philosophy of *Political Justice.*

Hannah More in ' The History of Mr. Fantom, the New Fashioned Philosopher, and His Man William,' [13] and the anonymous author of *The History of Sir George Warring-ton; or the Political Quixote* (London, 1797) both dwell on the professions of universal benevolence of philoso-phers who are unwilling to aid a friend in distress or feed a starving beggar. ' It is provinces, empires, continents,' cries Mr. Fantom, ' that the benevolence of the philoso-pher embraces; every one can do a little paltry good to his neighbor.' [14] And the professions of Mr. Goldney in *The Political Quixote* are equally expansive and equally meaningless as far as deeds are concerned: ' I own I am

[12] Paul, *op. cit.,* I, 158-59. She wrote to Mary Wollstonecraft that every thing that she had ever seen for the first time had disappointed her ' except Mrs. Imlay and the Cumberland Lakes.' *Ibid.,* p. 158.
[13] In *Stories for the Middle Ranks of Society, Works,* 1830, III, 1 ff.
[14] ' The History of Mr. Fantom,' *loc. cit.,* p. 13.

a republican, and glory in the title. I have a Roman spirit; and the character of Brutus is my delight and my example. I would sacrifice, like him, my best friend to preserve my country; and my own life and fortune are as mere nothings in the scale; universal benevolence is my religion, and universal philanthropy my practice.' [15]

Hannah More is one of the few popular writers known to us who put out her anti-revolutionary stories, such as 'Village Politics' and 'The History of Mr. Fantom,' in as cheap a form as possible at a tremendous financial loss to herself, solely for the good of the conservative cause.[16] 'Village Politics' was her first venture in the field of propaganda for the 'vulgar class of people'; she undertook the experiment, at the instigation of the Bishop of London, with a good deal of reluctance. Her own description of the writing of it is an amusing testimony to the negative impression that the current doctrines of social equality were making on the English people. 'As soon as I came to Bath,' writes Hannah, 'our dear Bishop of London came to me with a dismal countenance, and told me that I should repent it on my death-bed, if I, who knew so much of the habits and sentiments of the lower order of people, did not write some little thing tending to open their eyes under their present wild impression of liberty and equality. It must be something level to their apprehensions, or it would be of no use. In an evil hour, against my will and my judgment, on one sick day, I scribbled a little pamphlet, called *Village Politics, by Will Chip*; and the very next morning after I had conceived the idea, I sent it off to Rivington, changing my bookseller, in order the more surely to escape detection. It is as vulgar as heart can wish; but it is only designed for the most vulgar

---

[15] *Op. cit.*, I, 200-1.
[16] Charlotte M. Yonge, *Hannah More,* Boston, 1888, p. 132.

class of readers.'[17] We are told that 'hundreds of thousands of copies' went into circulation, and that the author was encouraged to follow up her success with the *Cheap Repository Tracts,* addressed to the same audience.[18] The following sample dialogue from 'Village Politics' will satisfy the reader's curiosity as to what constitutes writing 'as vulgar as heart can wish.'

Jack. What book art reading? Why dost look so like a hang-dog?

Tom (looking on his book). Cause enough. Why, I find here that I am very unhappy, and very miserable; which I should never have known, if I had not had the good luck to meet this book. Oh! 'tis a precious book!

Jack. A good sign, tho'—that you can't find out your're unhappy, without looking into a book for it! What is the matter?

Tom. Matter? Why, I want liberty.

Jack. Liberty! That's bad indeed! What! has any one fetched a warrant for thee? Come, man, cheer up, I'll be bound for thee. Thou art an honest fellow in the main, tho' thou dost tipple and prate a little too much at the Rose and Crown.

Tom. No, no, I want a new constitution.

Jack. Indeed! Why, I thought thou hadst been a desperate healthy fellow. Send for the doctor directly.

Tom. I'm not sick; I want liberty and equality, and the rights of man.

Jack. Oh, now I understand thee. What! thou art a leveller and a republican, I warrant?

Tom. I am a friend of the people. I want a reform.

Jack. Then the shortest way is to mend thyself.

Tom. But I want a *general* reform.[19]

---

[17] William Roberts, *Memoirs of the Life of Mrs. Hannah More,* London, 1839, pp. 219-20.
[18] Yonge, *op. cit.,* pp. 127-31.
[19] *Works,* London, 1835, II, 221-22.

II

I have touched on these various satirical novels and stories to give some idea of the many angles of attack on the 'New Philosophy.' The field of radical and anti-radical fiction at the end of the eighteenth century is a large and complex one which would amply repay much fuller study than it has received. Our chief concern here is with one small strand in the intricate texture. It is the problem of what happens to the theories of progress when they are consciously handled in this controversial fiction that is now before us.

We need not be surprised to find an even greater confusion of ideas in the attacks on progress than in the books supporting it, for the popular attacks are written by the ultra-conservatives for whom in general there are just two classes of ideas: the familiar, tested, safe ideas that they have inherited from past generations,—and all other ideas. It goes without saying that the second class is an ill-assorted lot, and there are few attempts at anything like philosophical distinctions. Charles Lucas, it is true, in *The Infernal Quixote,* attempts a classification:

As in my humble opinion this New Philosophy has never been clearly explained, or systematically defined. I shall, *first,* distinguish it from the common Philosophy.

It may be called—"*A species of wisdom, which man discovers by the aid of his own individual powers, corporeal and mental, without owning the aid of any superior Being, directly or indirectly. . . .*"

. . . .

Secondly. To define this DIABOLISM systematically, it may be divided into nine Sects, the number of the Muses.

They may be thus called:

Stoics, Epicureans, Peripatetics, Virtuosos,	*Of ancient race, but modernized.*
The Illuminati, The Libertinians, The Naturals, The Reasoners, The Nothingers,	*Modern.*[20]

Of the first group, the last, or Virtuosos, are the only ones of interest to us. They are apparently the primitivists lumped together with the enthusiasts for classical models in politics. ' The Virtuosos, or Lovers of Wonder,' writes Lucas, ' are certainly *no ancient Philosophers modernized,* but more properly *modern Philosophers antiquated.* These are continually telling what has been. . . . All *modern* laws and customs they abominate. Lycurgus, Solon, and Numa are their models; and if they are even inclined to believe a Deity, they are determined his name shall be Jupiter. . . . The Virtuosos hate the Government because it is a *modern* fabric; and use all their might to overturn the State, that they may revive the blessings of primeval times. All their writings in Divinity, Science, or Politics, are in praise of the Golden Age.' [21]

In the second group, the Illuminati, though not given very specific definition, would seem to be progressivists: ' These despise the knowledge of what is *past,* but are quite at home in what is *to come.* Their belief is—that all the world were fools till the present generation, and that they themselves are the wisest of this.' [22] But the Libertinians are also of the revolutionary group: ' Their

[20] *The Infernal Quixote,* II, 222-25.
[21] *Ibid.,* pp. 246-47.
[22] *Ibid.,* p. 251.

language and their conduct are in continual opposition. Their *ambitious views* they call Equality; their *love of power*—Liberty; *depopulation* is with them Civilization; and *forced subsidies* a Voluntary Loan; the *sword* and the *pistol* are Argument and Reason; and *death*— Conviction.' [23]

So far everything has been clear sailing. The confusion comes with the next groups. The Naturals are, according to Lucas, the unthinking tools of the Reasoners, persuaded by them that everything that is, is the ' genuine offspring of Nature.' [24] One gathers from a sentence in the next section that the Naturals are those who listen to the language of the heart rather than to that of the reason. Rousseau is cited as an example of a compound of the Natural and the Reasoner.[25] The Reasoners, the formers of the sect of Naturals, ' take good care not to be of it themselves.' [26] They are apparently the rationalists, and Godwin is cited as the foremost example,[27] but the Reasoners turn out in the discussion to be primitivists of the deepest dye— defenders of primitive virtue who write dialogues between the Christian and the savage to the infinite disadvantage of the Christian: ' But the *argumentum invectum* of the Reasoner I must not omit, when, at his first onset, he disarms his adversary, and then—cut and slash without mercy. Thus—The Reasoner contends that the Hottentots, or the Men in the Moon (no matter which), have the truest notions of religion. The simple Christian denies the assertion. The Reasoner begins,—declares the religion of the Men in the Moon, or the Cape—and one by one picks out the most prominent virtues of Christianity, which, with a long feather, naked feet, and plenty of Nature, becomes a very pretty picture, and assumes a most pleasing appear-

[23] *Ibid.*, p. 258.
[24] *Ibid.*, p. 263.
[25] *Ibid.*, pp. 283-84, note.
[26] *Ibid.*, p. 264.
[27] *Ibid.*, pp. 254-5.

ance. . . . But the most common method of the Reasoner is to write a dialogue upon the subject between himself and the savage. He, very kindly, for Christianity; the Savage for himself. Oh! how the Savage cuts him up!' [28] Finally, the Nothingers seem likewise to be rationalists, with Godwin among their number. They are the necessitarians who excuse all their misdeeds with the comment, ' I can't help it, and there's an end of the business.' [29]

Confused as this philosophical classification is, Lucas recognizes in his contemporaries a confusion even greater: ' some there are, whose minds, confined by no object, no principle, and no rule, expand themselves over the divisions and subdivisions of every party, and nobly grasp at once the whole.' [30]

III

I have chosen, as most fruitful for a close analysis, George Walker's *The Vagabond,* and Elizabeth Hamilton's *Memoirs of Modern Philosophers,* both highly popular in their day. Walker mentions in the preface to the fourth edition of his novel that two previous editions had sold out within six months, and that he is now urged to ' print a *cheap* edition, which might be within the purchase of *all ranks,* and tend to open the eyes of many deluded followers of the *new* philosophers.' [31] E. O. Benger, the contemporary biographer of Elizabeth Hamilton, remarks of the reception of *Memoirs of Modern Philosophers,* ' The popularity of *The Modern Philosophers* was a passport to fame and distinction; and Miss Hamilton consequently found herself admired by the celebrated and the fashionable, and the object of curiosity and interest to the public. On the plan and execution of this

[28] *Ibid.,* pp. 278-79.
[29] *Ibid.,* p. 290.
[30] *Ibid.,* pp. 218-19.
[31] *Op. cit.,* p. viii.

work it would now be superfluous to offer any remarks: its favourite phrases have acquired popular authority; the name of the heroine is proverbial.' [32]

In dealing with the satires, especially with Walker's *The Vagabond*, there is some difficulty in distinguishing between a confusion and contradiction of ideas that is an intentional ridicule of the same thing in the philosophers themselves, and an unintentional lumping of all objectionable ideas together. Certainly Walker was aware of some of the contradictions in his sources. In a foot-note, for instance, appended to a sentence from the *Social Contract*, Walker remarks, ' This inconsistent sentence makes a brilliant figure in the Social Contract. The reader is not to be surprised if he finds these great men contradict themselves in the course of the work; if they did not, they would not be modern philosophers.' [33] Yet how far Walker himself goes in misunderstanding the true nature of the theory of perfectibility which he is attacking may be seen by the following note appended to the expression of a desire for the primitive life on the part of one of his leading progressivists: ' It is the practice of the new school to exalt everything savage. An Indian is with them the most virtuous of human beings; and they make him utter sentiments he never heard, and perform actions which never were witnessed.' [34]

Perhaps the best approach to the ideas of this particular book is through the narrative.

" . . . Property! property! thou art the bean [sic] of earthly good, an ulcer in society and a cancer in the political oeconomy."

As the Doctor stamped his foot on the ground in the attitude

---

[32] *Memoirs of the Late Mrs. Elizabeth Hamilton*, London, 1818, I, 132. Cf. Elwood, *op. cit.*, p. 116.

[33] *The Vagabond*, p. 13, note.

[34] *Ibid.*, p. 177, note.

of an orator, heated with the idea of revolution and equality, a young man in a very ragged dress leaped from a thicket of hazels, and holding a pistol to the Doctor's breast, demanded his money.

. . . " This," said he, " is not right in the nature of things; force tells me that your argument is wrong: you should have first convinced me of your wants, and then my purse would have been your just property."

"All property is a monopoly," cried the young metaphysician, " and the most laconic arguments are the best: . . . unless you can prove that some other has a greater claim to your property, I must have the contents of your pocket."

" You are a philosopher," said the Doctor.

" Yes," replied the youth; " my dear Stupeo used to tell me so: but philosophy is not rewarded in the present detestable system of things; virtue is ridiculed, and vice rides in gilded coaches."

" How much do you need? " said the Doctor, in transport. " You are a pupil of the *new school*; come along with me, and you shall find me a man who will esteem you exactly according to the quantity of merit you possess; your talents ought not to be thus lost."

" Stupeo was perfectly right," said the youth, " he told me that all men are equal: I will go with you."

This opening dialogue introduces the three principal actors in the comedy, the young neophyte, Frederick Fenton, Stupeo, his tutor, and Dr. Alogos, whose name characterizes his quality. Frederick Fenton, after being well grounded at college by Stupeo in the materialistic doctrines of the new school, renounces filial obedience and all moral and religious restraints, in the confidence that ' the time will come, when knowledge is disseminated in all ranks; when the ploughman shall sit on his plough reading the Rights of Man, and all books of law and religion shall be burnt by the magistrates.' [35] ' Morality,' he

[35] *Ibid.*, p. 21.

says, ' is political justice, which prefers the good of the whole to the good of a part; suffering partial evil, that the great work of truth may go forwards, and liberty and reason be paramount over selfishness, pride, superstition, and priest craft.' [36]

He is called home by his father, where he seduces the fiancée of his best friend and then lets her and her father burn to death while he holds a ladder in the air trying to decide which one is of the most use to society. ' I was shocked,' he confesses, ' at so dreadful an accident, which would not have happened had Stupeo been there: but in this present rascally system of government and society, virtue will not always succeed; and no man can be condemned, if evil should result from a good intention.' [37] Forced to flee from the anger of his neighbors, he goes to London where he participates in a radical insurrection and the storming of Newgate. ' I ran from one ward to the next, and from cell to cell, sounding the tidings of liberty, and receiving a thousand blessings from those tongues which had too often been turned to curses and execrations. Pickpockets, cutpurses, shoplifters, and felons of every denomination, hailed the dawn of returning freedom, and sprang forward to a glorious consummation, helping us to destroy this dreadful tomb to all who despise the laws, and claim the natural privilege of dividing property.' [38]

It is after the Newgate episode that Frederick meets Dr. Alogos, in whom he recognizes a kindred soul. He tries in vain to corrupt Laura, the niece of Dr. Alogos, and convinces himself by utilitarian principles that he is justified in using force: ' It is the universal good and greatest resulting benefit we are ever to have in view. . . . Besides, am not I a philosopher? Yes: I have, and I will

[36] *Ibid.*, p. 31.   [37] *Ibid.*, p. 33.   [38] *Ibid.*, p. 63.

rise far above human nature.—Have I not seduced the mistress of my friend? Have I not been the means of a pretty girl and her father perishing in the flames? Have I not led a mob to burn down the metropolis of Great Britain? Have I not induced a wife to betray her husband, which caused his own and his children's death? Have I not lost three teeth and half my little finger in the cause of liberty? Have I not murdered my own mother? And shall the tears and lamentings of a girl prevent my marching forward in the high road of all-irradiating science and peopling the world?' [39] Laura, however, is too clever for him and he is obliged to give up the attempt.

The theft of most of the doctor's wealth by men whom he had converted to the doctrine of equal distribution of property convinces the friends that their difficulties are due to the vile government under which they live. They decide to go to America where they can live a life of primitive simplicity. Taking Laura and Susan, the maid, and Stupeo, whom they meet on the way, they emigrate to a land where they expect to sit under the date and the olive trees and talk of love. But primitive life in Kentucky where they first settle develops unexpected rigors. They find that they have to labor to eat. '" I must grant," said Frederick, that we have too much labour: this is not a state congenial to human nature—this is solitude without its concomitants, plenty, liberty, and ease. What signifies my being at liberty to wander in a forest and shoot deer, when I must till the ground or starve: this is not genuine equality, and I am determined to seek it in a savage state." ' [40] But savage life is a disappointment also. '" I begin to think," ' remarks Frederick after they have

[39] *Ibid.*, pp. 120-21.
[40] *Ibid.*, p. 178.

been robbed by the Indians, ' " the savage state of man is not conducted on philosophical principles." ' [41]

Laura is carried off by the Indians and the philosophers stop their disputations to go in pursuit. Crossing a range of mountains they come upon an ideal community in which the principles of equality and political justice are in force. The streets are empty, the houses falling to pieces, and the people almost naked. Each man in this community works half an hour a day, but as he is likely to spend all of his time deciding whether it would be more for the good of the whole to help with the harvest or drive a few nails in the new public granary, very little is accomplished. ' " I don't know how it is," ' remarks one of the citizens, ' " since we are all equal, and all labourers, and all studying the public good, our country is going rapidly to decay. An house that used to be built in three months, is not now done in as many years; and as to works of genius, it was found utterly impossible for different sets of workmen to paint a picture, write a book, or finish a device . . . it is strange how stupid the people grow since one man knows every thing. " ' [42]

' " But truth, eternal truth," cried Stupeo, " is—"

' " What we have heard an hundred times," said Frederick, " in as many different definitions; for my part, I am disgusted with every thing." ' [43]

The philosophers retrace their steps across the mountains in the further pursuit of the forgotten Laura; they are captured by the Indians and Stupeo is burned at the stake, maintaining to the end that ' the light of nature is always pure, and the actions of simple men cannot fail to be just.' [44]

It will be seen that there is almost every ingredient in

[41] *Ibid.*, p. 184.
[42] *Ibid.*, p. 190.
[43] *Ibid.*, p. 205.
[44] *Ibid.*, p. 222.

this satire. Our old friend, the light of nature,[45] and immutability [46] come in for ridicule side by side with utilitarianism and materialistic determinism.[47] The progressivists are primitivists and the primitivists are Godwinians. The blending of ideas is nowhere more compactly illustrated than in the following passage:

"You are right," returned I. "Mankind has hitherto been in a state of child hood, but the new philosophy will teach them to go without leading strings. Stupeo has demonstrated, that when men are sufficiently enlightened, their chains will drop off as by magic; every man will hail his fellow as his brother and the copper-coloured Indian will clasp in his arms the white European. Can any heart not beat with rapture at the idea? Can any mind resist the torrent of omnipotent truth?"

"Your ideas are very strange, I must confess," said he, "but they are morally impracticable. If you destroy the arts, and return to pure nature, how will you teach men the new philosophy? How will you prevent them sinking into barbarous ignorance?"

"That is not my business," said I, "it is the greatest good we are to prefer, and not to be staggered by apparent and trifling evils." [48]

'No doubt,' the author defends himself in his preface, 'those who feel them selves *sore* will endeavour to cast upon the work the charge of exaggeration; but, on this subject it is *impossible* to exaggerate; so inimical are the doctrines of Godwin, Hume, Rousseau, etc. to all civil society, that, when the reader candidly reflects, he will perceive that the inferences I have drawn from *their* texts naturally result.' [49] Considering the popular identification of Rousseau with primitivism, one cannot wonder that a satire that attempts to ridicule at one and the same time

[45] *Ibid.*, pp. 22, 206.   [48] *Ibid.*, p. 50.
[46] *Ibid.*, p. 178.   [49] *Ibid.*, p. vi.
[47] *Ibid.*, pp. 20, 140.

' Godwin, Hume, Rousseau, etc.' should depict characters with remarkably addled brains.

This identification of progressivism and primitivism is not uncommon in the satires. Mrs. West, in *A Tale of the Times,* makes her Godwinian philosopher idealize the simple life of the people who live next to nature,[50] and *The Political Quixote* likewise cherishes primitivistic illusions.[51] Walker himself seems to have been somewhat wavering in his opinion of the simple life. He ridicules the primitivists without reservation in *The Vagabond,* and in *The Travels of Sylvester Tramper,*[52] but in *Theodore Cyphon* he has several passages of glowing praise of the life of nature.[53] In *Cinthelia,* again, he describes with a great deal of sympathy a simple community of backwoodsmen; but his final conclusion seems to be that such a life is too meagre for man—that ' though civilization has *ten thousand* bitters, your state of nature has *not one* sweet.' [54]

IV

There is an even more striking identification of progressivism and primitivism in Elizabeth Hamilton's *Memoirs of Modern Philosophers.* A group of radicals in England consisting of Bridgetina Botherim, the grotesque little cross-eyed heroine who could quote whole pages from *Political Justice,* Mr. Glib, the philosophical apothecary, Myope, a former itinerant preacher, The Goddess of Reason imported from the streets of Paris, and Vallaton, ex-London-waif and hairdresser—all of them Godwinian progressivists—are aroused to enthusiasm for the Hotten-

[50] Alexandria, 1801, I, 234-35.
[51] I, 187.
[52] London, 1813, p. 147.
[53] London, 1823, II, 207 ff. First ed., 1796.
[54] London, 1797, IV, 111.

tots by reading Le Vaillant's *Travels from the Cape of Good Hope into the Interior Parts of Africa,* the English translation of which had appeared in London in 1790. Here at last they think that they have found the Age of Reason and the development of human beings to perfection realized: ' " See here, Citizen Myope, all our wishes fulfilled! All our theory realized! Here is a whole nation of philosophers, all as wise as ourselves! All on the high road to perfectibility! All enjoying the proper dignity of man! Things just as they ought! No man working for another! All alike! All equal! No laws! No government! No coercion! Every one exerting his energies as he pleases! Take a wife today: leave her again tomorrow! It is the very essence of enjoyment! "

' " Alas! " replied Mr. Myope, " I fear this desirable state of things is reserved for futurity. Ages must elapse before mankind will be sufficiently enlightened to be sensible of the great advantages of living as you describe."

' " No, no," cried Glib, " ages need not elapse. It is all known to the Hottentots. All practised by the Gonaquais hoard. Only just listen." ' [55]

It must be confessed that Le Vaillant furnished plenty of primitivistic material for our philosophers, if they were really looking for ' innocence and amiable simplicity.' ' Could I after this be deceived in this particular; ' writes Le Vaillant after a demonstration of Hottentot goodness, ' or refuse to attribute virtue to those who never heard the name, or saw the immense commentaries composed on the idea it contains? This innate sentiment in the heart of man, that neither education has enlightened nor example corrupted, was conferred on him by way of distinction, and to mark the superiority of his nature . . . I dare assert, that if there is a corner of the world where pro-

[55] *Op. cit.,* I, 320-21.

priety of conduct and manners is to be adored, one must seek its temples in the midst of desarts. The savage has received his principles neither from education or prejudice, he owes them to simple nature. . . . ' [56] ' " Favored mortals! " have I exclaimed, " long, long, may you possess your precious innocence; but live unknown! Poor savages! regret not, being born under a burning sky, on a barren soil, which scarce produces the bramble and the heath; but rather consider your situation as a signal favour of Providence, your deserts will never tempt European cupidity; unite yourselves with those happy nations, who, like you, are strangers to them; bury, and efface even the smallest traces of that yellow dust which forms itself in your rocks and mingles with your streams, should it be discovered you are lost; know it is the scourge of the earth, the source of crimes, and dread above all things, the approach of an Almagro, a Pizarro, or a Fernando Cortez." ' [57] There is nothing in this, it will be observed, but straight primitivism; the association with the idea of progress is Miss Hamilton's own.

' " It is evident," cried Bridgetina, " that the author of our illustrious system [Godwin] is entirely indebted to the Hottentots for his sublime idea of the Age of Reason. Here is the Age of Reason exemplified; here is proof sufficient of the perfectibility of man! "

' " Yes," said Mr. Myope, " and as we well know mechanical and daily labour to be the deadliest foe to all that is great and admirable in the human mind, to what a glorious height of metaphysical knowledge may we expect a people to soar, where all are equally poor and equally idle! What attainments must they have doubtless made in science? What discoveries in philosophy? " ' [58]

[56] London, 1790, II, 139.
[57] *Ibid.*, p. 148.
[58] *Memoirs of Modern Philosophers,* I, 325.

The philosophers decide to emigrate to Africa to seek in the philosophical society of the Hottentots that happier field and purer air; where talents and sentiments may *expand into virtue, and germinate into general usefulness.*' [59] ' Fly this dismal, dirty hog stye of a depraved and corrupt civilization;' writes Bridgetina to the man she is pursuing, ' and let us join ourselves to the enlightened race, who already possess all of the essentials which philosophy teaches us to expect in the full meridian of the Age of Reason. Let us, my Henry, in the bosom of this happy people, who worship no God, who are free from the restraint of laws and forms of government, enjoy the blessings of equality and love.' [60]

Elizabeth Hamilton thus kills two birds with one stone, but her own preference seems nevertheless to be for a modified primitivism of the anti-luxury variety. She finds occasion to deplore the spread of commerce and luxury in Henry Sydney's description of his tour through Scotland.

"Alas! " replied Henry. " It must indeed be confessed, that wherever commerce and manufactures have spread their golden wings, innocence and simplicity of manners have fled before them. . . . When after the contemplation of such scenes as I have been describing, I have in the close of evening come to a manufacturing town, and observed the crouds of pallid wretches who issue from the huge piles of buildings that were its pride and boast—the men, riotous, profane and brutal; the women, bold, squalid, and shameless—all flying with eagerness to recruit their worn-out spirits by drafts of liquid fire; how often have I been tempted to deplore the introduction of these boasted blessings, which, while they bestowed wealth on a few fortunate individuals, were to thousands the destruction of health and innocence. How much better, have I said to myself, how much more usefully would these poor wretches have been employed, had the

[59] *Ibid.,* II, 40.   [60] *Ibid.,* p. 401.

men been engaged to cultivate some of the many thousand acres of waste land which presents its desart hue on every side! And the women—how had they been preserved from vice and misery in the bosom of domestic industry!" [61]

Great as is the confusion in social theory in *The Memoirs of Modern Philosophers,* the confusion of ethical ideas is still greater. To begin with, the book is almost a net-work of quotations from Godwin, both from *Political Justice* and *The Enquirer.* Bridgetina, Miss Hamilton's heroine, is the most fluent in Godwinian phrases. She had first met the divine words of *Political Justice* on some proof sheets that had been used as wrapping paper for snuff. ' " I read and sneezed, and sneezed and read," ' she tells us, ' " till the germ of philosophy began to fructify my soul. From that moment I became a philosopher, and need not inform you of the important consequences." ' [62] She has adopted both associationism [63] and utilitarianism. Following is her definition of goodness: ' " Goodness! " repeated Bridgetina, with a sneer; " from whence proceeds this boasted goodness? Does it flow from a conviction of general utility, pursued through the maze of abstract reasoning? If it does not, what, I pray you, is its value?" ' [64] Not only is Bridgetina a utilitarian of the most rationalistic kind, but she finds it ethically convenient to subscribe to the doctrine of necessity, as on the occasion when she defends herself thus: ' " I wonder, mamma, how you can speak so ridiculously? Have I not told you again and again, that I am under *the necessity* of preferring the motive that is most preferable? The company, if they are not very ignorant indeed, must know that my

[61] *Ibid.,* I, 243-44.   Cf. pp. 216, 220-21.
[62] *Ibid.,* II, 88.
[63] *Ibid.,* p. 81.
[64] *Ibid.,* p. 79; cf. I, 182.

going instantly to Mr. Glib's is a link in the chain of causation, generated in eternity, and which binds me now to
act exactly as I do." ' [65] There is little doubt that Elizabeth
Hamilton is here referring to the moral laxity of *Emma
Courtney,* to which she refers in footnotes.[66] She makes the
point that the doctrine of necessity leads to a loss of the
sense of moral responsibility even more strikingly in the
case of Vallaton, her villain. Hearing that the old man
whom he had betrayed to the revolutionary tribunal to
escape the consequences of theft had been guillotined, he
exclaimed: ' But what have I to say to it? I am but a
machine in the hand of fate. Nothing but what has happened, could have happened. Everything that is must inevitably be; and the causes of this old man's death were
generated in the eternity that preceded his birth. What
then have I to say to it? ' [67]

All of this is consistent enough satire on the Godwinian ethics, but Bridgetina must serve as an awful example
to her sex in every way possible. She is made, therefore,
not only a heartless rationalist, but a person of overpower-
ing sensibility as well, apparently with no comprehension
in the author's mind of the incongruity. Sometimes utility
and sensibility jostle each other in the same passage.
Bridgetina, for instance, argues that Henry ought to rush
to her daily in spite of the demands of a dying friend.
' The life of a *prejudiced* old woman was, in her estimation, of little value, when compared with the *importunate
sensations of exquisite sensibility.* These ought to have
brought Henry to the farm; nor should the illness of any
old woman, whose life could not promote the grand object
of *general utility,* have detained him for a moment.' [68]
Certainly Bridgetina herself is as charming an exponent of

[65] *Ibid.,* I, 28-29.
[66] *Ibid.,* II, 85, 400.
[67] *Ibid.,* I, 82.
[68] *Ibid.,* II, 110-11.

the energetic ecstasies of sensibility as one could find. ' I
passed the shop of Mr. Gubbles,' Bridgetina tells us,
speaking of a time when Gabriel Gubbles, the apothecary,
was the object of her affections; ' young Gabriel was
there; he was looking into the mouth of an old woman,
who sat upon the floor to have a tooth pulled out. The
attitude was charming; the scene was interesting; it was
impressive, tender, melancholy, sublime. My suffocating
sensibilities returned. I pursued my walk, leaning at times
upon the umbrella; careless of the observations of the
passengers, who, strangers to the same fine feelings of an
exquisitely-susceptible mind, wondered at my keeping
down the umbrella in such a heavy shower.' [69]

Elizabeth Hamilton is then a typical promoter of the
confusion of ideas. She knows that there are certain
ideas current that she does not like. She knows that these
have been spread by people whom she labels ' modern
philosophers.' But of different schools of thought she
knows nothing. One philosopher is as wicked as another
to her. Being oblivious of philosophical distinctions, she
is aware, therefore, of no incongruity in making Bridgetina at one and the same time a primitivist and a progressivist, a utilitarian, a rationalist, a necessitarian, and
an adherent of the ethics of feeling.

V

One has to turn to Thomas Love Peacock, whose delightful novels fall just outside of our period, for a clear-
cut satire on both the primitivists and the ' perfectibilians.'
His own sympathies lean perhaps slightly to the side of
the primitivists, at least in his first satire, *Headlong Hall*
(1816), but he makes uproarious fun of them in *Melin-*

[69] *Ibid.*, p. 90.

court (1817) in the character of Sir Oran Haut-ton, the gentlemanly orang-outang, whose friends are trying to make him an M. P. The characteristics of Sir Oran are carefully built up from the writings of the primitivists, especially those of Monboddo who is copiously quoted. He is a polished gentleman, kindly and generous in his instincts; he has an embarrassingly primitive sense of justice, and an impulsive manner of putting it into practice. His only short-coming, which, indeed, becomes almost an asset when he stands for parliament, is the fact that he has been unable to learn to talk!

In *Headlong Hall*, Peacock opposes the perfectibilian, Mr. Foster, to the deteriorationist, Mr. Escot. The issues throughout their long debates are kept refreshingly distinct, even the distinction between simplicity and diversity, which was so apt to be lost in the general scramble. Mr. Foster paints a glowing picture of the diversified development of a progressing society: 'The manufacturing system is not yet purified from some evils which necessarily attend it, but which I conceive are greatly overbalanced by their concomitant advantages. Contemplate the vast sum of human industry to which this system so essentially contributes: seas covered with vessels—ports resounding with life—profound researches—scientific inventions—complicated mechanism—canals carried over deep valleys and through bosoms of hills—employment and existence thus given to innumerable families, and the multiplied comforts and conveniences of life diffused over the whole community.' [70] 'You present to me a complicated picture of artificial life, and require me to admire it,' replies Mr. Escot, and matches the representation with a two-panel picture of the wretched factory worker and the happy

[70] *Headlong Hall*, London, 1816, pp. 101-2.

natural man. 'As Mr. Escot said this, a little rosy-cheeked girl, with a basket of heath on her head, came tripping down the side of one of the rocks on the left. The force of contrast struck even on the phlegmatic spirit of Mr. Jenkison [the statu-quo-ite], and he almost inclined for a moment to the doctrine of deterioration.' [71]

Mr. Escot further runs true to form by supporting the doctrine of universal and immutable truth; Mr. Foster replies that from the diversities of opinion produced by the progress of philosophical investigation may ultimately develop a science of morals ' susceptible of mathematical demonstration.' [72] Mr. Foster, again, is apprehensive of the stultifying effect that a doctrine of deterioration may have on society: ' " What could be its effect, but to check the ardour of investigation, to extinguish the zeal of philanthropy, to freeze the current of enterprizing hope, to bury in the torpor of scepticism and in the stagnation of despair, every better faculty of the human mind, which will necessarily become retrograde in ceasing to be progressive? "

' " I am inclined to think, on the contrary," said Mr. Escot, " that the deterioration of man is accelerated by his blindness—in many respects wilful blindness—to the truth of the fact itself, and to the causes which produce it; that there is no hope whatever of ameliorating his condition but in a total and radical change of the whole scheme of human life, and that the advocates of his indefinite perfectibility are in reality the greatest enemies to the practical possibility of their own system, by so strenuously labouring to impress on his attention, that he is going on in a good way, while he is really in a deplorably bad one.' [73]

[71] *Ibid.*, p. 104.　　[72] *Ibid.*, p. 108.　　[73] *Ibid.*, pp. 140-41.

The honor of expressing Peacock's own opinion is probably given to Mr. Fax, the Malthusian, in *Melincourt*: 'The state you have described, is adapted only to a small community, and to the infancy of human society. I shall make a very liberal concession to your views, if I admit it to be possible that the middle stage of the progress of man, is worse than either the point from which he started, or that at which he will arrive. But it is my decided opinion that we have passed that middle stage, and that every evil incident to the present condition of human society will be removed by the diffusion of moral and political knowledge, and the general increase of moral and political liberty.' [74]

[74] London, 1817, III, 174.

CHAPTER XI

AFTER-THOUGHTS

The preceding pages have demonstrated, if nothing else, that even the most abstruse of philosophical systems may finally get some sort of a popular hearing. Hume is a case in point. The most revolutionary of Hume's books were notoriously bad sellers in the eighteenth century. One need not take too literally his often quoted remark that his *Treatise* ' fell *dead-born from the Press,*' but even of the revision of the *Treatise* into the *Enquiry concerning Human Understanding* he wrote in discouragement, ' On my return from Italy, I had the Mortification to find all England in a Ferment on account of Dr. Middleton's Free Enquiry; while my Performance was entirely overlooked and neglected. A new Edition, which had been published at London of my Essays, moral and political, met not with much better reception.' In the fifties the sale of his works began to pick up slightly, but his public was still most distinctly a public of *literati*. And yet the popular novels of the nineties, both radical and anti-radical, refer familiarly to Hume and his ideas; Walker, for instance, speaks of him in *italics* throughout *The Vagabond* as the ' *fashionable Hume.*' Whence came the popular familiarity with this difficult author? Certainly not through a wide first-hand reading of his works, for though they eventually reached a fairly steady sale, they never became popular enough for that; it must of necessity have come through the work of literary middlemen. On the gradual dissemination of abstract ideas in the century Mackintosh remarked aptly in his *Vindiciae Gallicae,* ' The convictions of Philosophy insinuate themselves by a slow, but certain progress, into popular senti-

326

ment. It is vain for the arrogance of learning to condemn the people to ignorance by reprobating superficial knowledge—The people cannot be profound, but the truths which regulate the moral and political relations of man, are at no great distance from the surface. The great words in which discoveries are contained cannot be read by the people; but their substance passes through a variety of minute and circuitous channels, to the shop and the hamlet.'

In following the life-span of ideas in the eighteenth century, one cannot help wondering just how inevitable their deterioration during the course of their passage to the shop and the hamlet is. Certainly there are a few relevant facts that compel one's attention with all the force of constant reiteration. One of these is the universal fact of intellectual inconsistency. Swift never wrote a truer thing than when he jotted down in his notebook the remark that 'If a man would register all his opinions upon love, politics, religion, learning, &c. beginning from his youth, and so go on to old age, what a bundle of inconsistencies and contradictions would appear at last!' And I do not think that Swift would have put himself or any of his circle of brilliant friends in a higher order of consistent mortals; he knew men's minds too well for that. Our study of eighteenth-century minds has only confirmed the wisdom of Swift. In point of consistency, the only difference between the highly cultivated intellect and the mind of the popular writer is one of degree. The seeds of destruction are thus more often than not inherent in an ideology from the very beginning. However well a thinker in the retirement of his study supposes that he is guarding the clear flow of abstract thought, he is after all no more than a mortal, with human complexes, antipathies and preferences; some early prejudice or early enthusiasm, some pressure of current opinion, some fixed purpose, will exert its quiet influence on his system of thought—and even a believer in a mechanical universe will give an outlawed God the office of holding the fixed stars apart. And to my thinking it is fortunate that even the best minds are sometimes inconsistent, since the completely consistent mind would be a completely rigid and unadaptable mind, tending to sterility rather than richness of content. Certainly the history of ideas in the eighteenth century would have taken a far different course had each mind which took up and helped to pass on an idea been completely and rigidly logical. For of course it is absurd to think—what many persons seem to assume without thinking—that an idea has any life of its own outside of the mind, or the innumerable minds, that think it. While it may have latent in it some 'immanent logic' of its own, this is for the most part ineffective; as a factor in history the idea must, in the main, float unsteadily about on a fluctuating sea of human thought and feeling. Each individual mind which it enters in some degree distorts it or gives it a new coloring; so that by the time it reaches the myriad-minded public it is often a sorry sight indeed.

As to the determinants of the popularity of an idea, I do not think that any sound generalizations can be made that will cover the case for different ways of thinking at different periods of time. Each complex of ideas as it comes into fashion is so motivated by social and political and economic forces, by the complex of ideas preceding it, and by the temper of the people who take it up, that its popularity is, or should be, a separate problem in itself. But if we cannot generalize about the cause of popularity, we can watch the effect of popularization on ideas.

There were various ways in which fashion vitiated
thought in the eighteenth century. In the first place, most
of the more popular writers wrote for a living. Few of
them could afford to be as public spirited as Hannah More
and write for the good of a cause at a great financial
sacrifice to themselves. They had to write what would
sell. As Bage remarks in *Barham Downs,* ' The bulk of
authors now are become political; and seem to have
adopted the precept of Doctor Swift, " Suit your words
to your music well." The sweetest music to an author, is
undoubtedly the jingle of guineas; the exchequer furnishes the greatest number of concertos, and requires
nothing more, but to " suit your words to your music
well." '

Naturally a popular author will take advantage of a
mode of thought already in fashion and use it as long
as he can sell it to the public. That is one reason for
the tremendous lag in the progress of ideas in the public
mind. We saw, for instance, the roots of sensibility in
the Cambridge Platonists in the seventeenth century; but
the climax of the popular vogue came, I should say, in
the last quarter of the eighteenth century. In the nineties
one gets expressions of it so exaggerated as to border
on burlesque, side by side with actual burlesque of the
fashion and the pronouncement that it is already dead.
The popular writer in eighteenth-century England knew
that he was addressing an audience controlled largely by
caution and conservatism in its intellectual processes—
at least until the end of the century, when the stress of
poverty, govermental oppression, and the example of
France, provided temporarily a more radical audience.
As I have pointed out many times during the course of this
book, each new idea brought forth a host of popular
writers who expressed the sentiment of the people by

defending the old, tried, and familiar ideas against the attacks of the new. That was the case at the introduction of deism, of mechanism, the economic defence of luxury, biological evolutionism, Jacobin political theories, and utilitarianism. Fashions in thought changed slowly. Popular writers more often than not depended for novelty, not on new ideas, but on a more and more extreme and bizarre exemplification of the old. Hence the unreality, the absurdity of human behavior in so many of the novels of sensibility and benevolence, for instance. In time over-statement and exaggeration brought discredit on the ideology itself and helped in its destruction.

On the other hand there were of course some writers who had their eye out for the coming as well as the established fashion. They realized the truth of Mary Wollstonecraft's observation, made in 1794, that ' men almost always affect to possess the virtue, or quality, that is rising into estimation.' They seized on the catchwords of the new mode of thought before they fairly knew what it was about. Just as today people talk glibly about Freudianism who have never read Freud, and apply the language of relativity-theory to fields where it has no applicability, so in the eighteenth century people talked about mechanism or general utility who had no more than heard of Newton or Bentham. That the public in the eighteenth century was treated to pyrotechnical displays of imperfectly understood abstractions is delightfully witnessed by Walker's ridicule of the affectation in *The Vagabond*: ' When,' asks Frederick, ' shall the catenas of mankind be decrepitated by the furnace of truth, ignited by the bellows of reason? When shall the ingann-nations of prejudice be delacerated, and the catachrestical reasonings of facinorous aristocrats be dispanded by the zetetic spirit of the eighteenth century? '

Not only was there danger from affected and pretentious use of new terminology, but from the stereotyping of catchwords. From the reign of the language of the ' light of nature ' and ' the candle of the Lord ' at the beginning of the century to that of ' rights of man,' ' perfectibility,' ' the greatest good of the greatest number at the end, the English public was conducted by means of a series of clichés through a course of second-hand thought only remotely resembling the original. It will have been evident to the reader that of all omnibus terms of the century, the word ' nature ' suffered the most, for the advocates of *every* system appealed to ' nature ' with every variety of implication. Even some of the popular writers themselves became conscious in the course of time of the confusion among the very scholars which was arising from the use of this word. Holcroft, in his criticism of Dugald Stewart's use of the word, does not, it is true, distinguish anything like the sixty-odd applications of the term that Professor Lovejoy has found, but he shows a surprising amount of discrimination. And even Dr. Alogos in *The Vagabond* has discernment enough to exclaim: ' But what is the light of Nature? . . . We know the genuine meaning of the word, but you apply to nature a personality: you make a mere *action* an *active being*; such are the consequences of applying terms, when the real meaning of the word is not understood; . . . even a new philosopher would startle, if, in place of saying man can be no longer happy than while he lives according to nature, we were to say—man can be no longer happy than while he lives according to the *act of beginning.*'

Perhaps even greater harm to the integrity of ideas than that done by the imperfect comprehension of them by people who expounded and simplified them for the public came from the habit of keeping hold of as many fashions of thought at the same time as possible. I am not now referring to such writers as Samuel Jackson Pratt who took up each new idea successively without bothering whether it conflicted with the ideas he had formally expressed or not. I am referring rather to the writers who clung to all the public favorites at once: who made their North American Indians creatures of sensibility, who made their characters of sensibility also utilitarians and rationalists, and who gave their perfectionists a passion for the simplicities of primitive life. Such unnatural mating of ideas could not help bringing forth a curious hybrid generation in which the original lineaments of the parent ideas were largely lost. Of all the favorite ideas of the eighteenth century, for example, the one that best maintained its popularity and most frequently made its appearance in all sorts of unexpected associations was that of benevolence. There is something rather endearing in the way eighteenth-century England clung to the idea of benevolence through every sort of intellectual crisis. The phenomenon makes one wonder just how large a part inherited national preferences and antipathies play in the determination of the current of thought of a nation. 'What in fact is that original goodness or moral sense, so much boasted by the English?' exclaimed Helvétius. 'Nothing is more absurd than this theologic philosophy of Shaftesbury; and yet the greatest part of the English are as fond of it as the French were formerly of their music.' And well might he so exclaim, for not only did the Shaftesburians have the terminology of benevolence continually on their tongues, but all the rest, from the most rigid rationalists at the beginning of the century to the Jacobins and utilitarians at the end, professed so much enthusiasm for universal benevolence as to give a distinctly sentimental turn to English thought, which is less evident in the corresponding course of French thought.

The general blurring of the philosophical distinctions, then, the taking up of imperfectly understood new modes of thought, and the clinging at the same time to old ones, the individual bias of each writer who acted as interpreter, the temper of the English public to whom the popular literature was addressed—its caution and conservatism, its sentimentality, its sturdy belief in the traditions of the English commonwealth, at war though that belief was with the restlessness bred of the pressure of economic and political oppression—all these factors helped to modify and reshape the current of English thought in the eighteenth century before ever it became an effective social force. One is half inclined to agree with a contributor to the *Quarterly Review* who wrote in 1816: ' Were it not that the present state of popular knowledge is a necessary part of the process of society, a stage through which it must pass in its progress toward something better, it might reasonably be questioned whether the misinformation of these times be not worse than the ignorance of former ages. For people who are ignorant and know themselves to be so, will often judge rightly when they are called on to think at all, acting from common sense, and the unperverted instinct of equity. But there is a kind of half knowledge which seems to disable men even from forming a just opinion of the fact before them—a sort of squint in the understanding which prevents it from seeing straight forward, and by which all objects are distorted.'

INDEX